the hero
in the Earthly City

medieval & renaissance texts & studies

VOLUME 33

the hero
in the Earthly City

A Reading of Beowulf

BY

Bernard F. Huppé

Medieval & Renaissance texts & Studies
STATE UNIVERSITY OF NEW YORK AT BINGHAMTON
1984

Center for Medieval & Early Renaissance Studies
State University of New York at Binghamton

Library of Congress Cataloging in Publication Data

Huppé, Bernard Felix, 1911–
    The hero in the earthly city.

    (Medieval & Renaissance texts & studies ; v. 33)
    Includes a translation of Beowulf.
    1. Beowulf. 2. Augustine, Saint, Bishop of Hippo—
Influence. I. Beowulf. English. 1984. II. Title. III. Series.

PR1585.H86   1984   829'.3   84-674
ISBN 0-86698-067-9

Printed in the United States of America

For

Mary Lois

my dear,
while the sands o' life shall run

Contents

In an earthly city ... in the sphere of demise and succession, where the dead are succeeded by the dying — what else but glory should they love by which they wished even after death to live in the mouths of their admirers? The earthly city is divided against itself by wars ... and such victories as are either life-destroying or short-lived, victories which end in death or are merely momentary respites from further war.... Thus the founder of the earthly city was a fratricide.

— Augustine, *The City of God*
(V, 14, XV, 4, 5)
(translated by Marcus Dods)

preface

the aim of this reading of *Beowulf* is to present a coherent view of the theme and structure of the poem in the context of the poet's inescapable Augustinian frame of reference. For the reader with little or no acquaintance with *Beowulf*, this reading should serve to forestall mistaking the poem as a primitive work of art, and to stimulate further study of it in the depth it deserves. For the reader who is versed in the poem, the reading should provide cause for reconsideration, if not assent.

The translation is an essential part of the reading in revealing its consequences for the shape and form of the rhetorical, lexical, and thematic structuring of the poem. Any reading of an ancient work of literature is an act of translating one's own perceptions of it; if these are wrong, or misguided, translation will reveal this more readily than involved explanation can do. The translation, dependent for its coherence on the view taken of the poem, cannot stand without the argument for its being, as the argument must stand on the evidence of what results from it, the translation.

The straightforward synopsis of the story of *Beowulf* with which this study begins, presents baldly the reading argued for in Chapters Two through Four and given shape in the translation, Chapter Five. For the reader with little or no experience of the poem, it might be best to read the first chapter and go directly to Chapter Five, only then coming back to the remaining chapters, which should challenge or reinforce his reading. For the reader who comes equipped with a knowledge of the poem equal or superior to my own, the synoptic reading cannot tell him anything he doesn't already know, but it will serve to forewarn him of the perceptions and preconceptions that govern the ensuing argument.

The writing of this study has been a long labor of love, extending back many years to the time when I first read the poem with an excitement which has never dimmed, and it is my hope that my readers will share with me my delight in *Beowulf* and the pleasure I have had in tracing its intricate involutions, its tragic theme, its appeal to what is constant in the human experience. To read or re-read *Beowulf* with loving care is to encounter the reality of literary experience, and it is to this experience that I hope this book will lead.

During its writing I have been sustained by the responsive love of my children: my daughter, Anne, whose charm has been a constant source of delight; my son, Alex, who, cheerfully and wittily assisted me in my final research at Boston; my youngest son, Geoffrey, who cheerfully followed the old paths with me.

To my fellow scholars whose work has enlightened my path toward understanding *Beowulf* I have made acknowledgement, however inadequately, in my notes. To the library of Boston University I am grateful for assistance in my final research.

To my students I owe more than this mere acknowledgement can express. They have challenged me, have sharpened my perceptions, have forced me to rid myself of comfortable fuzziness, have taught me more than I have taught them. They are too many to mention all by name, but as representative I thank: Gary Rubin who encouraged me; Mary Jo Arn who urged me on; Judith Weise who provided me with a most useful critique of the translation; Sylvia Horowitz for her many, important insights and for her help in editing the manuscript; Allan Eller for many suggestions which I have incorporated in my text and for his editing of the manuscript.

Many of my colleagues at Binghamton have aided me, but in particular I wish to acknowledge: Aldo Bernardo for the great gift of his friendship and our shared delight in the founding of the Center for Medieval and Early Renaissance Studies; Mario Di Cesare who, in friendship, urged me to complete and submit my book for publication by Medieval & Renaissance Texts & Studies and who has supervised its publication; Paul Szarmach, my friend and colleague, for his reading of my manuscript; Lee DiCesare for her copy editing.

Sadly, I acknowledge two dear, departed friends: John Gardner whom I knew only in my last two years at Binghamton, but who in that short time gave me encouragement and the intellectual support I required; finally, in grief, my dear friend and beloved colleague for so long, John Weld, who did not live to continue to help me in the final realization of my work on *Beowulf*; no one but I can realize what my book suffers from not having his final reading of it, but if it has any worth may it be a memorial to the guiding and cheerful presence of one who has gone but has never left me.

BFH

Castine, Maine
June, 1983

the hero
in the Earthly City

Chapter One
Story

a straightforward account of the story of *Beowulf* must begin with its legendary background. The major figures in the poem are part of heroic legend although the hero himself has no known existence apart from the epic. They live lives of biblical scope; the lineage of Grendel is, in fact, biblical; the ancient kings, Hrothgar, Hrethel, Ongentheow — and the old hero Beowulf — live lives of patriarchal length.

The legendary story apparently starts with the Danish king, Heremod, the counterfoil to Beowulf, who begins in promise and ends, through his own heroic failings, as a burden to his people, betrayed into the hands of his enemies and slain by them. There follows a dark period of lordlessness for the Danes, from which they are freed mysteriously by the arrival of Scyld, a foundling who rises from nothing to imperial power. His success is continued in the reign of his son, Beowulf the Dane, and of his son, Healfdane. Healfdane is succeeded by his oldest son, Heorogar, of whom we learn nothing except that he was not succeeded by his son, Heoroweard, but by Heorogar's brother, Hrothgar. Of another brother, Halga, we learn nothing, except that he left a son, Hrothulf, whose only role in the poem is to portend an ominous future of treachery. We also learn nothing about Heorogar's son, Heoroweard, or why Hrothgar ascended the throne in his place.

In addition to Danish legend leading to Hrothgar's reign and Beowulf's first adventure, further legendary background must be detailed. On the Scandinavian mainland are the Swedes, ruled by the "ancient" Ongentheow, who has two sons, Ohthere and Onela, the latter conjecturally married to Hrothgar's sister. The Swedes

(901-13)*

4-52

53-63

(467-69)

64-85
(1017)
(1162-87)
(2155-62)

(2928-32)
(62)

---

* Line references are to the translation, Chapter Five. Line numbers in parentheses indicate disjunctive, non-synchronic narrative events.

are the enemies of the Geats who live in a legendary land placed
somewhere in Scandinavia, perhaps — since they attack the Swedes   (2472-73)
across the water — an island, perhaps the island of Gotland, the
legendary home of the Goths. The Geats are ruled by the "ancient"
Hrethel who apparently, like Hrothgar and like Ongentheow,
manages to keep a warlike peace. Hrethel has four children: three
sons, Herebeald, Hæthcyn, and Higelac, and a daughter who is
married to Ecgtheow, a Wægmunding and not a Geat. Ecgtheow   (372-75)
is the father of Beowulf who is thus, through his mother, of the
royal blood.

Herebeald, the oldest son, is accidentally slain by Hæthcyn. (2435-2498)
Hrethel, in ancient grief, dies of sheer frustration at his inability
to resolve the ethical dilemma presented by his need to avenge his
son and the impossibility of vengeance upon his other son. His death
is the signal for Ohthere and Onela, the sons of Swedish Ongentheow, to attack the Geats at Sorrows' Hill in the land of the Geats.
In retaliation, King Hæthcyn with his brother Higelac attacks
Sweden. Hæthcyn is at first successful, but is then routed and slain
by Ongentheow, who surrounds the surviving Geats at Ravenswood. Higelac comes to the rescue, puts Ongentheow to flight, and
overruns his stronghold. There Ongentheow meets his death at the
hands of Wulf and Eofor, two of Higelac's retainers; Higelac is given
Ongentheow's armor and is called the "slayer of Ongentheow,"   (1968)
the epithet which marks his appearance in the second part of the
poem.

Beowulf, at first held in little esteem, shows his prowess in a   (2183-88)
youthfully reckless contest at sea and in his slaying of five giants   (530-81)
as well as the sea monsters who troubled the Geats. He seems also   (418-24)
to have conducted himself with distinction at Ravenswood, for after
the battle, Higelac, who now posesses the armor of heroic Ongentheow, apparently gives Beowulf, his remaining blood relative,   (453-55)
the armor of his father, Hrethel, reserving for himself the patrimonial sword. Beowulf now has become Higelac's champion.

This background is given in the poem by allusion, by indirec-
tion, by "digression," in retrospect and in prophecy, but it is essential
that these minimal details be kept in mind in the following précis
of Beowulf's adventures.

By warlike deeds Hrothgar has gained prosperity and to cap his   64-188
triumph builds a great hall, Heorot. His self-satisfaction, however,
is short-lived, for the hall is at once attacked by a monster, Grendel,
a descendant of Cain and his progeny of giants. Grendel is triumphant; the hall, now encrusted with blood as well as with gold, is
abandoned each night, and the Danes are helpless — as are their

gods. Beowulf hears of Hrothgar's plight and decides to go to his ⟶ 189-228
aid. Higelac, as we later learn, is not pleased with the idea, but ⟶ (1992-97)
Beowulf gains consent after the omens have been consulted.

He comes to Denmark, is challenged by the coast warden; given ⟶ 229-319
permission to enter, he marches to Heorot where he is again chal- ⟶ 320-70
lenged by Wulfgar, Hrothgar's herald, who also approves his credentials. Hrothgar admits him hopefully, suggesting that he is not ⟶ 371-455
a mere interloper but that he comes out of duty, Hrothgar having
befriended his father. Beowulf enters, presents his credentials as
a slayer of monsters (he has killed five giants as well as a number
of sea monsters) and asks that he may face Grendel. Hrothgar is ⟶ 456-98
delighted and welcomes him as one sent by providence and by his
honor to repay the debt his father incurred.

However, the king's spokesman, Unferth, gives voice to the la- ⟶ 499-709
tent resentment of the Danes; he claims that Beowulf's only known
exploit was his defeat by Breca in a foolish endurance match on
the open sea. With dignity, but forcefully, Beowulf replies. He
agrees that his match with Breca was a piece of youthful folly, but
that he emerged from it not only as victor, but also as one who
had providentially found his vocation as a slayer of monsters (a
fact attested by the exploits he had already mentioned). His response
is sufficient; Hrothgar gladly accepts his credentials and leaves him
to guard the hall.

Grendel bursts into the hall where all the Geats are asleep, ex- ⟶ 710-836
cept for Beowulf, who watches as Grendel devours one of his men.
Grendel now approaches Beowulf, seizes him, but finds that his
grasping arm is caught in the grip of a man of prodigious strength.
(Curiously, Beowulf's physical appearance and stature are given
only indirectly and chiefly through the fact of his deeds; the coast ⟶ (247-51)
warden singles him out from his troop, and later we learn how huge
Grendel really is and how strong Beowulf from the fact that it takes ⟶ (1634-39)
four of the Geats simply to carry the monster's head, which they
do, even so, with great difficulty.) Although Grendel is a giant,
he is overmatched by Beowulf who is God's agent. The battle is
ended as soon as it begins, with Grendel's sudden, desperate desire
to escape. He is attacked ineffectually by the Geats. (Grendel is ⟶ (801-05)
protected from swords by magic, a fact which casts curious light
on Beowulf's boast that he will face Grendel unarmed, thus prov- ⟶ (677-87)
identially freeing himself from what might have proved a disastrous
encumbrance.) Grendel's arm is torn away and he flees to die in
the tarn.

In the morning the celebrations begin. Following Grendel's tracks, ⟶ 837-924
a company rides out, and on their return Beowulf is celebrated

by a comparison of his heroic glory with that of the legendary slayer
of the dragon, Sigemund, and by contrast with the failure in heroic
glory of the Danish king, Heremod. The celebrations continue in
the evening feast. Hrothgar rewards Beowulf in particular with the   925-1062
sword and armor of Healfdane, perhaps symbolic of his taking
Beowulf as his son. (At the feast there appears an ominous figure,
Hrothulf, Hrothgar's nephew, the son of Halga, who lives in apparent amity with his uncle, an amity made suspect by the cryptic
comment that the Danes "in the fated future" would do "treacherous
deeds."

At the heart of the feast is the foreboding tale of Finnsburh,   1063-1162
which is related to entertain the company. Some time in the past
a truce to the feud between the Danes and the Frisians had been
accomplished through the marriage of the Danish princess, Hild,
to the Frisian king, Finn. The truce was broken by fighting between a visiting band of Danes, headed by Hnæf, Hild's brother,
and their Frisian hosts. Although Hnæf was killed along with the
son of Hild and Finn, a stalemate resulted which led to a truce
sworn between Hengest, the Danish leader, and Finn. The bodies
of Hnæf and of Hild's son, along with the other dead, were consumed on the funeral pyre. The truce continued during the winter,
but in the spring was broken. Finn was slain and his wealth and
his queen were carried back to Denmark.

The tale of revenge and betrayed trust is obviously told in celebration of Danish heroism, but it has ominous relevance to the present show of amity at the feast, for at its conclusion Queen Wealh-   1162-1250
theow enters the hall and turns to Hrothulf, voicing her hope that
he will prove loyal and protect her sons in the event of Hrothgar's
death, an ill-founded hope as the subtle comment suggests: uncle
and nephew were "then *still* at peace." She now gives Beowulf a
legendary necklet, upon which gift an auctorial prophecy is made
that Higelac will wear it when he meets death in a raid on Frisia.
Finally, she again reveals her deep anxiety about her sons in ask-
ing Beowulf to act as their protector.

When the feast ends, the Danes take their old place in the hall,
but Beowulf is lodged in guest quarters. The sleeping Danes are   1251-1320
attacked by Grendel's mother, acting in accord with the accepted
heroic imperative of revenge. She does not linger, but seizes one
warrior, Æschere, Hrothgar's chief companion. She slays him and
carries his corpse to the tarn. Hrothgar and the Danes are plunged   1321-1382
into grief, and Hrothgar summons Beowulf to impose upon him
the duty of the feud. Beowulf accepts, and they go to the tarn, which   1383-1472
is described with Vergilian echoes as a hellishly terrifying place.

After a prelude in which Beowulf spears one of the water monsters, he plunges into the tarn, is assailed by water monsters, and when he reaches the bottom is seized by the dam, who carries him into her cave, which is watertight and lit by a fire. 1473-1528

He strikes at her with the sword lent to him by Unferth; this failing, he grapples with her and is thrown. Miraculously, he sees hanging on the wall a giant sword with which he is able to slay her and to behead the lifeless corpse of Grendel. Leaving behind the treasure in the cave, he carries away only Grendel's head and the hilt of the sword, its blade having melted in the monster's poisoned blood. He comes to the surface where his Geats are waiting hopelessly, the Danes having already departed. Four of his men carry the head with difficulty to the hall. There Hrothgar looks upon the hilt, inscribed with its biblical history of the first fratricide, of the race of giants and the name of the man for whom the sword was made. Looking on its cruciform shape, Hrothgar is inspired to a homily, warning Beowulf, in particular, of heroic self-reliance and of failure to heed duty above glory and treasure. 1529-1650 1651-1816

Beowulf, further rewarded, leaves the next morning with the promise to come to Hrothgar's aid if he is needed. He arrives home where Higelac and Hygd, his queen, await him. Hygd is described by oblique reference to the story of a queen who was a model of unrighteous self-will until married to the hero, Offa, who tamed her and made her, through love, into the kind of queen that Hygd is. (Whether or not Higelac is another Offa is not indicated.) Beowulf greets Higelac and recounts his adventures in Denmark, interrupting his narrative with a long digressive prophecy. Hrothgar has betrothed his daughter, Freawaru, to Ingeld, the Heathobard king, to secure peace between the Danes and the nation they had earlier conquered. He prophesies, however, that the duty of revenge will overcome the wish for peace and the love of the king for his bride. That Beowulf is right in his forecast is attested very early in the poem where the account of the building of Heorot is concluded with the foreboding statement that the hall awaits its future destruction by flames, the result of the hostility of the son-in-law. Once again, then, the story of the feud with Grendel's race is counterpointed by an ominous prophecy of the fragility of peace in a world governed by the ethics of the blood feud. 1817-87 1888-1962 1963-2143

Beowulf, when he concludes his story, gives to Higelac Hrothgar's gifts to him, in particular, Healfdane's sword and armor, saying that Hrothgar had wished that its story be recounted, how it came to him from Heorogar by his wish and despite the claims of his son. He also gives to Hygd Wealhtheow's reward. Special emphasis 2144-2220

is placed on the priceless necklet with its attendant prophecy that   (1202–09)
Higelac would lose it in death upon an ill-fated raid into Frisia.
The moment of Beowulf's glory is punctuated by an account of his
life, stressing the theme of fortune's change and the agency of Providence. Beowulf began without promise, but by nurturing his
strength, realizing it as a gift rather than a personal possession,
and aware of his role as agent of a higher purpose, he has gained
honor, unstained by Heremod-like evil. The feast then resumes
with Higelac's gift to Beowulf of Hrethel's sword, completing the
earlier gift of the armor and perhaps symbolizing the full acceptance of Beowulf into the royal line of succession. The symbolism
is underscored by the further gift of wealth and power sufficient
to make Beowulf almost the equal of the king. The scene of joyous
amity is abruptly ended as the story suddenly shifts to the future
and hurries over the years during which Higelac and his son are
killed, and Beowulf ascends the throne to rule for fifty years until
the dragon comes.

The dragon is aroused to attack by a runaway slave who creeps   2221–2459
into his cave and steals a cup, which he takes to Beowulf, whom
he asks to intercede between himself and his master. The dragon
attacks in retaliation, and Beowulf is brought the news of its devastation. Although the dragon has returned to its fastness, satisfied with
its revenge, Beowulf decides that it is his duty to seek vengeance
and the gold. His mind, however, is clouded by the thought that
he has somehow transgressed against ancient law, and as he advances to face the dragon, he thinks of the past. He remembers
the death of Higelac and his own escape, of his befriending the
young Heardred, Higelac's son. He remembers how he became
embroiled in the Swedish feud, which has continued after the death
of Ongentheow, who was succeeded by Ohthere. Upon his death
Ongentheow's second son, Onela, took the throne despite the claims
of Ohthere's sons, Eanmund and Eadgils, who rebelled and then
fled to find refuge with the Swede's enemy, Heardred the Geat.
Onela pursued them into the land of the Geats where he slew both
Heardred and Eanmund, but permitted Beowulf to become king.
Beowulf, however, kept hidden his determination to avenge his
blood relative, in pursuance of which he befriended the remaining
Swedish prince, Eadgils, and later helped him slay his uncle. Eadgils
became and still remains the Swedish king.

Beowulf seeks the dragon. Speaking to his men of his youth, he   2460–2601
recalls in particular how the ancient Hrethel died in the frustration of grief; he recalls how war with the Swedes broke out after
Hrethel's death. He tells of becoming Higelac's champion and con-

cludes with his determination to continue, as he always has, to fight
alone, except that now he will rely, though unwillingly, on his sword
and iron shield. In the ensuing battle, however, both sword and
shield fail him and he is left helpless before the dragon.

At this point the action of the battle is interrupted by the in-   2602-68
troduction of Wiglaf, who alone will come to Beowulf's rescue. Wiglaf is presented through the story of the sword and armor which
he will carry into battle. This royal armor, once worn by the Swedish prince, Eanmund, Onela had given to Wiglaf's father, Wihstan,
as reward for slaying his rebellious nephew. Apparently because
Wihstan is his Wægmunding kinsman, Beowulf befriended him
when he was forced to flee from the successful Eadgils, Eanmund's
brother and Beowulf's ally. After Wihstan's death, Wiglaf inherited   2669-2723
the armor which he now carries into battle in aid of Beowulf. He
rescues his king by striking the underbelly of the dragon with his   2724-2820
dagger and thus mortally wounding him. Beowulf, too, is mortally wounded. Dying, he asks Wiglaf to enter the cave and bring
him a portion of the treasure for which he has given his life so that
he may feast his eyes on the visible evidence that his death was
not in vain. Wiglaf brings the treasure; Beowulf dies, and in dying leaves the rule of the Geats to Wiglaf, a Wægmunding and his
only remaining blood relative. The exchange of power is symbolized
by the transferance of his armor, presumably that of Hrethel which
Higelac had given Beowulf.

After Beowulf dies, Wiglaf again berates the craven retainers   2821-91
and sends a messenger back to the Geatish stronghold. The messen-   2892-3057
ger not only announces the death of the king, but in a long speech
pictures the plight of the Geats because of his death: they are
threatened by the Franks and Frisians seeking to avenge Higelac's
raid, and more immediately by the Swedes who will resume the
long feud, of which he gives an account; he does not explain why
Eadgils, Beowulf's ally, should wish to attack. The explanation is,
of course, implicit in the account of Wiglaf's lineage. The sacred
duty of revenge demands that Eadgils slay Wiglaf, whose father
slew his brother, and that he punish the Geats, whose dead king
had befriended the father and made the son his successor.

The company has joined Wiglaf in viewing the dead bodies of   3058-3136
Beowulf and the dragon, an action interrupted by extended auctorial commentary on the curse placed upon the treasure and the
deadliness of the desire to gain and keep the treasure. Wiglaf now
speaks, declaring that he and others had tried to persuade Beowulf
to leave the dragon alone, not to seek revenge and the treasure,
but that Beowulf was driven by some relentless force to seek his

doom. He laments the fact that the self-will of great men is the cause of disaster to their people. He then bids that a company go with him to take the treasure from the cave, and that, while they are gone, the rest make ready a bier to transport the gold and the king for burial. This is done. The dragon is then shoved off the cliff in a sort of parody of the solemn burial at sea of Scyld at the beginning of the poem.

Beowulf is brought home. A funeral pyre is prepared; he is placed   3137–end
upon it, and, as in the Finnsburh tale, is consumed in the flames. He is buried in the barrow which he had ordered made, and along with him the treasure, worthless as it was before. Beowulf is lamented by his people:

> they said he was   of the kings of the world
> the most gentle   and mildest of men,
> most kind to his people   and keenest for glory.

This summary of the plot of *Beowulf* represents my understanding of it. As the *Beowulf* scholar will recognize, it includes, without comment, much that remains controversial, but which will be defended in the ensuing chapters and in the notes to the translation. It should act for the scholar as forewarning. For the reader unversed in the scholarship, it should serve as orientation to my reading without the immediate encumbrance of scholarly apparatus. For both scholar and novice, however, the function of this summary is to enforce, or re-enforce, a necessary awareness of the complexity of the narrative method of *Beowulf*, as involuted in development as it is simple in outline.

The story advances in puzzlements, and the straight line of narrative is constantly interrupted by references to events not yet recorded, by a background of Germanic myth, heroic legend, history, and by biblical allusions as well.[1] This background the poet shared with his audience, as he shared with them a biblically oriented understanding that the word and event of heroic legend may recapitulate the spiritual history of man. Indeed, when allegorically understood, heroic legend may provide a typology of providential design. These views shaped the poet's handling of his story and perhaps account for his narrative method. His method is designed to involve the reader in the thematic unfolding of the story, not through knowledge of legendary background so much as through recognition that unexplained events either foreshadow the future or are the result of past events which will be narrated later in the poem. The story is self-contained; what appears as puzzlement is intended to alert the reader to the thematic unfolding of significant events, and to underscore his need to keep in mind a counterpoint of past and future as he follows the narrative present.

One such example of puzzlement appears at the beginning of the poem with the celebration of the founding, by the mysterious Scyld, of a new Danish royal line after a time of trouble for the "lordless" Danes. There are the three puzzles left unanswered here. Why were the Danes left "lordless"? Who is Scyld? Finally, why should an epic about a Geatish hero begin with the celebration of Danish kings who disappear from the story once Beowulf has completed his adventures in Denmark? The answer to the first question is given much later in the poem, as we have seen, when Beowulf is praised by contrasting him to the Danish king, Heremod, who became a tyrant to his people, was betrayed into the hands of his foes, and slain by them. Here the time of the Danes' lordless trouble is explained, and, in consequence, why Scyld came as a blessing to them. Who Scyld is we never learn, but the reason for his anonymity rests in the poem itself: it is necessary that he remain mysterious to emphasize his role as an agent of Providence. Because he is sent by God, he is mysteriously inexplicable. This role the poet also stresses by interjecting into the story of Scyld an account of the succession of his son, Beowulf the Dane. God sent this son to Scyld and the Danes (14–17), because of the sorrow they had suffered from being lordless.

Scyld is simply an agent of an always mysterious design which permits a merciful relief to long suffering. The peace Scyld brings, however, is gained and maintained through war. Thus, although Scyld's peace reflects God's mercy, it also reveals the impossibility of the worldly achievement of true peace. It is in this observation that one may understand why Scyld and his succession are appropriate as introduction to an epic celebrating Beowulf the Geat. Scyld's role has unmistakeable thematic significance and serves to provide a thematic context by which the hero may be judged. To understand Scyld is to understand something about the world and the values of the world to which the hero belongs.

The story of *Beowulf* is further complicated by the characteristic device of disjunction. Disjunction (tmesis) involves the disruption of temporal sequence or separation of contiguous narrative elements to achieve an overall design, usually at the service of theme. In this method, the narrative is advanced in a series of interlaced forward-backward-forward movements and is well illustrated by the story of Scyld and his succession (4–67). This first of the poem's puzzlements moves forward and backward in a series of disjunctures of the temporal sequence. The narrative begins with Scyld's rise to power, returns to his mysterious beginnings, then back to his rise to power and dominion. Before describing his death and burial, the narrative looks forward to his successor, Beowulf the Dane[2], as the description of the son's rise to fame looks back to the time of Danish suffering prior to Scyld's mysterious arrival. The paragraph describing Scyld's burial includes references back to his beginnings as well as to his future in eternity. The accession and reign of Scyld's son Beowulf follows, but between this and the accession of Beowulf's son, Healfdane, the narrative returns briefly to the death of Scyld. After Healfdane's sons and daughter are introduced, the expected sequence is curiously broken. No mention is made of the reign of the oldest son, Heorogar; instead the narrative turns puzzlingly to an account *in medias res* of Hrothgar and his triumphs in war. The missing link in the chain of succession receives no notice until lines 467–69 and 2158–62.

Such narrative devices are characteristic of the whole poem.[3] Some other examples of puzzlement may be cited from the summary given above: the discrepancy in the accounts of the Geatish response to Beowulf's going to Denmark; his unexplained wearing of Hrethel's armor; the oblique and elliptical references to Beowulf's giant stature and Grendel's magical powers; Higelac's being termed, "the slayer of Ongentheow" at his first appearance; the elaborate development of the description of Wiglaf's armor. Some other examples of disjunction may also be cited: the accounts of Beowulf's earlier life and long reign; accounts of the Swedish wars and of Higelac's raid on Frisia and of his death; finally, the accounts of the dragon, the hoard and the curse laid upon it. Detailed discussion of the poet's contrapuntal narrative method will be given in a later chapter, but a glance at the examples cited will serve to indicate how the story of *Beowulf* must be approached, how essential it is in the course of reading to keep details in mind and to be prepared for back reference. The story of *Beowulf* is a web of words to be apprehended as an interlaced unity controlled by thematic design.

Notes

1. The pattern of allusion to heroic legend, story and history which underpins the narrative of *Beowulf* bristles with problems which the great scholars, upon whose shoulders we sit, have done much to solve. The best introduction is through Frederick Klaeber, *Beowulf*, 3rd. edition (Boston: Heath, 1950) and R. W. Chambers, *Beowulf: an Introduction*, 3rd. edition with supplement by C. L. Wrenn (Cambridge: University Press, 1967). Still stimulating is William Lawrence, *Beowulf and the Epic Tradition* (1928; reprint ed., New York: Hafner, 1961). For a general study of Germanic legend, H. Munro Chadwick, *The Heroic Age* (Cambridge: University Press, 1912), along with later work in collaboration with Nora Chadwick, is basic. Jane Leake, *The Geats of Beowulf* (Madison: University of Wisconsin Press, 1967), provides an understanding of the intellectual milieu of the poet's conception of the history and legend of his race.

Recently, Douglas Short, '*Beowulf* Scholarship: an Annotated Bibliography' (New York: Garland, 1980) affords an invaluable aid to further study.

2. A more likely name for the son of Scyld Scefing (shield/sheaf) would appear to be Beow (grain); see R. W. Chambers (note 1), pp. 87–88 and Klaeber (note 1) pp. xxiii–

xxvii. The variation the poet chooses, *Beowulf*, as Klaeber notes, "has caused much perplexity to students of the poem" (p. xxiv). But the choice may be deliberate. The theme of succession is a dominant one in the poem, as even the basic plot summary would suggest. Beowulf the Dane's succession is orderly as is that of his son, Healfdane. Beowulf, to the contrary, succeeds to the Geatish throne as a result of Higelac's reckless adventure and the death of his son in violent feud. And Beowulf, in dying, laments the lack of a son to succeed him.

3. Klaeber, pp. lvii–lviii. John Leyerle, "The Interlace Structure of *Beowulf*," *University of Toronto Quarterly* 37 (1967–68): 1–17, introduced the term "interlace," i.e., "narrative threads, intersected by other material," which is a form of tmesis. He illustrates, "with Hygelac's Frisian expedition ... segmented into four episodes, 1202–14, 2354–68, 2501–9 and 2913–21, in which chronology is ignored," p. 7. Lewis Nicholson, "The Art of Interlace in *Beowulf*," *Studia Neophilologica* 52 (1980): 237–49, among other valuable observations, traces the interlace of the threatened doom by fire of Heorot throughout the poem. (See Chapter Five, note to line 84.) W. F. Bolton, "Boethius and a Topos in *Beowulf*," *Saints, Scholars and Heroes*, edited by Margot King and Wesley Stevens (Collegeville, Minn.: St John's Abbey, 1979), pp. 15–43, feels that the term "interlace" is probably misleading," but he is fundamentally in agreement that the narrative "in generally chronological sequence, is dissynchronized through frequent retrospect, anticipation, and repetition," p. 17. To Leyerle's parallels with the decorative arts I have added a further observation in "Nature in *Beowulf* and Roland," *Approaches to Nature in the Middle Ages*, edited by Lawrence Roberts, Medieval & Renaissance Texts & Studies, vol. 16 (Binghamton, N.Y., 1982), pp. 3–40, especially pp. 3–5.

Chapter Two
Thematic Polarity[1]

The contrapuntal narrative method of *Beowulf* demands close attention to the interweaving of the threads that make up the story of the hero. The narrative moves from puzzles to answers which raise further questions. Thus, the poem begins with the puzzle of Scyld and his succession. Although answers are later given, they leave a mystery to be understood only in the realization that Scyld is an agent of destinal or divine purpose, which man cannot comprehend any more than he can the mystery of death. The function of narrative puzzlement, in short, is thematic.[2]

The epic life of Beowulf unfolds by puzzlement and shadowy recall of the deeds he has done. An ultimate question, however, is not answered. Why does Beowulf, heroically virtuous in death, leave a legacy of worthless gold and a future of unrelieved misery for his people? Although he is the heroic antithesis of Heremod, both leave their people wretched. Why? When Beowulf determines to fight the dragon, why is he filled, not with fear, but with doubt? Why does he have misgivings about transgressing the ancient law when in dying he is aware only of having lived with pious regard to the right uses of the strenth given him for destinal purposes? In short, why does the second part of the poem not move to triumphant affirmation of the glory of Beowulf's heroic death, but rather to lamentation over its waste?

These questions, as with Scyld, can only be answered thematically. The answers to them rest in the meaning that is given to the hero's life, and that meaning is based on the poet's concept of the heroic, which, in turn, must reflect a then-current climate of belief. Thus, it would appear essential to discover what this attitude was, a seemingly impossible task since the date of *Beowulf* has not been determined. It may have been written during the early, missionary stages of Christianity in England when the triumph of the new religion required apology and vigorous defense (seventh century). It may have been written when Christianity was firmly established and English energies were directed, for example, to the conversion of the continental Saxons (eighth century). Finally, it may have been written after the Viking invasions when

English intellectual energies would have been responsive to Scandinavian paganism or, conversely, would have been influenced by Scandinavian Christianity (ninth, tenth, or even eleventh centuries).[3]

All these varying dates, however, belong as a whole to the Christian era when the intellectual life of England was dominated by Augustinian and monastic conceptions and constructs. This temporal-intellectual fact provides the opportunity and governs the attempt to recapture some approximate understanding of the preconceptions of an earlier age, the meta-linguistic imperatives that directed the poet's concept of his hero, Beowulf.

In this attempt to rediscover the territory of the poet's mind, we are like the makers of historical maps who plot the routes of communication of a forgotten past. They cannot use the grid of the modern highway system; rather they must disregard the modern to discover obliterated roads leading to obliterated villages, camouflaged and covered by the modern grid. Once we find the ancient road, however, we are met with the puzzle of a road sign pointing in two opposite directions. One directs us to the paganism of the poem that appears to govern its forms and the motivation of its characters. The other points to the Christianity of the poem. The authenticity of the signpost is attested by contemporary evidence. Thus Alcuin, Charlemagne's English school-master, asks the vital question, "Why Ingeld with Christ?"[4] If Alcuin, in the poet's own monastic era, was troubled, surely the modern scholars who began the serious study of *Beowulf* appeared to be on the right track in assuming the poem to be basically Germanic and pagan, with interpolations designed to allow Ingeld to live more comfortably with Christ; that is, to give the basic paganism of the poem the coloring, if not the substance, of Christianity.

This satisfying direction, however, does not suffice in the face of the most recalcitrant of all facts, the poem itself. For Klaeber long ago observed, and modern scholarship is in agreement, that the pagan and Christian threads of the poem are too intertwined to be disentangled. If the Christian threads were removed from the poem, its unity would be destroyed. Thus it may be that our modern perception of what troubled Alcuin is at fault, for it is likely in the context of the Augustinian theory of literature to which he subscribed that Alcuin was no more disturbed by the juxtaposition itself than he would have been in finding God called Jove in a Latin Christian poem. What he was troubled by was not the juxtaposition, rhetorically permissible, but the need *in a monastery* to fashion Christian truths in poetic guise. Augustine had defended the use of literature as providing nourishment for babies in faith — until they could feed on the sturdy meat of doctrine itself. Alcuin, in turn, would not have questioned the use of pagan fable to inculcate Christian truth in neophytes and worldly men, but he might well have questioned the need of such a pedagogic device for monks who would presumably have been both knowledgeable and otherworldly.

The Christian moralizations of *Beowulf* may appear jarringly anachronistic, tangential to, and incompatible with the basic paganism of its story, language, and motivations. However, such a reaction is modern, a signpost hiding the old Janus-faced one which points in the direction of the intertwined existence of pagan and Christian in the poem. There is a reason for the bivalent sign, and this reason may be sought in the literary evidence of English attitudes toward the heroic.

Since we cannot be sure when the poet lived, it seems best to trace this evidence backwards from that expressed in the late tenth, early eleventh centuries, by Ælfric and in the *Battle of Maldon*. In dealing with Ælfric's conception of the hero, we face the problem that his heroes are saints, in particular the kingly martyrs, Oswald and Edmund.[5] These two are first of all saints, and only thus are heroes: they are examples of perfect living and perfect dying. The clash of swords, the bang of shields are missing in their stories — and the loss is essential. The hero, to be anything like Beowulf, must do battle as did Aeneas, one obvious prototype for the medieval hero.

Of prime importance in the conception of a hero like Aeneas is that he served an inner direction. Aeneas is governed by fate, in the Christian interpretation an emblem of divine providence directing man to his true home, the heavenly Jerusalem. But such a hero is not simply driven; he must himself act, and act heroically. It is only through his personal discovery of the right road, frequently after misdirection, that the operation of the divine plan can be seen. The saint, on the other hand, in his actions too clearly exemplifies the operation of divine providence. The saint's life is a miracle and is punctuated by miracles, the embodied evidence of things unseen. The saint is defined as a manifestation of divine purpose, whereas the hero, however superhuman, lives in a frequently strained relationship between himself as human agent and the larger purpose he must learn to serve. Except where his conversion may be involved, the saint knows his way and is devoid of strain in submitting to the will of God.

Thus Ælfric's saints, though they are heroic, are not Beowulfian heroes simply because they are too exemplary. They are living miracles: not superhuman as Beowulf is, but supra-human. Their battlefields are totally spiritual, and they are divinely, not humanly, motivated. Nothing more clearly illustrates the distinction between saint and hero than Ælfric's two martyred warrior kings. Oswald's reign is punctuated by a pair of heroic battles, his victory over the heathen Cedwalla and his death and defeat at the hands of the apostate Penda. The battles demand heroic treatment; they are the substance of the epic. But Ælfric sees Oswald not as a hero, but as a saint, so that the battles are deliberately slighted in favor of the development of the charity of his reign and of the miracles that followed his death. For example, the story of the sick horse who is cured after it wandered over Oswald's place of death is more developed than are both battles put together.

The first battle is described with startling brevity:

Oswald then raised up a cross to the honor of God before he came to battle and called out to his companions, "Let us kneel before the rood and pray to the Almighty that He protect us against the haughty enemy who wishes to slay us: God himself knows readily that we contend rightfully against this fierce king to protect our people." They all then knelt with Oswald in prayer and afterwards in the early morning went to battle and won the victory as God aided them because of Oswald's faith, and they laid low their enemy, the proud Cedwalla with his great army, he who thought that no army might withstand him.

In essence the battle consists in the raising and worshipping of the cross; the victory is that of God's power and Oswald's faith — no shields are raised, no spears brandished. In the second battle "celebrated" by Ælfric, high heroic tragedy is implicit in the defeat and slaying of Oswald by the apostate Penda. Yet Ælfric, with conscious artistry, erases from the scene all but the motif of Oswald's saintly martyrdom:

It came to pass that Penda waged war on him, Penda the king of the Mercians who had aided Cedwalla at the slaying sometime before of Oswald's kinsman, Edwin the king; and Penda understood nothing about Christ, and all the Mercian people were still unbaptized. They came then to battle at Maserfield and met together until the Christians fell and the heathens approached the holy Oswald. Then he saw the end of his life approach and prayed for his people who there fell in death and commended their souls and himself to God, and thus called out in his dying, "God have mercy on their souls!" Then the heathen king commanded that his head be cut off, and his right arm, and that they be set up as a sign.

Even the background for the action raises Beowulfian expectations of the heroic with the evocation of the motif of vengeance for a kinsman. Ælfric, however, merely notes as a matter of fact that Penda had been allied with Cedwalla when he slew Oswald's kinsman, Edwin. Apparently, the thought of vengeance is as foreign to Oswald as it was natural for Beowulf to consider vengeance as the highest of duties. Ælfric's failure to exploit the possibilities inherent in the motif of vengeance and in the battle is deliberately designed to stress the saintliness of Oswald's character. The organization of Ælfric's account of the battle suggests that he was conscious of the contrast between saintly and heroic ideals, and that he deliberately plays one against the other, counterpointing expectations of the heroic against the actuality of saintly conduct.

The death of Edmund, as Ælfric narrates it, even more clearly exemplifies his conscious disavowal of the heroic and emphasis on the saintly. In the scene, the saintly martyr facing the heathen Hingwar deliberately discards the heroic response to which he is naturally attracted. He rejects it to follow Christ's injunction literally:

> Lo then when Hingwar came, King Edmund stood within his home mindful of the Savior and cast aside his weapons. He wished to imitate the example of Christ who forbade Peter to contend with weapons against the bloodthirsty Jews. Lo the heathens bound and humiliated Edmund shamefully and and beat him with cudgels and then led the confessorking to an earth-rooted tree and tied him thereto with strong bonds and beat him then for a long time with whips; and he always called out between the blows with true faith to the Savior Christ; and the heathens became madly angry because in his faith he called upon Christ for aid. They shot at him then with spears as if in a game until he was all covered with their shafts as if with the bristles of a porcupine, just as Sebastian had been. When Hingwar, the heathen pirate, saw that the noble king would not abandon Christ but with steadfast belief ever called upon Him, he commanded that he be beheaded, and the heathens did so. While still he called upon Christ the heathens drew the saint to slaughter and with one blow cut off his head, and his soul voyaged blessed to Christ.

In this scene Ælfric has Edmund deliberately reject the heroic response, a rejection prepared for earlier by juxtaposing Christian and heroic ideals in the king's mind as he deliberates his response to the invasion. True to the patterns of heroic conduct, the king declares his wish not to survive the death of his dear retainers and continues:

> It was never my custom to turn to flight; for if I must I would readily die for my country, and the Almighty God knows that I will never turn from His worship, nor from His true love, whether I live or die.

The king is motivated both by Christian and by heroic ideals, but at the crisis recognizes that they cannot coexist; he rejects heroic death for triumphant martyrdom in imitation of his Master's unheroic surrender to the enemy. His death, even to the image of the porcupine and the heathen game-playing, is made humiliating to reflect the ignominious victory of Christ's Passion and St. Sebastian's martyrdom. Edmund becomes saint and Christian hero in the act of rejecting the heroic.

Ælfric's awareness of the heroic tradition and his rhetorical use of it for antithesis is anticipated about a century earlier in the Old High German *Ludwigslied*.[6] This poem, written in late 881 or early 882, celebrated the victory of the king of the Franks, Louis, over the Vikings, but the heroic potentials of the subject are realized only as antithesis to the king's Christian triumph through God. The poet concentrates his attention on celebrating Louis as the vicar of God, executing divine purpose. Louis has no personality in the poem except for his relationship to God. The king served God, we are told; indeed when Louis lost his father, God adopted him as His own son, became his foster father. However, for their sins, God visited punishment upon the Franks by permitting the attack of the Vikings, but then called on Louis to defend them: "Louis, my king, help my people." In response Louis gathers his men to face the Northmen; he takes shield and spear, but this heroic gesture is followed by his singing the praise of God. To his saintly battle-cry, his men respond "Kyrie eleison!" The battle begins and victory and honor are immediately awarded to Louis. The potential for the heroic in such a battle is left unrealized except as it provides implicit counterpoint to the tendentiously Christian.

A tradition of rhetorical use of heroic motifs in antithesis to the Christian ideal appears to exist, as is attested by the *Dream of the Rood*, a poem written perhaps as early as the beginning of the eighth century. In it the Cross itself narrates the Crucifixion in terms appropriate to heroic battle:

> I saw mankind's Protector
most manfully hasten   to ascend me;
I did not dare   in disobedience
to bow or crack   though I saw the bounds
of earth trembling;   truly I had the might
to fell these foes   — yet I stood fast.
The young hero prepared   — He was Almighty God —
great and gallant to ascend   the gallow's abject height,
wishing as many watched   magnanimously to free mankind.
Trembling in the Son's clasp   I dared not crouch on the ground
or fall to earth's boundaries   — I had need to stand fast;
erected as a cross   I raised the King
of the heavens above   — I dared not bow.
They pierced me with dark nails;   on me appear the wounds,
the gaping blows of hate   — I dared not hurt them in return.
They besmirched us both;   I was besmeared with the blood
which poured from the Man's side   after he surrendered his soul.

The rhetoric of the passage is complex, involving metaphorical extension, metonymy, oxymoron, and antithesis. For the present purpose, however, what is important is the metaphor of battle, with Christ pictured as a warrior preparing for battle and the Cross as the Lord's retainer, torn between his desire to attack and the compulsion to obedience. The effect of the poet's heroic metaphor is to emphasize the antithesis between the degradation of the crucifixion and the language of heroic battle employed to describe it. His bold rhetoric may be explained as serving the ends of missionary apology. By this hypothesis, the poet would have had the specific intention of engaging the imagination of an audience brought up on heroic poetry and responsive to it, so that they could perceive through the epic diction the higher heroism of the penitential life, the way of the cross.

The heroic, then, would have been employed to celebrate its antithesis, Christian humility. The poet's vision serves as apologia for an ideal in conflict with what was customary in a warrior society. It does so by suggesting that the penitential life has affinities with that of the warrior, who also must suffer privation that he may win triumph and glory; only the definition of what constitutes glory is changed. That is why, in *The Dream of the Rood*, both Christ and Cross appear as soldiers engaged in a conflict with victory as its goal. Like good soldiers, they are absolutely obedient to a command that calls upon them not to strike but to endure, not to be heroic but to be humble. The Cross tells the story of the Crucifixion as if he were a warrior who has had placed upon him a soldierly obligation not to be heroic. In so doing, the Cross reveals the tensions inherent in a warrior society, the ultimate values of which have been put in question by the new dispensation that refutes the heroic ideal by redefining glory, the reward of victory. Thus the Cross yearning for heroic battle is enjoined to the higher fortitude of humble suffering in order to gain Christian glory, the crown of victory in the kingdom of Heaven. This reward the Cross promises to all who forego worldly glory to follow the penitential way to heavenly glory.

The currency of the use of the heroic by antithesis to celebrate its opposite is attested in other poems. In *The Wonder of Creation*, of undetermined date, a striking equation is made between the contemplative (monastic) life and the life of fortitude. By redefinition, it claims for Christian contemplation a virtue which in the heroic warrior's definition was his alone. In *Judith*, perhaps of the ninth century, a battle scene appears celebrating the victory of the Hebrews over the Assyrians. The narrative mode is heroic: the banners move forward; the shields clash at dawn; the carrion wolf and raven are aroused and the eagle sings the battle song; the warriors advance under their shields, discharge arrows, cast spears, draw their swords and attack hand-to-hand. The battle, however, has no part in the Vulgate source, which expressly states that no battle took place, only the threat of attack and the consequent flight of the Assyrians. Thus the battle scene, rendered in the traditional formulaic patterns of heroic verse, involves an extended use of hysteron-proteron, the thematic function of which is to emphasize the presence of God's hand and to establish the spiritual, providential nature of the Hebrew victory. The Hebrew warriors, like Judith, are the agents of God, His executioners, as it were. Again, the heroic serves as emblem of its antithesis, Christian victory through faith.[7]

The battle in *Judith* is very like the symbolic battles between Abraham and the nine kings in *Genesis A*, a poem unquestionably among the earliest in the Old English poetic corpus. The account of the battles is lengthy and is characteristically heroic (lines 1960–2095). The northern kings are at first victorious, so that "many a fearful maiden had trembling to go to a stranger's embrace," and the defenders perish, "sick with wounds." In a second battle,

the kings again attack; "the spears sing, the raven croaks, greedy for prey."
The "battleplay" is hard but the kings "possess the place of slaughter." Abraham
now gathers a small band, symbolically numbering three hundred and eighteen; he comforts his band by declaring his faith that "the Eternal Lord may
easily grant good speed in the spear strife." In the ensuing battle, "Abraham
gave war as a ransom for his nephew [Lot], not the wound gold." Finally,
the army of the kings is left to be torn by the carrion birds. This heroic battle
scene, however, both echoes and was written against standard interpretation
of the Bible, where it was considered to be, as Bede puts it, an emblem of
"a very great miracle of divine power." The numbers of the kings and of
Abraham's band are symbolic, so that the battle is, in its significance, a
psychomachia in which Abraham's victory is "symbolic of the Christian soldier's
victory over worldly temptation."[8] The poet's heroic battle scenes do not
celebrate the memories of heathen poetry; rather by symbolic antithesis they
celebrate the triumph of faith. The intended effect was through the use of traditional heroic idiom by antithesis to affirm Christian doctrine. The figure of
Abraham does not evoke the pagan warrior but rather the ideal of Christian
faith.

Judging from all this literary evidence, which spans the entire period in
which *Beowulf* could have been written, the heroic tradition appears to have
been very much alive, however negatively, in the consciousness of the early
medieval poet and writer.[9] Further, the antithesis between heroic and Christian ideals, it must be assumed, presented a primary social problem. The strain
caused by the coexistence of Christian and pagan traditions in a war-like society
may be shown by two examples, one from the court of Theodoric, the other
from Charlemagne's court. Theodoric's successor, Athalaric, under the influence of his mother, was given clerical training in the arts. This effort,
however, was successfully resisted by the unreconstructed nobility who considered such clerkly instruction to be opposed, as Reto Bezzola puts it, "to
the spirit of the Ostrogoths." It was not an education, they argued, suitable
to "a young king of their race destined for a warrior and heroic career." In
short, Christianity was for priests and women, the heroic was for the warrior. The second example comes from a poem by Theodulf, a clerk and poet
in Charlemagne's court. He tells how his verses pleased the court except for
a certain "Wibrodus heros." He, as Bezzola summarizes, "shook his huge head
in a menacing and ferocious manner," until Charlemagne himself was forced
to stop him. The strain evident early in Theodoric's court remains in
Charlemagne's court in the ninth century in the confrontation between the
clerk and the warrior, so significantly termed "heros."[10]

The conflict of ideals would also have presented a basic problem to Christian writers in England from the time of the Conversion until after the Viking
invasions. After the Conversion they faced the dilemma of teaching Christianity to an audience brought up with, or vividly remembering, the heroic

poetry of their pagan ancestors. Thus we hear of Aldhelm in the seventh century, according to William of Malmesbury, composing secular verses in the accustomed manner, but with the purpose of leading his listeners to doctrinal truth "by interweaving among foolish things, the words of Scripture."[11] In the ninth century, Alcuin, it will be recalled, was aware of the commonplace interweaving of Ingeld with Christ. After the Viking incursions, the English poet, by definition Christian and probably monastic, would have written for a society facing the pagan Vikings whose attack upon Christendom required both prayer and, more importantly, a heroic, warrior-like response. It would have been the task of the poet somehow to reconcile the two ideals of the heroic and the Christian, not merely to use the heroic to serve by rhetorical antithesis as metaphor for penitential fortitude. This is the task, of the poet of *The Battle of Maldon*, and it was also that of the poet of *Beowulf*, as will be argued, whether he wrote at the same time as *The Dream of the Rood* or much later.

The problem these poets faced cannot be glossed over by hypothesizing the side-by-side existence of two cultures, that of the warrior and that of the clerk, in which the heroic poem is simply covered with a veneer of Christian moralization.[12] There may have been in fact a division in society, but the poetry that remains to us is inevitably the product of clerks, that is to say, at that time of monks. Yet, though the poetry is monastic, the heroic in *Maldon* and in *Beowulf* cannot be explained away simply as rhetorical manipulation, as is true of *The Dream of the Rood*. The heroic in the two poems under question cannot be transformed into Christian statement, for example, by allegorization.[13] Rather, the poets were trying, according to my hypothesis, to effect a reconciliation, trying to bring together the split halves of their society. These were great poets writing about what was most profoundly important in their own times; there could have been nothing more important for them than to deal with the meaning of the Christian soldier in actuality, not merely metaphorically. The dilemma they faced is clear: the only valid life was that led in the *imitatio Christi*, yet meek surrender to the heathen could not have been contemplated in the actual world. Ælfric was aware of the dilemma and offered a traditional solution: that military (heroic) action with the intention of humble service to Christendom is justified. Thus, in commenting on his metrical version of the biblical Judith, he cites her both as an example of the triumph of humility and as "an example to you men that you with weapons should protect your land against the attacking enemy."[14] One way or another the Christian writers of *Maldon* and *Beowulf* were dealing with the problem of the relation between the parts of the equation, Christian and heroic.

The *Battle of Maldon* is a Christian poem of monastic provenance. In the traditional manner, it narrates a battle in which the English, led by the pious yet heroic Byrhthnoth, were defeated by the heathen Vikings.[15] Two matters are of special interest in the attempt to discover how the poet conceived of

the heroic in Byrhthnoth's conduct of the battle. First of all, it should be clear
that *Maldon* is a poem, not an historical account to be judged by the principles of accurate representation. In all likelihood, the poet felt free to take
what might be called poetic license with the accounts of the battle which he
had heard. At any rate, he contrives his narrative so that the death of the
hero, Byrhthnoth, appears not as the climax but as the center of his poem,
as in Ælfric's homilies on Oswald and Edmund. The first half of *Maldon* leads
up to his death; the last part narrates the treachery of some of Byrhthnoth's
followers and the faithfulness to death of the remainder. In consequence, the
poem appears to enclose, to set off Byrhthnoth's dying speech:

> I give Thee thanks,   God of nations,
> for my well-being   here in the world;
> now my greatest need,   Gracious Lord,
> is that You grant   this grace to me
> that now my soul   may ascend to Thee,
> Ruler of angels,   and into your realm
> may come in peace;   upon Thee I call
> to hold it safe   from the devils of hell.

His speech is Edmund-like. He is a martyr turning to God in the full expectation of protection from devils and of eternal life because he is dying in battle against human devils, the Vikings. Yet, as the poet has made clear earlier,
Byrhthnoth's own heroic actions contribute in a decisive way to his defeat and
death and that of his men, when he recklessly abandons the advantageous
position he holds at the ford. Out of heroic pride, *for his ofermode*, Byrhthnoth
agrees to permit the Vikings to mass their forces on the shore instead of having to cross the ford singly. Then he taunts them and tempts God:[16]

> Room has been made;   now speed you men
> to give us battle   — God alone knows
> who will be the victor   on the battle-field

Byrhthnoth's action and his speech are governed by an heroic ideal of warrior
conduct; in sharpest contrast, his death is pictured as that of a Christian martyr. The antithesis the poet establishes is similar to that found in *The Dream
of the Rood* and Ælfric's homilies, but with a crucial difference. Here the antithesis is embodied in a single Christian hero, Byrhthnoth. Apparently the
poet must have felt that in his portrait of Byrhthnoth he had achieved a reconciliation of the antithetical halves of his character. Relying upon a shared climate
of belief, he found no need for explanation, so that his reconciliation of the
Christian and the heroic must be examined to provide some clue to the concept of the Christian hero that he and his audience held.

Byrhthnoth's heroic recklessness in permitting the Vikings to fight on equal
terms may be likened to that of Beowulf's in determining to battle Grendel

on even terms by abandoning his sword and armor. Such conduct, however, though it may be appropriate to a pagan hero, seems ill-suited to the character of a Christian hero. The poet is aware of this in equating his heroism with pride, *ofermode*, the sin of Satan who is also given heroic stature in two poems, *Genesis* and *Christ and Satan*. At the same time, however, the poet appears to accept Byrhthnoth's heroic pride as an essential characteristic, in this case, not of a satanic heathen but of a pious Christian warrior. Byrhthnoth's decision to follow heroic precepts in giving away his advantage on the battlefield, accompanied by an heroic boast (*beot*), does not represent a sudden change, but is of a piece with his earlier defiant reply to the Viking messenger's demand for tribute. Here in epic formulas he reveals his heroic resolve (*anræd*):

> Seaman do you hear   what this people say?
> They willingly give   a gift of spears
> to you in battle   and profitless booty
> of poisoned point   of patrimonial sword.
> Viking messenger,   bring to your men
> a loathsome tale   in the telling:
> here in loyalty   a leader with his troop
> stands to keep safe   his native soil,
> the land of his king,   Lord Æthelred's
> fields and his folk.   The heathens shall fall
> in battle here;   it seems to me base
> that without battle   you board your ships
> with our treasure   now you have traveled
> the long way here   into our land.
> Without trouble   you'll not gain treasure;
> the point and the edge   will be our appeasement,
> rough battle-play   before we pay tribute.

The heroic resolve of this speech anticipates the heroic pride involved in his giving fighting room to the heathen enemy. In heeding an heroic imperative he becomes responsible for disaster, so that in Byrhthnoth's heroism lies something akin to the tragic flaw. Conversely, he appears also to be governed by faith and Christian piety, as in his thanks to God for victory in his first skirmishes after he had drawn back to give the Vikings room:

> The doughty earl
> was happy and laughed,   gave thanks to heaven
> for the day's labor   the Lord gave him.

As his boast to the Viking messenger leads to his fatal heroic action, this speech of Christian thanksgiving, revealing the steadfastness of his Christian faith and purpose, leads to his dying speech in which as a martyr he expresses his hope of salvation.

In *Maldon*, Christian and heroic exist as antitheses, yet are reconciled in Byrhthnoth. His death as a martyr apparently absolves, for the poet, the fatal flaw of pride in his obeying the dictates of heroic conduct. The poet's line of reasoning is not difficult to follow because it flows from the rudimenatry Christian doctrine of grace. The heroic is human, thus part of man's estate, the result of original sin. But the heroic in Byrhthnoth, the taint of fallen humanity, is absolved because it has been placed in the service of the Faith, and, through grace, becomes good work. In his heroic bravado he falls, but in his death he imitates Christ and becomes a martyr. Because Byrhthnoth's martyrdom is an emblem of Christ's death, it shares in the mystery of grace by which erring humanity is reconciled with God. In the Christian interpretation of the *Aeneid*, the hero serves a divine purpose which he does not recognize; Byrhthnoth in *Maldon*, though flawed by his heroic recklessness, serves God's purpose, which he recognizes. Byrhthnoth's human heroism leads to defeat, but his heroic effort serves Christendom, so that his defeat reveals a high, providential purpose by providing a Christian example of a warrior's holy dying.

Implicit in the poem is the recognition that the human condition requires men to do battle. Such men are likely to be self-reliant, proud of their valor and, in their fallen humanity, heroic. The hero *qua* hero is without grace; his heroism, however, may be redeemed by its service to Christendom, and he may thus achieve the status of the saint through grace, right faith and holy dying. The concept is analogous to that of the *felix culpa*, the sin which through providence becomes the happy redemption. Though the dictates of the heroic lead to the sin of self-reliant pride, the heroic may be transformed in obedience to divine will. The act of doing battle with heathens in the defense of Christendom partakes of the penitential, and if death follows from the act it becomes martyrdom which exculpates the sinfulness of heroic conduct. Thus the battle for the Faith and the martyr's death transform heroic conduct into a model of salvation,and Byrhthnoth's folly is reconciled with his Christian life.

This concept provides an adequate explanation for the heroic in Byrhthnoth but may be of less value in explaining Beowulf, a pagan for whom the heroic imperatives are the essential motivations of his conduct. It is tempting to solve this difficutly by resort to the notion that *Beowulf* essentially conveys a pagan heroic ethic which cannot be explained by recourse to the concept of the Christian hero. In such a view the Christian, as merely external coloring, cannot lead to the heart of the poem. Such a solution will not suffice, however, because the Christianity of *Beowulf* has been shown to be an essential part of its form and structure, although its subject and the motivations of its characters are pagan. It would be naive to assume that the poet was not aware of the paganism of his hero and of his society. It would be equally naive to assume that he would have celebrated a society which lacked the knowledge of the truths of Christianity.[17] The values of such a society, lacking in the saving grace of the theological virtues, he would have deplored.

However, even if a pagan hero were blessed with piety and the cardinal virtues, he could not thereby attain the status of Christian hero, which involves the possession of the three theological virtues of Faith, Hope and Charity. Like Aeneas, the pagan hero in Christian interpretation, may reveal the way in which providential design makes use of the hero, or may even typify the Christian search for the heavenly home.[18] Nonetheless the pagan hero remains a pagan, blind himself to the real meaning of his life. Christian doctrine alone provides the key to such meaning; in and for themselves the epic adventures of a pagan hero can only reveal his limitations and those of his society, for he, without faith, is a blind man leading the blind. Yet this very antithesis between the Christian and pagan understanding of the epic hero provides an hypothesis for the understanding of how *Beowulf* was intended to be read by its Christian audience. The hypothesis assumes that the fictional world of *Beowulf* is pagan, its point of view Christian. From the Christian point of view, the pagan events of the poem reveal the limits of heathen society, the limits of the righteous pagan, and the limits of the heroic ideal.[19] Such Christian revelation is the primary thematic function of the poem.

This hypothesis serves to explain much that is otherwise puzzling in the poem: for one major example, its descending line of mood and action, so that the omens of disaster in the first half of the poem are fulfilled and completed in the last half. After Beowulf returns home and gives his account of his exploits in Denmark, there is a scene of joyous, prosperous amity jarringly concluded without interruption by the twenty-line narrative of ensuing disasters leading to Beowulf's reign, which culminates in the coming of the dragon. Amidst forebodings of disaster, Beowulf decides to revenge the dragon's onslaught and gain the treasure. His mind, however, is darkened by ethical doubt and is filled with memories of past battles. He recalls the tangled net of Higelac's adventures and the internecine Swedish wars in which he became involved. Finally, he recalls the death in grief of ancient Hrethel, fatally unable to solve the dilemma to which his heroic ethic could give no answer: his duty to avenge his son; his duty not to be guilty of the death of his son. In the battle, Beowulf is fatally wounded and averts defeat only through the aid of Wiglaf. In his dying speech, Beowulf places his hope for the future upon the gold he has won. His speech, as he gazes upon the gold, recalls in counterpoint the lament of the last survivor as he looked on the useless treasure he was about to bury, a counterpoint of doom and disaster which dominates the last part of the poem. After Beowulf's death the mood is further darkened, not so much by grief over his passing as by forebodings of impending doom. The messenger retells the story of Higelac's fatal raid and of the deadly Swedish wars, not to celebrate the hero, but to foretell the disastrous legacy of lordless grief, suffering, and exile that Beowulf will leave to his people.

Further underscoring the dismal view of his death is the contrast between youthful Wiglaf and aged Beowulf. Wiglaf recalls the young Beowulf in Denmark as, concomitantly, Beowulf recalls the aged Hrothgar. Hrothgar, with his self-deceiving trust in the security provided by his power to reward through treasure, has his counterpart in Beowulf, with his equally self-deceiving trust in the security provided his nation by the dragon's treasure. Wiglaf, however, is not the exact counterpart of the young Beowulf. If he were, he would be expected to lighten the oppressive gloom in providing some hope for the future. Such expectation the poet takes pains not to fulfill. Beowulf transfers his kingship to Wiglaf who has proved his heroic quality, but Wiglaf does not respond with the assurance of the young Beowulf. He provides no expected show of determination to emulate his dead hero-king; rather he shares completely in the messenger's sense of inevitable disaster. He refuses to share Beowulf's trust in the dragon's treasure, but agrees that it should again be buried to remain as worthless as it was before. Further, he openly declares that Beowulf's encounter with the dragon was the result of a doomed, reckless heroism, a recklessness which will have the ruin of his people as a consequence. Wiglaf's grief is understandable; the failure of his will to succeed is not. The hope implicit in his heroic youth is not realized. Because he considers Beowulf's death only as a disaster brought about through heroic pride, and because he has no apparent hope for the future, Wiglaf reveals the ineffectual emptiness of his society, the failure of its ideal hero and of the heroic. Far from lightening the darkness, Wiglaf's bright, heroic youth intensifies it. From the cycle of trust in treasure and the heroic response there is no escape. *Beowulf* does not end in tragic celebration of the hero but in lament over the doomed waste of his youth and valor.

The heroic in *Maldon* is represented as a tragic flaw which precipitates disaster but leads through the mystery of the *felix culpa* to the good of redemption through martyrdom. Byrhthnoth's death is the tragic cause for celebration; Beowulf's is not. The heroic in *Beowulf* is self-contained; it is the ethos of a culture, of the heroic past as the poet envisioned it; it must be self-justified because it cannot, as in *Maldon*, appeal to redeeming grace. That is why the last words about Beowulf are about his search for glory, the empty ideal of a pagan, heroic world. To the contrary, the poet's attitude toward the heroic ethos and its goal of glory is Christian and critical.[20] That is why the direction of the poem is inevitably toward doom and disaster unrelieved by any sense of hope and redemption. Beowulf's flaw is tragic precisely because there are no means available to him by which the flaw may be redeemed. Thus his tragedy rests in his inability to rise above the ethos of his society, the mores of revenge and war which govern his actions. In the first part of the poem, in contrast to the aged and ineffectual Hrothgar and to the vigorously evil Heremod, Beowulf appears as a savior, a cleanser of evil; in the last part, Beowulf appears to echo and reflect not beginnings but endings. He has become involved in his world and in the ethos of the feud. Though he remains heroic, his heroism is no more effective than is Hrothgar's helplessness. Like Hrothgar he looks toward the past, as does also the last survivor, lamenting the glory that is gone.

The hero's role, as with Aeneas, is to be an agent of fate, that is, Divine Providence in Christian understanding. The beginning of *Beowulf* introduces the theme of agency in the figure of Scyld who appears mysteriously to succor the Danes and disappears in death into the unknown. His mystery is that of the agent of God by whom he has been sent, though a pagan, to alleviate pagan suffering. Yet, in counterpoint to this Christian understanding of his role is that of his pagan followers who see in him only the mystery of his coming and of his leaving. That is to say, Scyld's pagan followers reveal the limitations of their paganism, the limitations of an understanding lacking the truth of faith.

Beowulf, thus introduced, is also an agent of God, as is seen most clearly in his battles against Grendel and particularly against the mother whom he slays with a giant sword to which he is divinely guided.[21] Beowulf brings back the hilt of this sword upon which is recorded the biblical tale of the downfall of the giants, the race of Cain. One effect of the story is to cast Beowulf in the role of God's avenger who eradicates a residue of Cain's generation of monsters. In turn, Hrothgar, gazing on the hilt, is inspired to utter a homily which reaches to the edges of Christian truth. The homily provides a warning to Beowulf against heroic self-reliance whereby his subsequent actions may be judged.[22] Beowulf's own judgment of himself is clouded. On the one hand, when he determines to attack the dragon he is concerned about having violated the old law; on the other hand, in dying he finds comfort in knowing that he has not violated the code by which he has lived. His wavering between moral doubt and certainty results from his being both righteous and pagan. He strives for the truth but cannot escape from the necessary error of all who are without the grace of knowing through faith. Beowulf's striving for righteousness is blocked by the very ethical code which he has piously observed. He cannot understand his feeling that he has transgressed against the old law because he does not know the new law. He has no referent for righteousness except the heroic code, which has revenge as its most sacred obligation, glory and gold as its ultimate reward.[23] The futility of such a code is made evident in Hrethel's fatal ethical dilemma. From the Christian perspective, to seek revenge is sinful error; thus Hrethel, who accepts revenge as ethical obligation, cannot solve his dilemma because he seeks to find his answer in a false faith.

How Beowulf is himself caught in the iron circle of heroic error is evidenced in his inward determination to avenge the death of his nephew, Heardred, Higelac's son, by securing the death of his slayer, Onela, the Swedish king, who had entrusted Beowulf with the Geatish throne, presumably after appropriate swearing of oaths. Beowulf, however, does not perceive that his secret determination to betray Onela is dishonorable because he feels he is being morally obedient to the sacred and paramount duty of revenge.[24] This appears from his dying assertion that he has not dishonored himself with false oaths. Finally, his reasons for attacking the dragon flow from his allegiance to a false moral ideal. He need not have sought revenge; the dragon would have remained in his barrow unless he were again disturbed. For the hero, however, who strives for the ultimate goal of such abiding glory as Sigemund had attained, revenge is an absolute imperative which takes no count of practicalities. Further, the attack on the dragon holds the promise of another ultimate reward, the treasure, visible evidence of glory. In short, as Wiglaf puts it, Beowulf is driven by "relentless doom" because of his own will he seeks the two goals of worldly men living in error, glory and its visible sign, gold. He is doomed because his will now serves a faulty human end.[25] Before, in Denmark, he served as agent of a merciful design, though without understanding; now as king he serves only himself by seeking a heroic goal. In pursuing gold and glory Beowulf becomes the victim of fate because he has accepted the error of his society, and has lost his youthful role as agent of providence.

Thus the final action of the poem takes place not providentially but fatalistically. This fatalism reveals that Beowulf, governed by the law of revenge, is self-doomed, and it reveals the futility of a society not governed and directed by the goal of salvation. The movement of the poem is downward toward a fatally tragic end. Beowulf and the dragon are the victims, the first in seeking the gold, the other in keeping it, and Beowulf's doomed descent is that of all who lack saving grace. The poem ends, to be sure, with Beowulf's people celebrating him as the mildest of kings and the most worthy of praise. He is worthy of praise, however, as the last words of the poem reveal, because he was "most eager for glory." That is, they praise him in terms that would befit any good pagan hero and apply equally well to Aeneas, to Hector, to Odysseus. Their praise is defined by purely human limitations and specifically lacks any of the Christian overtones of *Maldon*. For in direct contrast to Byrhthnoth, Beowulf in dying reveals no movement toward redemption. His death is completely unlike that of the Christian hero because it lacks the sense of revealed understanding suggested by Byrhthnoth's dying plea that his soul be brought home safely to his God.

Beowulf ends with the death and burial of the hero, which is precisely what might be expected in heroic epic, except that no sense of triumph is imparted.[26] The oddity is in the *Battle of Maldon* where the death of the hero comes at the center of the poem, with the result that his death is not the main point toward which the poem is leading. Rather his death serves to reveal the fulfillment of God's design, of which the hero's death is but part. The real point of *Maldon* does not rest in the battlefield death. Conversely, the death of the hero *is* the point of *Beowulf*. The first part of the poem reveals and celebrates the workings of God's hand; the death of the hero reveals the emptiness of Beowulf's heroic life when it serves the hero's own ends of glory rather than God's purpose. His death suggests that the heroic ideal is ineffectual and futile, that its supreme embodiment in a Beowulf or an Aeneas lacks any real dignity when compared with the ideal of the Christian as embodied in Byrhthnoth who serves the Lord in faith. In this implicit contrast, the tragic implications of *Beowulf* may most clearly be realized; its pathos rests in the irony of its conclusion where the Geats celebrate a hero who has left them literally nothing but the legacy of debts to be collected.

To conclude, for the author of *Beowulf* and his audience there can be but one ultimate hero, and he is Christ. Whatever is truly heroic comes from the imitation of Him, and the saint is the true hero. St. Edmund imitated Christ truly and is the saintly hero and martyr. Byrhthnoth is a hero who follows Christ and in so doing redeems that which is merely heroic within him. Beowulf is a hero who lacks Christ and reveals that the heroic in itself is an empty ideal. The contrast suggests the obvious, that *Beowulf* may have served as Christian apologetic, revealing the error of the ancestral way of the English, however eager for glory it was, and, in contrast, suggesting the truth and validity of Christian faith. Thus a central thematic function of *Beowulf* as Christian apologetic is, through the tragedy of its great and virtuous heathen hero, to promote by antithesis the concept of the Christian hero, true to himself in being true to Christ in seeking not glory but salvation. In the poet's intention the hero to emulate is not a Beowulf but a Byrhthnoth.

Notes

1. This chapter has been developed from a paper delivered in 1970 at the Fourth Annual Conference of the Center for Medieval and Early Renaissance Studies, Binghamton, N.Y. which appears in *Concepts of the Hero in the Middle Ages and Renaissance*, edited by Norman Burns and Christopher Reagan (Albany: State University of New York Press, 1975), pp. 1–26. Documentation has been up-dated through 1980 and less exhaustively through 1981.

2. W. F. Bolton, "Boethius and a Topos in Beowulf" (see Chapter One, note 2), illustrates the thematic role of what I have termed "polarity" by examination of the Boethian "topos, 'one of two things,' " showing how for the hero "while the topos expresses a static view, the view is increasingly in error about the situation it observes and summarizes.... The pervasive dualism of Beowulf schematizes the conflicts that lie at the surface of the narrative.... Tragedy, accordingly, is not reversal of fortune but rather commitment to Fortune's sphere.... Beowulf's thrice repeated 'one of two things' predictions in the alternative-fatal mode just before each of his three great fights express his grasp of his role in the world. The poet's concern is not with this world, however, but with man's understanding of it;

epistemology is the central concern of *Beowulf,* and in this lie both its basic structure and close affinities with the *Consolation,*" pp. 16 ff. J. D. A. Ogilvy, "Beowulf, Alfred, and Christianity," *Saints, Scholars and Heroes* (see Chapter One, note 2), observes the polarity and concludes that the poet "may have regarded Beowulf as a good pagan, like Dante's Vergil. At any rate, being a good Christian himself, he endowed Beowulf with such Christian virtues as were compatible with the heroic code. When Christian virtue and the code diverged, however — as in the matter of vengeance or of worldly fame — the Christian view came out a poor second (p. 64). Ogilvy is misled, I believe, by his failure to distinguish between the poet's attitude and that of his narrator and his characters. As Joseph Baird, "Unferth the Thyle," *Medium Aevum* 39 (1970): 1-7, cogently observes, "The presence of conscious paganism in a poem has nothing to do with whether or not it is the work of a Christian poet"; rather it is "the *attitude* which he evinces toward this pagan subject matter." *Beowulf,* indeed, splendidly exemplifies the heroic, but it is precisely the heroic which is being examined and found wanting on its own terms.

Barbara Raw, *The Art and Background of Old English Poetry* (New York: St. Martin's Press, 1978), observes the polarity but superimposes on it a modern point-of-view, coming to a somewhat anti-climatic view: "Heroism may be a glorious thing in poetry, but in real life it is seen to lead to nothing but misery. Moreover, by juxtaposing the mythical Beowulf, a type of the heroic ideal, with the real-life events of the digressions, the poet has shown the ideal for what it is: something splendid but impractical," p. 96.

Adelaide Hardy, "Historical Perspective and the 'Beowulf-poet,'" *Neophilologus* 63 (1979): 430-49, from an historical perspective attempts an impossible reconciliation of the antitheses: "Through his hero the poet shows that faith in the Ruler of Man has immeasurable value because it inspires the esteemed Germanic ideal of absolute courage and loyalty," 439. To consider that faith is justified by its reconciliation with the heroic is to posit a "historical perspective" which is closer by far to that of "ethical culture" than it is to either Germanic paganism (whatever that may have been) or Augustinian Christianity (whose limits of tolerance are not elastic). Only a resolute modernism could think of a Christian poet finding ultimate value in the ideal of the *comitatus.* It is such a view which leads to her conclusion: "The *Beowulf*-poet has accepted the challenge of conveying in formulaic verse the tension between old and new religions, evoking at the same time continuity through the complex theme of the *comitatus*—a court which is superficially noble, yet essentially ignoble, a vision of the human condition in which men enjoy the warmth and security of close-knit fellowship, yet are essentially alone in their freedom to choose alliance with a God they cannot see or touch" (pp. 445-46). This eloquent and perceptive conclusion cannot fail to evoke a responsive modern reaction; unfortunately, from the perspective of intellectual history, it is simply heretical and no part of an Augustinian frame of reference. A good corrective to Hardy's view is Anne Payne's "The Dane's Prayer to the 'gastbona' in *Beowulf,*" *Neuphilologische Mitteilungen* 80 (1979), which provides the right historical perspective on the poet's universality in observing that in his employment of the Christian-heathen polarity, he makes his audience aware that Christianity provides an antidote to the heroic, not a total cure, since man is always liable to mistake the values of the world for those of reality: "The poet was consciously drawing on the Christian-heathen dichotomy for a convenient metaphor to describe a state of mind which he found perpetually possible, perpetually destructive to his own society as well as to the heroic society he writes about" (pp. 508-9). W. F. Bolton, *Alcuin and Beowulf* (New Brunswick, N.J.: Rutgers University Press, 1975), also provides a salutary reminder of what must be borne in mind when assessing the Christian poet's viewpoint on heroic virtue. "Beowulf has virtue, but virtues alone do not make a Christian; on the contrary, Alcuin insists, what makes a Christian — and hence saves a soul — is baptism and faith" (p. 155). Marijane Osborn, "The Great Feud: Scriptural History and Strife in *Beowulf,*" *PMLA* 93 (1978): 973-98, argues cogently for the need to maintain "two separate frames of reference" (p. 980), that is, the heroic against Augustine's two worlds.

Finally, it should be noted that J. R. R. Tolkien, "*Beowulf*: the Monsters and the Critics," *Proceedings of the British Academy* 22 (1936): 245–95, marks the beginning of the serious study of the thematics of *Beowulf*, and that Dorothy Whitelock, *The Audience of Beowulf* (Oxford: the Clarendon Press, 1951), has laid the groundwork for our understanding of the intellectual milieu in which the poet wrote.

3. For citations see Douglas Short's bibliography (Chapter One, note 1.) The parameters are given recent illustration. Louise Wright, "*Merewioingas* and the Dating of *Beowulf*: a Reconsideration," *Nottingham Medieval Studies* 42 (1980): 1–6, argues that the word gives a *terminus a quo* of possibly 751, but more likely early 800. Norman Blake, "The Dating of Old English Poetry," *An English Miscellany Presented to W. S. Mackie*, edited by Brian Lee (Cape Town: Oxford University Press, 1977), pp. 14–27, argues for a date in the Alfredian period, and Nicolas Jacob, "Anglo-Danish Relations: Poetic Archaisms and the Date of *Beowulf*: a Reconsideration of the Evidence," *Poetica* 8 (Tokyo, 1977): 23–43, also argues for the ninth century. In two recent books, which I have not had the opportunity to consult, the dating of *Beowulf* has been reconsidered: Kevin S. Kiernan, *Beowulf and the Beowulf Manuscript* (New Brunswick: Rutgers University Press, 1981) has apparently presented a vigorously-argued dating of the poem in the eleventh century, but we are best advised to consider the matter as still open, a conclusion which folllows from the collection of essays by various hands, *The Dating of Beowulf*, edited by Colin Chase (Toronto: University of Toronto Press, 1981). In the light of what I have found in Ælfric, Kiernan's dating would suit admirably my thesis that the poet's intellectual milieu is Augustinian, but is not essential to it since, early or late, the viewpoint is traditional and is based on an unchanging theological point of reference. Whatever the immediate context of the poet's own time may be, he remains within the parameters of the Christian view. Kiernan appears also to have presented important observations on the structure of *Beowulf* which, unfortunately must be left for later consideration in the detail they deserve.

4. *Monumenta Alcuina*, edited by Wattenbach and Duemmler (Berlin, 1873), p. 357.

5. Both lives are edited by G. I. Needham, *Lives of Three English Saints* (New York: Methuen, 1966). Translations are my own except where indicated.

6. *Ludwigslied*, edited by T. Schauffer in *Althochdeutsche Litteratur*, 2nd edition (Leipzig, 1900), pp. 119–23.

7. For *The Dream of the Rood, Wonder of Creation* and *Judith* see my *Web of Words* (Albany: State University of New York Press, 1970), pp. 85–88, 103–4, 173–78.

8. See my *Doctrine and Poetry* (Albany: State University of New York Press, 1959): 195–200; 237–38.

9. *Widsith, Deor* and *Beowulf* themselves testify, for example to the lively survival of the "heroic" literary conventions.

10. Reto Bezzola, *Les Origines et la Formation de la Litterature Courtoise en Occident*, Part I (Paris: Champion, 1958), pp. 19–21 and 98.

11. William of Malmesbury, *Gesta Pontificum Anglorum*, Vol. 5, edited by N. Hamilton (London, 1870), p. 38.

12. Just such an attempt is apparently made by Jon Kasik, "The Use of the Term 'Wyrd' in 'Beowulf,' " *Neophilologus* 63 (1979): 128–35. He concludes that his "analysis shows that the *Beowulf*-poet used the term 'Wyrd' in neither a purely pagan nor a purely Christian sense" (p. 132). Although he does examine each example of 'wyrd' in the poem, his conclusion results from the primary critical error of failing to distinguish between a character's use of the term and the author's. Further, he totally ignores the background of intellectual history which must undergird any attempt at semantic analysis. For a somewhat similar

attempt, see Adelaide Hardy, note 5 above, and Robert L. Kindrick, "Germanic *Sapientia* and the Heroic Ethos of *Beowulf*," *Medievalia et Humanistica* 10 (1981): 1–17, who concludes that *Beowulf* "represents a genuine advancement in the development of social consciousness" (p. 14), a comfortable conclusion whatever it may mean. Robert Levine, "Ingeld and Christ: a Medieval Problem," *Viator* 2 (1971): 105–28, solved the problem *ignotum per obscurum* by finding a "compassable ambiguity" (p. 117).

13. M. B. McNamee, "*Beowulf* — an Allegory of Salvation," *Journal of English and Germanic Philology* 59 (1960): 190–207, demonstrates that almost anything can be allegorized, but that it is another matter to show that *Beowulf* is actually allegorical. Charles Donahue, "*Beowulf* and Christian Doctrine: a Reconsideration from a Celtic Stance." *Traditio* 27 (1965): 55–116, although denying that allegory is involved (p. 116), would, however, make Beowulf a kind of type of Christ. His argument fails in not taking into account the downward movement of the poem. For an important study of typology in *Beowulf*, see Margaret Goldsmith, *The Mode and Meaning of Beowulf* (London: Athlone Press, 1970). John Halverson, "*Beowulf* and the Pitfalls of Piety," *The University of Toronto Quarterly* 35 (1965-66): 260–78, with a certain amount of gleeful accuracy smashes the arguments for transforming *Beowulf* through allegory, significantly concluding against "an optimistic view of what happens in *Beowulf*," that "its power ... lies precisely in the fact that it represents a world without salvation" (p. 277). Curiously, however, he also considers that it is tragic because it is not Christian, failing again to distinguish the poet from his story.

To conclude, *Beowulf* is not Christian allegory, but this is not to deny what Margaret Goldsmith and recently Sylvia Horowitz, "Beowulf, Samson, David and Christ," *Studies in Medieval Culture* 12 (1978): 17–23, have demonstrated — that biblical typology exists in *Beowulf*. A distinction must be kept in mind, however, as Sylvia Horowitz makes clear in her conclusion that "in Beowulf we have a post-Christ figure who symbolizes Christ in the way that Samson and David did" (p. 22). David and Christ may be typologically similar in being agents of God, but David, through grace, may prefigure Christ; Beowulf cannot. He can, with reservations, symbolize David and through him Christ. Because he is outside grace, a basic limitation is in effect, and when he ceases to act as God's agent, he ceases to typify David. He is the dark mirror in which is reflected both of Augustine's cities; as God's agent in Denmark he typifies the citizen of Jerusalem, as heroic warrior facing the dragon he typifies the citizen of Babylon.

14. *Web of Words*, p. 146. Ælfric's adjuration is based on traditional view, for a summary of which see my "The Concept of the Hero," (note 1 above), pp. 24–25, note 10.

15. *The Battle of Maldon*, edited by Eric Gordon (New York: Methuen, 1966).

16. As Morton Bloomfield, "Beowulf, Byrthnoth, and the Judgment of God: Trial by Combat in Anglo-Saxon England," *Speculum* 44 (1969): 547–48, observed. George Clark, "The Hero of *Maldon*: Vir Pius et Strenuus," *Speculum* 44 (1979): 257–82, unconvincingly attempts to show that Byrhthnoth's decision to let the Vikings cross was sensible and thus that Byrhthnoth is an unsullied hero. It should be observed, however, that for the poet, Byrhthnoth was not less a hero because of his heroic pride, which is, indeed, essential to his being an heroic figure. But in finding him a true hero, he does not exonerate him from the Christian condemnation of the heroic ethic; from this he is exonerated through the operation of grace and his conscious service of God. Fred Robinson, "God, Death, and Loyalty in the *Battle of Maldon*," *J. R. R. Tolkien, Scholar and Story Teller*, edited by Mary Salu and Robert Farrell (Ithaca: Cornell University Press, 1979), pp. 64–75, provides a convenient review of the controversy. He correctly observes "that Maldon was written out of a culture whose fundamental assumptions about God and death were incompatible with a heroic sense of life" (p. 77), but places the reconciliation of Christianity and the heroic (that is, the poet's universality), upon the pivot of the loyalty of Byrhthnoth's doomed men. This appears to me to miss the point of what is argued here and earlier in "Concepts,"

(see note 1 above) of which he has not taken note.

17. This represents, in essence, the view of Patrick Wormald, "Bede, *Beowulf* and the Conversion of the Anglo-Saxon Aristocracy," *Bede and Anglo-Saxon England*, edited by Robert Farrell (Oxford: British Archaeology Reports, 1978), pp. 32–95. He finds that "the early English Church was, in a sense, dominated by aristocratic values," so that "the coming of Christianity displaced the old Gods, and diverted traditional values into new postures, but it did not change these values" (p. 67). He further considers that the dualism of Christianity and paganism "springs from a fundamental tension within the poet's soul" (p. 67). Tension, however, is not reconciliation of discordant views of value; such reconciliation can be found only in the concept of martyrdom.

18. See *Doctrine and Poetry* (note 8 above), pp. 28–29, 66–67. John Gardner, "Fulgentius' 'Expositio Vergiliana Continentia' and the Plan of *Beowulf*: an Approach to the Poem's Style and Structure," *Papers on Language and Literature* 6 (1970): 227–62, provides an appealing suggestion of the influence of just such Christian allegorization on *Beowulf*.

19. Robert Finnegan, "Beowulf at the Mere (and elsewhere)," *Mosaic* 11, no. 4 (1978): 45–54, makes the point that in *Beowulf* "the characters within the artistic frame" do not have the Christian "perspective and cannot have it" (p. 48). He concludes that the hero "is the good man, manqué from the Christian point of view, struggling to defeat forces he cannot fully understand with weapons that often do not function at need ... and becomes increasingly entrammeled in the meshes of the society of which he is part.... The society which as king he represents is judged and found wanting" (p. 54). Edmund Reiss, "Nationalism and Cosmopolitanism as Subject and Theme in Medieval Narrative," *Proceedings of the IVth Congress of the International Comparative Literature Association*, edited by François Jost (The Hague: Mouton, 1966) 1: 619–22, finds Augustine's doctrine of the Two Cities reflected in Beowulf: as agent of God he reflects the heavenly, but in his pride when he attacks the dragon he reflects the worldly city.

20. Robert Hanning, "*Beowulf* as Heroic History," *Medievalia et Humanistica*, New Series 5 (1974): 77–102, independently and from a different perspective arrived at conclusions encouragingly similar to my own. *Beowulf*, he cogently argues, "functions as a post-conversion essay in pre-conversion heroic history" (p. 88). Of Beowulf's death he says the poet "completely reverses all tendencies toward harmony in heroic history, and offers instead a soured, ironic version of what has gone on before, embodying a final assessment of a world without God as a world in which time and history are themselves negative concepts"; he further notes that the poet uses "the metaphor of treasure ... as an image of flawed achievement and human limitation" (p. 94).

21. Robert Morrison, "*Beowulf* 698a: 'frofor ond fultum,' " *Notes and Queries*, New Series 27 (1980): 193–94 in a detailed analysis of the biblical influence on the phrase supplies further evidence for Beowulf's being considered as God's agent in his adventures in Denmark.

22. See Chapter Five note to lines 1705–8.

23. A. J. Bliss, "*Beowulf*, Lines 3074–75," *J. R. R. Tolkien* (see note 16 above), in his analysis of the much-debated curse on the treasure, which he finds symbolic (see Chapter Five, note to lines 3074–75), makes clear Beowulf's flaw. The curse, he states, "symbolizes the corrupting power of the gold (*hæðen gold* as it is called in line 2276), which the poet has described explicitly in lines 2764–66.... Far from being arbitrary, the curse is the direct consequence of Beowulf's avarice" (p. 60), and "in lines 2345–47, a verbal reminiscence emphasizes the fact that Beowulf ... did succumb to arrogance" (p. 61). (See Chapter Five, note to line 2345.) Thus, "far from being a hero without tragic flaw' [Arthur Brodeur, *The Art of Beowulf*, p. 105], he is a hero with two tragic flaws." John Gardner, "Guilt and the World's Complexity: the Murder of Ongentheow and the Slaying of the Dragon," *Anglo-Saxon Poetry: Essays in Appreciation for John C. McGalliard*, edited by Lewis Nicholson and Dolores Frese (Notre Dame: University Press, 1975), pp. 14–22, comes to a somewhat

similar conclusion (pp. 21-22). Robert Burlin, however, comes to a startlingly different one, in "Inner Weather and Interlace: A Note on the Semantic value of Structure in *Beowulf*," *Old English Studies in Honor of John C. Pope*, edited by Robert Burlin and Edward Irving (Toronto: University Press, 1974). The poet "does not need to find some flaw—Augustinian or Aristotelian—in his hero or some inherent deficiency in the heroic society he embodies, to envision the death of Beowulf and its consequences." He arrives at this conclusion without effective massing of evidence, as with Bliss, but I suspect that the dichotomy rests on almost inarguable premises. Both feel the force of the poet's "universality," but Burlin, I would venture, feels that such universality is cabined and confined by reference to an historical frame, where I (and I assume Gardner and Bliss) feel that universality is thereby enhanced.

24. Norman Eliason, "Beowulf, Wiglaf and the Wægmundings," *Anglo-Saxon England* 7 (1978): 95-118, puts the matter clearly: "The Wægmundings [through Weohstan] had earned Onela's gratitude.... Later when the Swedish king's gratitude was extended to Beowulf [in offering him the throne], we are surely to understand that this was because of Beowulf's connection with the Wægmunding family." Beowulf attacks Onela, however, "to avenge the death of Heardred.... The moral is plain: man's transcendent duty is to avenge the killing of his kinsman or his king" (p. 100).

25. Anne Payne, "Three Aspects of Wyrd in *Beowulf*," *Old English Studies in Honor of John C. Pope* (see note 23), presents the issue with clarity: "The nature of Beowulf's violation puts him in a narrow place where no universal forces reflect and magnify his energies.... He is not able to project in this episode an adequate understanding against the challenge, so as to put himself immediately in touch with what he should have done; he is too close to his error," and thus his boast before the dragon battle "is characterized by a desperate search for a comprehensible mode of action and fulfillment" (p. 23). "The heroic code, even if followed at the highest of all ethical levels, is not sufficiently inclusive to materialize clearly the divine order of things for man to follow" (p. 26).

26. Larry Benson, "The Originality of *Beowulf*," *The Interpretation of Narrative*, edited by Morton Bloomfield (Harvard English Studies 1, Cambridge: Harvard University Press, 1970), places Beowulf's death with accuracy as "an unusual death for a hero, for though heroes must die they die gloriously; their death is their victory. Not so with Beowulf.... The poet goes out of his way to stress the futility, the ultimate defeat that Beowulf suffers" (p. 32). See also his "The Pagan Coloring of Beowulf," in *Old English Poetry*, edited by Robert Creed (Providence, R. I.: Brown University Press, 1967), pp. 193-213.

Chapter Three
Narrative Polarities

The theme of *Beowulf* is developed contrapuntally, and its hero acts between illusory polarities. As agent of God's mercy Beowulf may bring peace, but in God's justice he is doomed because even as God's agent he is himself directed by the desire for glory, not faith, and the reward he seeks and gains is not spiritual, but earthly treasure. In a society governed by an heroic ethos, peace results from war and brings war, as in the endless feud of the Geats and the Swedes. In such a world, unguided by the goal of salvation, the security of peace is the prelude to disaster, as Heorot is to Grendel, and Beowulf's reign is to the dragon. It is a world without faith where present amity breeds festering hate, illustrated in the Finnsburh and Ingeld tales. In a society limited by pagan ignorance of eternity, death is the counterpoint to life, as with Hrethel and his sons, as with Beowulf and Wiglaf. Finally, the pagan hero who seeks, as his final reward, glory and its evidence in treasure, seeks that which must be given to the waters, as with Scyld, or consumed in the flames and returned to the dust, as with Beowulf. Thus, in the Augustinian view, heroic society, being without grace, cannot perceive that war and peace are not true polarities, but simply counterpoints in a cycle where "the dead are succeeded by the dying."

A. Lexicon

The polarity of theme is realized in *Beowulf* by contrapuntal narrative development. Its structure, as will be seen in the next chapter, gives evidence of this. So, too, does its narrative technique as for example, in its lexicon, a striking feature of which is verbal ambiguity and antithesis. The word, *æglæca*, "adversary," provides a good instance in its polarity of meaning, generally "fiendish foe," but also "hero," 893, and in the plural designating both the dragon and Beowulf, 2592.[1] The effect of the ambiguity is to suggest an association between hero and enemy. As adversaries, Beowulf and Grendel share supernatural stature. Beowulf is gigantic, as is his semi-historical kinsman, Higelac, who found his way into the medieval legendary of monsters. Beowulf's size is hinted at by the coastguard's singling him out from his men, 247-51, and is implied by his hand-to-hand combat with the sea monsters and with Grendel. It becomes evident in a detail from the later account of the carrying of Grendel's head from the tarn; what Beowulf could do by himself four of his men could do only "with great difficulty by prodigious effort," 1636. The affinity between gigantic hero and gigantic adversary is thematic. Grendel is the "glory demon," 86, and Beowulf lives for glory; the dragon dies in protecting his treasure as Beowulf dies in gaining it. The pagan hero has both a light and a dark side, so that Beowulf's radiance has its counterpart in the demonic darkness.

Another example of lexical antithesis is the word, *fah*, translated "encrusted" throughout but in context meaning either "stained" or "decorated." The word is employed frequently and deployed with far-reaching effectiveness. One instance of this omnipresent interlace will serve as an example. Heorot is called *sincfage*, "dearly encrusted," 167, but, occupied by Grendel in "the dark nights," it has become *dreorfah*, "encrusted with gore," 485. This hall encrusted with gold and gore is seen externally and at a distance by Beowulf and his men as *goldfah*, 308, when they see it for the first time.[2] They, wearing helmets *fah* with gold, find their way to it by a *stanfah*, "stone-encrusted," street, 320. In counterpoint, Grendel, approaching, sees the *fættum fahne*, "gold-encrusted," hall, 716, where Beowulf waits as Grendel crosses its *fagne flor*. With what is the floor encrusted? tiles? the blood resulting from Grendel's earlier forays? or, in premonition, the blood of the Geat he will kill and with his own blood when his arm will be ripped from his shoulder? Probably all these meanings are implicit in the term, as well as an extended meaning, "hostile," found in the designation of Grendel in the ensuing battle as *fag with God*, the encrusted floor of Heorot being the scene of Grendel's earlier hostile aggression, as it will be of the hostile meeting between the giant adversaries.

There are many other uses of *fah* clustering around Heorot, particularly in word-play combination with *fæge*, doomed, and *fæhð*, "feud."[3] These need not be examined here, but such lexical interlace running through the poem may be further exemplified in tracing two words *fæþm* and *bearm*, through the course of the poem.[4] Both have the root meaning, "bosom": *bearm*, which always appears in the singular, is thus translated throughout, while *fæþm*, which also appears in the plural, is translated "bosom" for the singular and "embrace" for the plural. Both have varied contextual connotations. In the sententia concluding the story of Scyld's reign and succession, it is observed that a wise prince will give liberally "from his father's bosom," *on fæder (bea)rme*, that is, either "from his father's treasure" or "while under his father's protection." In line 35, Scyld's body is placed "in the bosom," *on bearme*, of the ship, and treasure is placed "upon his bosom," *on bearme*, 40. The triumph of Grendel is concluded with a sententia providing a striking contrast between the evil who will be consumed in "the fire's bosom," *fyres fæþm*, 185, and the good who will find peace in the "Father's embrace," *fæder fæþmum*, 188. The loading of war gear onto Scyld's funeral ship is next counterpointed by the loading of war gear "upon the bosom," *on bearm*, of Beowulf's ship as he sets out for Denmark, 214. Then, when the Danes look upon Heorot as it is being shaken to its foundations by the furious battle between Beowulf and Grendel, they lose their assurance that the hall could never be broken, only consumed "in the fire's bosom," *liges fæþm*, 781. *Bearm* is again used in the context of the loading of a ship, as Sigemund, in the scop's tale, loads the treasure of the dragon he has slain onto the bosom, *on bearm*, of his ship, 896. In the Finnsburh tale, *bearm* reappears in counterpoint: "earth's bosom," *foldan bearm*, 1137, is made fair by the Spring which ironically releases Hengest's ice-locked desire for revenge, signalled by the placing of a sword "upon his bosom," *on bearm*, 1144. After this tale is told, the feast continues with further gift-giving, culminating in Wealhtheow's presentation of a legendary necklet, which provides the occasion for the foretelling of Higelac's loss of it in death. In this foretelling, *fæþm* reappears with extended meaning; Higelac's body and treasure will pass "to Frankish bosom," *in Francna fæþm*, 1210. The referent for *fæþm* is again the earth in Beowulf's vow that Æschere's slayer will not escape unavenged "upon the bosom of earth," *on foldan fæþm*, 1393. The words do not reappear until line 2128 in Beowulf's report on his adventures in Denmark where he tells how Grendel's dam had deprived the Danes of the consolation of giving Æschere's body to the funeral fire because she had taken it away in her "fiendish embrace," *feondes fæþ (mum)*, 2128. In 2194 Higelac places Hrethel's sword on Beowulf's "bosom," *bearm*, an echo of line 1144. Next the cup stolen from the dragon comes to Beowulf's "bosom," *bearme*, 2404; the battle with the dragon over, Wiglaf gathers the treasure in the barrow upon his "bosom," *bearm*, 2775, to bring it to the dying Beowulf. Finally, 3049, Wiglaf and his men look at the treasure which has been buried a thousand years in the "bosom of earth," *eorðan fæþm*.

The words function thematically, the basic polarity being established by the repetition of *fæþm*, 185,188, anagogically counterpointing two embraces, that of the eternal fire and that of the Father. From this ensues a contrapuntal pattern reflecting the polarities of earthly treasure and the dust of death: Scyld's body is laid in the ship's *bearm* and upon his *bearm* the treasure of war is laid. Beowulf on his way to gaining his treasure of reward loads his war gear in the *bearm* of his ship, as Sigemund loads his reward of treasure upon his. The *bearm* of earth is renewed in God's design, but in the earthly estate only to unleash hate as the sword is placed on Hengest's *bearm*. In turn Higelac places Hrethel's sword on Beowulf's *bearm*, and quickly the narrative moves to Beowulf's doom as he seeks revenge and the dragon's gold after the cup is brought to his *bearm*. The treasure is gathered in Wiglaf's *bearm* to be shown to the dying Beowulf, the treasure which has lain buried in the *fæþm* for a thousand years and which will again be buried along with the hero who died to gain it and glory.

B. Point of view

Examples of such counterpointing in the lexicon of *Beowulf* could be tediously multiplied, but what has been examined is sufficient to establish that polarity is at the center of the poet's narrative technique.[5] This polarity also governs his intricate handling of point of view and narrative voice. The poet's problem is obvious; in his hero the ideals of his society are realized, but his tragic flaw springs precisely from his exemplification of ideals which, in the withering Augustinian analysis, are wrong and contain no guide to right behavior. Nevertheless, the hero must appear praiseworthy and his world must appear worthy of belief. The solution the poet found to this problem of point of view may have been suggested by the Christian reading of the *Aeneid.* Vergil, without the revelation of faith and celebrating the way to Rome, was considered by Christian commentators to have been inspired to create, though without ultimate comprehension, an allegory of the way to Jerusalem. The narrator or persona of *Beowulf* appears a fictive Germanic Vergil, telling an epic story of his race which reveals the truth about the earthly city which he believes he is celebrating.

The persona speaks in his own fictional voice eighteen times, employing the *gefrignan, hyran* formula.[6] Of these, eleven are concerned with the theme of treasure (38, 74, 776, 1011, 1027, 1196, 2163, 2172, 2752, 2773, 2837; three with fame (1, 837, 1955); a cluster of two with heroism (2685, 2694), and one with royal marriage, 62. These assertions of the narrator's voice serve, as has elsewhere been noted, as an "authenticating voice," supplying a "ring of verisimilitude," a "willing suspension of disbelief," even a "willing suspension of disapproval."[7] The literal validity of the story is enforced by accepting the pagan values of its characters and not juxtaposing them against the truths of Faith. The narrative voice thus distinguishes the "Vergilian" persona from the Christian author.

The third person commentaries with which the poem abounds are generally consonant with those in the first person in providing a sense of historical authenticity and distancing, but they also serve to provide, as has been noted, a sense of contemporary moral "relevance to the poet's own time."[8] These third person comments are more elusive than those of the first person because inherent in them is a polarity of viewpoint, that of the Vergilian persona and that shared by the Christian poet and his audience. Thus the comments fluctuate between the voice of worldly wisdom, as in lines 24–25, and the voice of spiritual perception, as in lines 183–88.

At times the comments contain their own polarities, which may be illustrated by two which both pertain to Wiglaf. First when he determines that he must come to Beowulf's aid, the comment is made, "who holds to the right / will never betray the ties of kinship," 2600–1. Here is enunciated the highest ideal of heroic society—blood loyalty. But in this ideal, as it is presented in the poem, lies a dilemma, which Beowulf reveals in his reminiscences as he prepares to face the dragon. As I mentioned in Chapter Two, he remembers "the death in grief of Hrethel, fatally unable to solve the dilemma to which his heroic ethic could give no answer: his duty to avenge his son; his duty not to be guilty of the death of his son." Beowulf cannot solve the dilemma because he, too, is caught in the iron chains of an ethic which, in giving ultimate value to the finite ideal of loyalty, in effect sanctions what from the Christian viewpoint is the sinful error of blood revenge. Implicit in the praise of Wiglaf for his fidelity to the heroic ideal is its counterpoint, the futility of that ideal. Second, Wiglaf's entry, "proudly exulting" into the treasure barrow is followed by the comment, "Treasure of gold ... may easily overcome any human being," 2764–66, an adage clearly consonant with Hrothgar's viewpoint in his homily on pride which served as warning to Beowulf, as this must serve for Wiglaf.[9]

In this heroic ethic, as it is expressed in the poem, the hero is true to the ideal if he is directed by the aim of glory in his violent amassing of treasure (Sigemund); he is false if he seeks only self-gratification in his violent amassing of treasure (Heremod). The flaw in such an ethic, from the Christian view, is that its polarities provide for no mean because they disguise their essential identity: the search for glory is as much a manifestation of pride as the search for self-gratification. The true ethical polarity rests in the contrast between heavenly and earthly reward. Because the search for glory has a form of earthly reward as its end, it provides as dusty an answer as does the search for self-gratification; both are forms of self-love, differing only in outward appearances. In the light of such understanding, the ethical warning to Wiglaf becomes a comment on Beowulf who was driven to give battle to the dragon, as Wiglaf declares," by relentless doom," a doom of his own making "because of his own will he seeks the two goals of worldly men living in error, glory and its visible sign, treasure."

The narrative voice has a further interior level since much of the story is told by the characters themselves. Praising Beowulf by comparison and contrast, Hrothgar's scop, a kind of interior persona, from his store of "heroic tales and timeless legends," 870, tells of Sigemund and Heremod. In setting the polarities of the heroic ideal, this foreshadows Beowulf's battle with the dragon and provides a clue to the mysterious time of trouble preceding the coming of Scyld, also provided by Hrothgar, 1709–22. Accounts of Beowulf's father are provided by Beowulf, 263–66, and by Hrothgar, 372–75, 458–72. On the latter occasion Hrothgar also makes mention of the hitherto ignored reign of Heorogar and of his own succession, an account which he supplements when he presents Healfdane's armor to Beowulf, as the latter reports, 2155–62. The legendary tale of Finnsburh is related by an interior persona, Hrothgar's minstrel, a tale which with far-reaching effectiveness touches on the major motifs of the poem: the powerlessness of a woman's love, the funeral pyre, revenge, and the bringing away of treasure.

Beowulf himself retells the narrator's account of the adventures in Denmark, with somewhat different emphases and with added details. In the course of this retelling he prophesies the fall of a love-made peace because of the demands of filial revenge. Later in his mournful recollections of the past as he goes to meet the dragon, Beowulf gives a first-hand account of Higelac's raid on the Franks and of his death, first foretold in third-person comment on Wealhtheow's gift of the necklet. In these reminiscences, employing the narrator's *gefrignan* formula, he also gives, 2484, an account of the feud between the Geats and Swedes that preceded his Danish adventures, continued into his own long reign, and will resume on his death. A different version of these events is also given by the messenger who reports Beowulf's death and concludes that the feud will be renewed and that the Geats are doomed.

Finally, the narrator's tendency to sententious comment is echoed by Hrothgar, by Beowulf, and by Wiglaf. Looking on the hilt of the sword, the blade of which had melted in Grendel's blood, a hilt which contains biblical history, Hrothgar is inspired to give his sermon on pride. Beowulf, thinking of the death in despair of Hrethel, is led to give his moving, philosophical analogue on the father's helpless despair when his son is hanged, and Wiglaf, disregarding any conventional statement of heroic resolve, laments the disaster that "one man's will ... and relentless doom" has brought upon the Geats, 3077-82. The voices of the interior personas and of the major characters thus reflect the narrator's voice, both celebrating the glory, and lamenting the doom of the heroic. This polarity is also reflected in the treatment of nature in *Beowulf*.[10]

C. Nature

Although examples of sustained or special development of nature descriptions in the poem are surprisingly few, in all of them appears a polar counterpoint between the exorcizing power of God's providence and the hostility of man's natural surroundings with lurking monsters and dangerous dark, gripping cold and violent storm.[11] The first passage of sustained natural description in the poem is in the scop's song in Heorot, 87-114. Here Creation and Fall are interlocked as primordial cause and model of man's beleaguered estate in a hostile world, and it appears designed to produce the recognition that the ensuing demonic attack on Heorot is a typological repetition of the attack on Eden.[12] God's creation, nature, is everywhere beautiful, like Eden, but the Fall has caused the perversity of human life at war with itself and with nature. Cold and heat are not enemies in the temperate zone of God's love, and the darkness does not threaten the light in God's day; but the threatening monsters do overcome the false Eden of worldly prosperity, except as they may be overcome by redeeming grace or providential design. God's natural order and man's corruption of it is epitomized in the history of Heorot. It is erected as an emblem of man's pride. At its inauguration, it falls to a demonic attack from which it is saved by an agent of God's mercy, Beowulf. Finally, it will be consumed in the flames of a feud, an event prophesied at the moment of its completion. In picturing post-lapsarian Nature as hostile to man except through the intervention of providential design, this first extended passage of nature description is the contextual paradigm of all the remaining passages. These consist of descriptions of (a) Grendel's tarn, (b) the sea, (c) the dragon, (d) sea journeys and (e) metaphors of light and dark.

a) *Grendel's Tarn.* Grendel's tarn is the occasion for the most developed and expanded "nature" description or metaphor in the poem. The detailed descriptions are foreshadowed in the passage where the men, following Grendel's track in the morning after his battle with Beowulf, come to the mere, 847-52. Then, in the narrative of the attack of Grendel's mother, mention is made "of her enforced dwelling in the dread waters of frozen streams," 1260-65, as a descendant of Cain who had fled from men "to inhabit the wasteland." After her attack she returns "to the moor," 1295. The first full description is reserved, however, for Hrothgar's report of what he has heard of the monsters' dwelling in "tales told by my people." From the distance of folklore the unnatural nature of the tarn is developed in a long set piece portraying hellish and menacing nature, 1345-76. It is the habitation of monsters of mysterious origin, a hideous, windswept fenland at the heart of which is the tarn of such alien hostility that a deer pursued by hounds "would stand and die rather than dare / to plunge within." The frightening report is followed by the equally vivid approach to the actuality of the tarn, 1402-41. Tracking Grendel's dam with difficulty "by ways unknown," over "stony cliffs" and "looming headlands," suddenly the company comes upon "the grisly pool"—and Æschere's head. In grief and horror they watch the sea monsters departing at the sound of the trumpet. The description is concluded, however, with the startling reversal: Beowulf and his men become hunters, he slaying one of the monsters with an arrow and they hauling it ashore with boarspears. Implicit in the image of the deadly hunting game is the reflection of the menace of the monstrous in the mutual menace of man; the very futility of the hunt of the one sea monster serves further as an ominous foreshadowing of Beowulf's subsequent invasion of the tarn where he is, in turn, hunted by the sea monsters.

In contrast, Beowulf's descent and his encounter with Grendel's mother in the cave below are told with minimal descriptive detail. As against his earlier prowess as a hunter he is here powerless. Attacked by "the sea-wolf" and by "many sea monsters with their fierce tusks," he cannot retaliate; only his armor saves him, 1506-12. He is carried into "a hall hostile in its mystery," the only description of which is that "the rushing flood" does not enter it and that it is "pallidly lit / by the flames of a bright fire," 1512-17. In the ensuing battle in the cave and its sequel the only passage of natural description, 1608-11, is metaphoric and is best left for discussion as part of the pattern of such detail interwoven into the structure of the poem as a whole. With the slaying of the dam and the beheading of Grendel, the monsters are overcome and the tarn is purified. Then in Hrothgar's ensuing reflections on the hilt of the purifying sword, the waters which the monsters inhabit are related to the Flood, thus in God's just design becoming symbolic both of purification and of the dwelling in damnation of that which must be punished, 1687–93.

b) *The Sea.* The elaborate description of watery menace and sea monsters in Beowulf's descent is lacking, perhaps because it was preempted by the preceding developed description of the tarn and by earlier descriptions of battling sea monsters in the Breca episode. There Unferth's account makes mention only of the folly involved in facing the perils of the deep, 506–15. Beowulf's own account emphasizes the theme of menace; he speaks of cold, of storm, of night, and in addition tells of his conquest of sea monsters, the providential outcome of his youthful folly, 539–67. Only through its perversion does nature become fiercely hostile, and in Beowulf's narration, this perversion is imaged in the grimly ironic picture of the foiled feast of the monsters, 561–67:

> I waited upon them   as was their due;
> seated at the board   at the bottom of the sea
> looking forward   to their fill of me,
> the evil fiends   had no joy in the feast,
> for in the dawn   cut down by my sword
> in the sleep of death   they lay on the surface
> beside the shore.

The monsters are given the human role of being seated at a feast, the main course of which is human; Beowulf, however, through his strength and God's grace, provides them with the sleep of death, not of repletion. Because of the prominence given feasting in the poem, this image, even more than that of the hunt of the sea beasts, suggests how man has become involved in the monstrousness of nature; the beastly intention of feasting is a reflection of fallen man, and the foiling of it is a sign of how, through grace, he may overcome the horror of evil. The scene ends with a related counterpoint between the dark and the light of day, "the light came in the East, / God's bright beacon," 569–70. This imagery, however, like that in the battle with Grendel's dam, is best treated as part of the recurrent pattern of such imagery, which is discussed later.

c) *The Dragon.* Although the dragon, like the other monsters, is introduced as ruling "in the dark night," 2211, and its barrow lies, like the tarn, in a place remote from man's knowing, the dragon attacks only when its refuge is penetrated; moreover, the description of the barrow and the dragon, unlike that of the mere and its monsters, is developed in brief and scattered passages which only cumulatively give a sense of alien antiquity and of the heart of darkness which man penetrates only in deadly peril. Even before the first mention of the dragon, there was a brief foreshadowing of it and of its barrow in the tale of Sigemund, 884–97. There, too, the dragon was "keeper of the treasure," lived "under the gray stone," in death "melted in its heat," and lost its treasure to the hero. The first brief passage actually dealing with the dragon that Beowulf must face, and with its dwelling, appears when the awakening of the dragon is suddenly introduced; it lived "on the high heath / in a lofty stone barrow." The way to it is "unknown to the people," 2212–14. The next descriptive details appear only when the narrative has turned back to the story of the ancient burial of the treasure; the barrow is "near the seashore," and was secured "through skillful concealment" by an unknown race, 2241–43.

The dragon itself is described later in the act of finding the barrow "unguarded by the ancient foe." Its nature is to fly "in the night," "bound in flames" in search of "the buried hoard where hoary in age / it guards heathen gold though it gains nothing." This it has done "for three hundred winters" until aroused "by the theft of the cup," 2270–77. There follows a grimly humorous description of the dragon's angry circling of the barrow in search of the intruder, of its returning within to make sure of its loss, and finally of its wait for the dark, 2287–2311. Here the only descriptive detail given is of the dragon's discovering no one "in the desert waste." Emphasis is given, however, to the passing of day, the coming of night and the dragon's fiery menace. In turn, the brief description of the dragon's attack, 2312–23, is dominated by images of fire, of burning, and of the concluding coming of day.

The dragon and the barrow are next described, but without added detail, when Beowulf, with the thief as guide, goes to do battle with it, 2410–16. When Beowulf sees the barrow for the first time, detail is added; Beowulf sees "the stone arch rising"; from the barrow a stream "of murderous fire" rushes. Beowulf roars his challenge, "the sound of battle / resounding clearly within the gray cliff." In response from the cave comes the blast of "the adversary's breath inflamed for battle," 2542–59. Of note here is the evocative intertwining of images. The stream issuing from the rock becomes one with the fiery stream issuing from the dragon, and Beowulf's battle cry penetrating within the barrow is interwoven with the emerging, answering breath of the dragon. The metaphoric effect of this interweaving of images is striking, and may have relation to the darkening tone of the final adventure. Earlier Beowulf was shown to act as an agent of God in slaying the monstrous Grendel, whose triumphant onslaught was occasioned by the building of Heorot, the product of the pride of fallen man. Because of his role as providential agent, Beowulf's adventures in Denmark with their interweaving of the human and the monstrous largely served to underscore the hero's triumph over an evil begotten by humanity. Now, however, in facing another monster, the dragon, Beowulf feels a sense of having transgressed against "ancient law" and of having angered "the eternal Lord," 2330, whom he thought to serve. As has been observed earlier, he cannot find an answer to his unease because he "devised revenge," 2336, and sought not only to gain "glory / from the feud," 2513–54, but also "to win the gold," 2535, as he did not in his feud with Grendel and his dam. These motives he considers "worthy," 2535, and, thus, in pagan error, Beowulf becomes estranged from God. He ceases to act as His agent, though he does not known why. Concomitantly he becomes profoundly involved in the hostility of Nature, as the interweaving of images in the description of his approach to the dragon's barrow implies.

Except for minimal narrative requirements, neither dragon nor locale is described in detail in the ensuing battle; after it is over, however, the barrow, an "imperishable work of giants," 2717–18, is viewed again by the dying Beowulf, and its interior by Wiglaf in seeking treasure to show to his lord, 2756–82. Here description is of the "ancient wealth" of the "ancient night-flying dragon," the absence of which in death makes the barrow possible to plunder. Now there is "no trace" of its "protector" which "for a long time in fiery terror, / fiercely flaming had fought for the hoard." The alien menace of the antique dragon is gone, but the human menace of the antique treasure remains. The dragon's death does not lift the curse from the treasure; instead, it releases the power of the curse. The dragon, the greatest of nature's monstrosities, and the accursed treasure, the greatest of human possessions, are mysteriously intertwined. Earthly treasure gives function to the dragon; its avarice makes the curse of earthly treasure ineffective. But man's cupidity overcomes the keeper, and in consequence releases the curse which brings death and destruction.

Because the alien horror of the dragon is intertwined with the human treasure, in death Beowulf and the dragon lie side by side, along with the treasure, as Wiglaf views them, 2821–45, a passage ending with this perti-nent comment:

>   For Beowulf's death
>   the treasure in part   was payment;
>   through both their doing   it had brought an end
>   to their transitory life.

Monster, hero and treasure are again linked when Beowulf's returning troop looks upon them.[13] They see their king in "awesome death," but before this they see the dragon "lying opposite," "scorched by the flames / monstrously horrible and measuring the length / of fifty feet," which once "flew joyously / in the dark sky," but now "had come to the end of its use of caves." Alongside lies the treasure, "eaten through with the rust of the thousand years / of its burial in the bosom of the earth," 3033–50. This final view of the dead adver-saries is followed, in turn, by comment on the curse of the treasure, which reveals that it is through God's design that the dragon who hoarded the treasure and Beowulf who sought it are counterpointed in death.[14] Unnatural nature, hostile and inimical, is part of the estate of fallen man.

d) *Sea Journeys*. In the accounts of Beowulf's journeys to and from Denmark a different kind of nature description appears, for Nature seems to be, as it were, smiling. In both passages, 210-88 and 1903-13, however, this effect does not result from any expressed pleasure in journeying on the sea; rather it results from a sense of relief that the journey has been passed in safety. The Geats put off from the shore; with joy they come to the end of the voyage. What is emphasized is the beautiful sturdiness of the ship, the swiftness of the passage unhindered by storms, and most particularly their safe arrival. The sea has not shown its accustomed enmity, but that is not because nature smiles; rather its menace has been for the moment exorcized because Beowulf is the agent of God's mercy, within which he and his men are safe.

e) *Metaphors*. There remain the brief metaphorical passages of nature description. These center on the opposition between sunlight and dark, warmth and cold or fierce flame. There are also two intertwined examples of animal imagery. The sun and night imagery is pervasive. The monsters, for example, are creatures of the dark and cold; they all wait for the sun to leave before they attack; conversely they are all associated with flame.

Grendel is introduced as a creature of darkness, inimical to day, 87-89, and in the narrative of his attack on the Danes is so developed by selective, though scattered, descriptive details. His attack begins "after night had fallen," 115; the coming of day serves simply to bring loud lamentation as the horror is revealed, 126-29. The sun brings no comfort; Grendel attacks "the very next night," 135, and the "dark adversary and deadly shadow," who "in darkness held the misty moors," then "occupied Heorot in the dark of night," 159-67. Finally, the tale of his "tyranny / nightly inflicted," 192-93, comes to Beowulf's ears. Grendel in his battle with Beowulf is again described in scattered images of dark, 702-3, 705-11, 730-36, 755-56, 762-64, 805-8, 819-21, 844-46, and, 726-27, "a fearful light / most like to fire flared from his eyes."

In the Breca episode, discussed earlier, the descriptive details emphasize the cold, the night, and the water as the milieu of monsters. In counterpoint, "in the dawn" after the monsters have been disappointed of they prey and the seas made secure of passage, the sun appears, 565-70. Beowulf, in calling it "God's bright beacon," makes of the sun not a mere index of time but a symbol of destinal design that has kept him secure against the monstrous dark. He gives further emphasis to the symbolism of the motif in repeating it at the conclusion of the Breca tale, where he promises Hrothgar that after he has defeated Grendel "the radiant sun" will "bring morning light to the sons of men," 605-6, and it will be evident that the hall is secure from the dark.

In the Finnsburh lay, nature description is employed with striking symbolic effect.[15] After the "funeral flames," 1119, there comes a winter's truce until the spring unlocks the possibility of revenge. The splendor of the poet's rhetoric is brilliantly illustrated in this image of the winter of peace made "murderous" by discontent and by his inversion of customary associations: peace is maintained in the icy winter; war will break out in the peace of spring. It is, of course, man with his revengeful mind who causes the inversion of nature. The icy bonds of winter are the fetters of revenge unfulfilled; the ice of human hatred is melted only to release its fury.

In the battle with Grendel's dam, as has been noted, there appears another set of images of fire and sun. Within the cave, before he had grappled with the monster, Beowulf saw that the cave "was pallidly lit / by the flames of a bright fire," 1516-17. He discovered that his sword, "the battle flame had no power to bite," 1523, and he was almost defeated in his hand-to-hand encounter. The light, however, enabled him to see the sword by which, through God's grace, he was able to triumph. After he had slain the dam, a light guides him, "even as heaven's candle in clear radiance / shines from on high," 1570-72, to complete his act of purification by cutting off Grendel's head. The sword melts like "icicles" in the Spring when "the deadly fetters of the binding frost" are freed by "the True Father / Who holds in His sway time and season," 1605-11. The simile of "heaven's candle," as in the Breca episode, suggests God's mercy; the simile of the icicle, in counterpoint to the inverted imagery of winter in the Finnsburh lay, suggests God's mercy and justice. The sword melts to signify the completion of God's justice in the eradication of the monster; the hilt remains because in God's mercy, the ice of hatred is, for this time, melted.

Finally, upon Beowulf's arrival home, "the world candle shone," 1965. He begins his account of his adventures in Denmark with his boast that none of Grendel's "bestial race" survives to "boast at dawn," 2005-9, and resumes with the coming of Grendel in the night "after heaven's jewel / had coursed the earth," 2072-74, continuing with the tale of the battle and of the rejoicing on the following day "until the darkness of night / came again to man," followed by the lamentation "after morning came, 2103-24.

Two passages of bird imagery remain to be discussed. The first is a curious one that appears at the end of the feast celebrating Beowulf's victory over Grendel's dam; after "the shadow of night / darkened over the courtiers," Beowulf took his rest "until the black raven blithe-hearted announced / the bliss of heaven," the sunrise, 1789-1804. The effect of the raven, conventionally ominous, announcing the day is startling. In the interlocking design of the poem it seems surely related to the later appearance of the raven, next to be discussed. Its function would be thematic in suggesting that in the city of the world, moments of triumphant glory are omens of inevitable disaster to come.[16] It is a foreshadowing of the descending movement of the last part of the poem.

There the raven does reappear under much more usual circumstances to conclude the messenger's announcement of Beowulf's death and prophecy of disaster to follow, 3021-27:

                                                    Therefore many a spear,
          cold in the morning,   fingers must clasp
          and hands must raise;   the song of the harp
          will never rouse the warrior,   but the black raven,
          settling on the doomed,   will have much to say
          in relating to the eagle   his luck at the feast
          while he and the wolf   worried the corpses.

In this final piece of nature description the festal song of the harp is counterpointed against the unnatural song of the raven relishing its feast on the feasters.
This counterpoint of human and animal serves to recapitulate the poet's treatment of nature, the polarity of which appears to stem from some kind of meta-
linguistic, metavisual level of experience possessed by a people too close to
nature not to feel its icy terror but, at the same time, sustained by Christian
faith.

This sensibility reflected in *Beowulf* is most aptly expressed by Bede in his
Historia where he recounts a pagan noble's reaction to the promise of Christianity. This well-known passage is particularly serviceable in elucidating the
attitude toward nature in *Beowulf*. Because its straightforward narrative style
is markedly different from that of the poem, the fact that the burden of its
message is the same appears to point to an ultimate climate of belief expressed
both in convoluted and straightforward styles:

> 'Your majesty, when we compare the present life of man with that time
> of which we have no knowledge, it seems to me like the swift flight of
> a lone sparrow through the banqueting hall where you sit in the winter
> months to dine with your thanes and counsellors. Inside there is a com-
> forting fire to warm the room; outside, the wintry storms of snow and
> rain are raging. The sparrow flies swiftly through one door of the hall,
> and out another. While he is inside, he is safe from the winter storms;
> but after a few moments of comfort, he vanishes from sight into the
> darkness whence he came. Similarly, man appears on earth for a little
> while, but we know nothing of what went before this life, and what follows.
> Therefore, if this new teaching can reveal any more certain kowledge,
> it seems right that we should follow it.'

In *Beowulf*, then, the treatment of nature, its involuted narrative method,
lexical ambiguities, and complexities of point-of-view are all contrapuntal and
function to reflect the complex polarity of its theme. The poem juxtaposes
the unity and clarity of Christian life against the unresolved polarities of pagan
life, which is circumscribed by the darkness of an unknown eternity and bound
to the cycle of the dead succeeding the dying.

Notes

1. Doreen Gillam, "The Use of the Term 'Æglæca' in *Beowulf*," *Studia Germanica Ganden-sia* 3 (1961): 162–69, has provided a detailed study of the word. Marion Lois Huffines, "O.E. *aglæce*: Magic and Moral Decline of Monsters and Men," *Semasia* 1 (1974): 71–81, who apparently overlooked the Gillam study, attempts to define the term as "a being who inspires fear by magical powers" (p. 72). Although her attempt is based on etymological conjectures which do not sustain solid definition, her suggested connotation for the word seems plausible, particularly as she traces its use in the poem and finds that it reflects a movement toward an increasing interweaving of the hero and the monsters (p. 80). E. G. Stanley, "Two Old English Terms Insufficiently Understood for Literary Criticism: *Þing Gehegan* and *Seonoþ Gehegan*," *Old English Poetry*, edited by Daniel Calder (Berkeley: University of California Press, 1979), pp.75–76, makes clear the neutrality of the term. Allan Eller, "Semantic Ambiguity as a Structural Element in Beowulf" (Ph. D. Dissertation, State University of New York at Binghamton, 1978), pp. 25–28, supplements and develops Gillam's work. He also provides an important study of the ambiguous elements in the poet's lexicon, which makes possible the rapid and selective survey made here.

2. Patricia Silber, "Gold and its Significance in *Beowulf*," *Annuale Mediaevale* 18 (1977), in surveying the uses of gold in the poem, notes that "our first sight of gold is the light flashing off the helmets of Beowulf and his retainers" (p. 9). She further notes the distinction between the association of gold "with light" in the first part of the poem, whereas "after line 2200" gold "never appears in a context of festivity or victory" (pp. 10–11).

3. See Allan Eller (note 1 above), 47–146. For a study of *fæhðe ond fyrene* see Stanley Kahrl, "Feuds in *Beowulf*: a Tragic Necessity," *Modern Philology* 69 (1972): 189–98. J. Edwin Whitesell, "Intentional Ambiguities in *Beowulf*," *Tennessee Studies in Literature and Language* 11 (1966): 145–49, provides a list of words containing possible word-play.

4. John Gardner, "Guilt and the World's Complexity" (Chapter Two, note 23), points out the repetition of *bearm* and *fæþm*, p. 15.

5. See, for example, Louise Corso, "Some Considerations of the Concept of 'Nið' in *Beowulf*," *Neophilologus* 64 (1980): 121–26. Although chiefly concerned with establishing the meaning of the word, she traces effectively the thematic interlace provided by *nið*: it first appears in line 184, where it serves as generalized moral warning against evil, and is echoed in Hrothgar's homily, 1785; in line 2206 it appears as prelude to Beowulf's ascent to the throne, and in 2714 it is used in the description of Beowulf's mortal wound; finally it is deployed in the significant contrast between Beowulf's dying declaration, 2738, that he *ne sohte searoniðas* and Wiglaf's assertion that he died precisely because he *sohte searoniðas*, 3067. See also, Arnold Talentino, "Fitting *Guðgewæde*: Use of Compounds in *Beowulf*," *Neophilologus* 63 (1979): pp. 592–96.

6. T. C. Rumble, "The *Hyran-Gefrignan* formula in *Beowulf*," *Annuale Mediaevale* 5 (1964): 13–20, counts sixteen examples as against my eighteen, omitting that in line 1, presumably because it is in the plural although clearly the editorial first person, and that in line 18 which appears to be a clear-cut example of the formula.

7. Respectively, Stanley Greenfield, "The Authenticating Voice of *Beowulf*," *Anglo-Saxon England* 5 (1976): 60–61; T. C. Rumble (see note 9); Sylvia Horowitz, "The Sword Imagery in *Beowulf*," (Ph. D. Dissertation, State University of New York at Binghamton, 1978), p. 204. Horowitz gives a reasoned and convincing view of this "ambivalent" voice. As Peter Clemoes, "Action in *Beowulf* and Our Perception of it," *Old English Poetry* (note 1): 149–50, puts it, "The narrator mediates between events and us.... His voice is that of traditional corporate wisdom, indistinguishable from the kind the protagonists utter

themselves." John McGailiard, "The Poet's Comments in *Beowulf*," *Studies in Philology* 75 (1978): 243–70, classifies the comments in six categories and concludes that "no reproach is attached to the hero in any of this" (p. 270), a conclusion which appears not to distinguish between author and narrator.

8. Stanley Greenfield (note 7), p. 60.

9. Sylvia Horowitz (note 7), pp. 208–9.

10. The comments on nature in *Beowulf* are derived from a paper I presented in 1977 at the Tenth Annual Conference of the Center for Medieval and Renaissance Studies, published in *Approaches to Nature in the Middle Ages*, edited by Lawrence Roberts, Medieval & Renaissance Texts & Studies, vol. 16 (Binghamton, N.Y., 1982), pp. 3–40.

11. For the relation of this view of nature to Anglo-Celtic pictorial arts, with documentation, see my study in *Approaches* (note 10), pp. 3–5.

12. Alvin Lee, *The Guest Hall of Eden* (New Haven: Yale University Press, 1972), pp. 178–82. For the punctuation of the passage see Chapter Five, note to lines 90–101.

13. Alan Brown, "The Firedrake in *Beowulf*," *Neophilologus* 64 (1980): 439–60, perceptively observes the thematic force of the linking of dragon and hero in death. The "diminished Leviathan lying stripped of all its natural and supernatural distinctions," serves as a commentary on Beowulf's death. For a related motif see John Gardner's observation, "Guilt and the World's Complexity" (Chapter Two, note 23), of a parallel between the death of Ongentheow and that of the dragon, "so close" that it can "hardly be accidental," p. 14. The significance of this parallel, as he cogently notes, is to link thematically Higelac and Beowulf in heroic recklessness. His observation might be extended to include the theme of treasure: Higelac-Beowulf are linked in seeking it; Ongentheow-the dragon in guarding it.

14. See Chapter Five, note to lines 3074–75.

15. See Chapter Five, note to line 1129.

16. Sylvia Horowitz, "The Ravens in *Beowulf*," *Journal of English and Germanic Philology* 80 (1981): 502–11, observes that "the blithe-hearted raven is set in a context of other expressions that say something optimistic and secure and suggest something fearful and dangerous," (p. 506). In particular, the raven here suggests that Beowulf's "unquestioning acceptance of the rewards of this life is the beginning of his death" (p. 507).

Chapter four
Structure

althoug the design suggested by the narrative involutions, digressions and verbal ambiguities of *Beowulf* should be reflected in its formal structure, what this is has not as yet been determined. Klaeber's hypothesis, the prevalent one, is that the poem has two parts, The Adventures in Denmark and The Dragon,[1] but this has been challenged by the argument that the incremental development of the three adventures suggests a structure of three parts.[2] Both hypotheses are equally plausible, yet neither is susceptible of proof because each is subjectively based. In consequence, no real advance toward definitive structuring of the poem has been made in recent editions and translations, so that Klaeber's perceptive attempt to deal with the problem in his great edition (with revisions) still remains the best starting place for serious study.

Klaeber, in opting for a two-part structure, indicates the beginning of the second part by spacing at line 2200. In his introduction he also suggests an episodic structure within each of the two parts, although this design is not reflected in his text, which is sequentially paragraphed, with fitt numberings indicated marginally, but without the spacing of the manuscript. Thus Klaeber has apparently concluded that because proposals for the ordering of the poem must be subjective, they are best simply noted and dismissed.[3] His misgivings are reflected by all editors of the poem, down to the present, as with Chickering and Bolton (in his revision of Wrenn). They review various proposals, but come to no conclusion and present texts which are fundamentally the same as that of Klaeber, although even more conservative in that they refrain from indicating a two-part structure by Klaeber's division at line 2200.[4] Recent translations also tend to treat the ordering of the poem as an entirely subjective matter.[5]

An understanding of the formal structure of *Beowulf*, however, is too crucial to the appreciation of the poem to permit dismissing the problem as insoluble. This is particularly true because objective criteria do exist by which an approach to a solution may be attempted. The objective criteria consist first in the fitt segments given in the manuscript, and second in the ascertainable conventions of rhetorical patterning that elsewhere serve a structural function. The rhetorical components of the Old English narrative poem are, in general, period, verse paragraph, fitt, episode, and part, each respectively a constituent of the next larger segment. These segments, in particular the verse paragraphs, are consistently signalled by the objective evidence of various rhetorical devices.[6]

On the objective evidence of the manuscript, *Beowulf* is segmented into forty-three fitts. These segments, however, did not appear to Klaeber and most others a viable means for getting at the formal structure of the poem because they concluded that the fitts are peripheral to, and unreliable as, guides to the inner design of *Beowulf*. One reason for this conclusion is that the fitts are misnumbered in the manuscript. This misnumbering however, should give no real cause for uneasiness because it is easily explained.[7] Furthermore, whatever the explanation, there are forty-three fitts clearly indicated in the manuscript, whether the first fitt is numbered or not. (In the following the fitts are numbered seriatim in italicized Arabic, *1* through *43*, so that fitts i–xxviii in the manuscript appear as *2* through *29*.)

A more basic reason for considering the fitt segments to be of marginal importance in determining structure is that they frequently appear to clash with the narrative ordering demanded by common sense. For example, although lines 188–93 recapitulate Hrothgar's abject grief, the subject of fitt *3*, they do not serve to conclude this fitt, but to introduce fitt *4*, the subject of which is the appearance of the hero, Beowulf.

Because rational ordering and fitt section appear at variance and because such examples of apparently irrational division abound in the poem, Klaeber, after carefully weighing the fitt segments, found them insufficient guides to inner structure. His conclusions are, as usual, both perceptive and instructive:

> Though sometimes appearing arbitrary and inappropriate, these divisions are not unnaturally to be attributed to the author himself, who may have considered his literary product incomplete without such formal markings of sections. Of course, it must be borne in mind that his conceptions of structure were different from our modern ones. He felt at liberty to pause at places where we would not, and to proceed without stop where we would think a pause indispensable. He cared more for a succession of separate pictures than for a steady progress of narration by orderly stages. Thus he interrupts, e.g., the three great combats by sectional divisions, but he plainly indicates by the character of the closing lines that he did so on purpose (lines 788–90, 1555f., 2600f.). He even halts in the middle of a sentence, but the conjunction *oð þæt* which opens the ensuing sections, *xxv*, [*26*] *xxviii*, [*30*] was not considered an inadequate means of introducing a new item of importance.... On the

other hand, the last great adventure is not separated by any pause from the events that happened fifty years before (see line 2200). A closer inspection reveals certain general principles that guided the originator of these divisions. He likes to conclude a canto with a maxim, a general reflection, a summarizing statement, an allusion to a turn in the events. He is apt to begin a canto with a formal speech, a resumptive paragraph, or the announcement of an action, especially of the 'motion' of individuals or groups of men.... Altogether there is too much method in the arrangements of 'fits' to regard it as merely a matter of chance or caprice.

(Beowulf, ci)

Unwilling to dismiss the fitt segments and aware that they represent a sense of structure different from ours, Klaeber nevertheless considered them only as rhetorical embellishment, peripheral to the formal organization of the narrative, and he came to the conclusion that *Beowulf* "consists of two distinct parts joined in a very loose manner and held together only by the person of the hero" (li).

Since Klaeber made these tantalizing comments, attempts to show that the fitt segments are truly functional — while not gaining general acceptance — have given impetus to a re-examination of Klaeber's perception that there are "general principles that guided the originator of these divisions."[8] Certainly these principles, however "different from our modern ones," are in practice nothing if not consistent. Thus the beginning of fitt *4* with recapitulation is not an aberration, but is found also at the beginnings of fitts *10* and *31*. Particularly striking is the insistent division of continuous action, which Klaeber noted. Arbitrary and inexplicable as these may seem, they appear entirely deliberate since all the significant actions of the poem are so divided, even subdivided: Beowulf's account of his contention with Breca, *9* and *10*; his battle with Grendel, *12* and *13*; the scop's tale of Finnsburh, *17* and *18*; the battle in the tarn, *23* and *24*; Hrothgar's homily, *25* and *26*; Beowulf's account of his adventures begins in *29*, is interrupted by his Ingeld prophecy, *29* and *30*, and is concluded at the beginning of *31*; Beowulf's remembrance of things past as he goes to meet the dragon extends over *33, 34* and *35*; his battle with the dragon begins in *35*, is interrupted by fitt *36* at the end of which it is resumed, to be concluded in *37*; the messenger's dire prophecy is divided between *40* and *41*; the sententious reflection on the curse of the treasure hoard begins at the end of *41* and is concluded in *42*.

Such consistency of pattern suggests auctorial design that may, however, have a rhetorically decorative, not a structural function. To determine which function is served, an examination of the poet's handling of the introductions and conclusions to fitts may provide a clue if these can be shown to conform to a decipherable pattern of selection which reflects inner structure. First, as Constance Hieatt has shown, the beginnings and conclusions of about a fourth of the fitts do serve an interior function as circumscribing envelopes.[9] These envelopes are largely concentrated in the first part of the poem, through *24*, but evidence of other significant general deployment can be demonstrated.[10]

Thus, twenty fitts (almost half) begin in constructions with transitional *Pa*, "then," plus durative, inchoative or inceptive verbs. Ten fitts (a fourth) are introduced with the formulaic *maþelode*, "spoke," including fitt *5*, the variant *andswarode*. Five fitts are introduced by transitional connectives, *Swa*, "So," and *Oð þæt*, "Then finally." Two are introduced with nominative clauses. Four begin with *Wæs* as simplex or auxiliary.[11] The two exceptions to the repetitive pattern are easily explicable. The introduction to the poem by the formulaic *Hwæt ... we gefrunon* appears a deliberate variation for rhetorical emphasis. Although *Hwæt* is employed frequently in the poem as other than fitt introduction, *gefrunon* does not appear again in the first person plural; significantly, however, *gefrignan* is employed as fitt introduction with *Pa* in the first person singular, fitts *37* and *38*, where the climax of the poem is reached with the death of the hero. The single variant, *Nolde*, which introduces fitt *13* divides Beowulf's battle with Grendel, the exception from pattern giving emphasis to the hero's strength of purpose.

This selective limitation of introductory verbal formulas is matched by selective restraint on the number of functions served. These are limited to three, fairly equal in number although not evenly distributed. Twelve serve to introduce action or speech and are found only in the first twenty-seven fitts, where the speech introductions appear in clusters. Thirteen function to introduce the abrupt divisions of continuous action, which are a notable feature of the rhetorical structure of the poem. Seven of these twelve appear in the last quarter of *Beowulf*, where they are concentrated in clusters. Eighteen serve a transitional function and also tend to appear in clusters.[12]

The conclusions are also limited in type and function. Four fitts end in formal *sententiae*. Twenty-four appear in clusters and end with generalized statements of thematic import (God's power, Beowulf's might, reward, glory), or thematic analogue. Fifteen, also in clusters, have purely narrative conclusions. These three types of conclusion are clustered to serve three functions, concomitant with those served by the introductory formulas. Thus fourteen, coupled with the corresponding fitt introductions, serve as abrupt divisions of continuous action. Eleven conclude speeches, or actions. The remaining eighteen serve as transitions.[13]

These patterns of selection, particularly of introductory formulas, do appear to offer clues to the design of the poem. Most striking is the curiously persistent repetition and variation of the introductory formula of *3, Gewat þa*, "He went then," announcing the coming of Grendel. This is next repeated in *11, Pa ... gewat*, but with some irony to announce the hasty departure of Hrothgar from Heorot, leaving Beowulf to face the coming of Grendel, which is announced to introduce the next fitt with the variant *Pa com*. Next the division of the tale of Finn is introduced by the variant, *Gewiton ... þa, 18*. This describes the departure of the Frisians to their homes in false security, a motif which is counterpointed two fitts later, *20, Sigon þa*, describing the Danes remaining in Heorot in false security now that Grendel is dead, and also unaware of impending bloodshed. Considerably later, fitt *28* begins with *Cwom þa* and *29* with *Gewat him þa*, bracketing Beowulf's departure from Denmark and debarkation at home. The introduction to fitt *35, Gewiteð þonne*, is a variation used to divide Beowulf's analogue of the despairing father. Finally, another variant, *Þa se gæst ongan*, introduces *33* to announce the coming of the last monster, the dragon, and *Þa wæs gegongen, 39*, to announce the immediate sequel to Beowulf's death.

Three introductory patterns, each found only twice in the poem, also appear to be part of a design. Thus, in the juxtaposition of the two fitts, *6* and *41*, each introduced with the simplex *wæs*, a wide-ranging irony emerges: *Stræt wæs stanfah— Wæs sio swatswaðu ... wide gesyne*. The street "encrusted with stone," leads to glorious Heorot, now "encrusted with gore," *dreorfah*, because of Grendel's feud with the Danes; the widely visible track of deadly feud between Swedes and Geats is bloody, *swatswaðu*, in the messenger's gloomy tale of Beowulf's death and his bequest to his people of fatal feud. The two fitts introduced with nominative clauses, *32* and *34*, are almost contiguous, with the former introducing the arousal of the dragon and the latter dividing Beowulf's recollections as he goes to face it. In the last of the unique pairing of introductory formulas, *Oð þæt*, the conjuction is used first to divide Hrothgar's philosophical reflections on the destructiveness of self-sufficient pride, *26*, and second to divide Beowulf's prophecy of how filial pride will destroy Hrothgar's attempt at peace through a marriage of love(*30*).

Finally to be noted is the very striking deployment of the fitts introduced by *maþelode*. There are ten of these, including the variant, *andswarode*, and they are found only in the twenty-four fitts, *4-27*, comprising the Adventures in Denmark, where they are deployed in distinct clusters: *5, 7, 8, 9,— 15,— 21, 22, 23, 25, 27*. The positioning of the final use of the *maþelode* formula to introduce fitt *27* appears to reinforce a narrative division between the Adventures in Denmark and the Adventure in Geatland, since fitt *27* deals with Beowulf's departure from Denmark and the close of this adventures there.[14]

That this deployment of introductory formula is intended to mark a partition of the narrative at *27* is reinforced by the conclusion to the fitt with its praise of Hrothgar's generosity and comment on the ravages of old age, 1884-87:

> Often in leaving   they lavished praise
> upon Hrothgar's gifts   — here was a king
> who ruled without flaw   until the ravages of age
> deprived him like many   of the pleasures of power.

The praise of Hrothgar's generosity provides a suitable conclusion to Beowulf's adventure in Denmark in suggesting the magnitude of his reward, which is the visible evidence of heroic glory. In turn the concluding comment on old age looks forward to the dragon episode; as the aged Hrothgar needed Beowulf's youth, so aged Beowulf will need the youthful Wiglaf. Further, the linking of old age and treasure appears to anticipate the theme basic to the ensuing narrative: Beowulf returns in glory and disposes of his reward but the celebration is immediately followed by his old age and death in seeking vengeance and the dragon's gold.

The conclusion to fitts by formal sententiae provides another indication of narrative partition. There are, somewhat surprisingly, only four of these, and the first, concluding 3, is sharply distinguished from the rest, not only in being the most developed by far of the four, but in its overt expression of Christian truth. In fitt 7, Beowulf concludes his speech, 455, "Fate goes as it will"; 35 is concluded with sententious approval of Wiglaf's decision to aid Beowulf, "who holds to the right / will never betray the ties of kinship," 2600–1; in fitt 39 Wiglaf sententiously concludes his reproof of Beowulf's craven retainers, 2890–91, "death is better / for any lord than life of ignominy." Thus, in distinction from 3 the remaining three concluding sententiae as a group express the ultimate constituents of a pagan ethos: fate as ruler, kinships as sacred imperative, fame as the ultimate good.

Furthermore, the Christian sententia of 3 provides the conclusion to a thematic progression: fitt 1 ends with a generalization on the limits of the pagan understanding of eternity, 50; 2 ends with a biblically-derived generalization on the monstrous folly of defying God, 113; the conclusion to 3 expresses the Christian truth that in eternity the evil are doomed to Hell and the good are rewarded with peace in "the Father's embrace," 183–88. The thematic progression, which moves from pagan ignorance through perception of God's Justice to an anagogical awareness of God's Justice and Mercy, suggests the possibility that the first three fitts may be a unit serving as prologue.

As prologue, the movement from lordless distress in 1 to glorious triumph in 2 and back to distress in 3 establishes the movement of the entire narrative, where distress is ended by Beowulf's glorious triumph, which is followed finally by the dark doom of the dragon. Further, as prologue, the first three fitts establish the theme of reversal in the affairs of the world. The earthly prosperity granted to the Danes by a merciful God through the agency of Scyld culminates in the building of Heorot, symbol, like the tower of Babel, of security in worldly possession, that must inevitably be followed by doom, represented by Grendel, the glory-demon. The theme thus presented is a paradigm of Augustine's view of the earthly city — its prosperity granted by God, its doom implicit in its earth-bound satisfaction.[15]

Finding such clear possibilities of division in the narrative proper, however, presents a problem. Rhetorical signals, noted above, appear to suggest a partition at fitt *27* between Beowulf's adventures in Denmark and the story of his return and his fatal battle in old age with the dragon. However, the division thus suggested appears to contradict narrative logic since fitts *28*–31 deal with Beowulf's homecoming and his account of his Danish adventures, to which they would appear to provide an appropriate conclusion, not an introduction to the story of the dragon. Thus the conventional sense of narrative structure has tended to consider the dragon episode as beginning in fitt *31*, and, accordingly Klaeber mades a break at line 2200, dividing the two parts of the poem within the fitt.

His perception that narrative considerations demand disregarding the integrity of a fitt raises a basic issue. For if narrative logic demands that a structural division be made within a fitt, it must follow that the fitts are the purely rhetorical, non-structural entities which Klaeber considered them. In consequence, the divisions postulated on rhetorical evidence need not be considered as being structurally significant, and the ordering of the poem must be left to subjective judgment. At cursory glance, fitt *31* does indeed appear to break at line 2200 with the sudden, abrupt and apparently unprepared for shift from the present of glorious amity to the disasters of "the days to come." Closer examination, however, reveals that the shift, however abrupt, is an integral part of the movement of the fitt. The clue to this movement is to be found in the motif of "reversal," *edwenden*, 2188, which the poet finds exemplified in Beowulf's life. It is this motif which governs the fitt and explains why the abrupt shift from present prosperity to future disaster in the final paragraph of the fitt is an essential part of its narrative strategy. Because reversal is inevitable, prosperity may follow disaster, and disaster must follow prosperity. This is an iron law which governs man in his fallen state.

This theme of reversal (to be examined in detail later in this chapter), is developed as the fitt moves to the climactic gift by Higelac to Beowulf of Hrethel's sword, a gift introduced in the period which precedes it by the explicit announcement of the theme of *edwenden*, "reversal." For fitt *31* and the entire episode of the homecoming lead to Higelac's gift, and from this act follow the disasters of the "days to come" that are foretold in the final paragraph of the fitt. Beowulf's achievement of glory is epitomized in the gift to him of Hrethel's patrimonial sword, but his achievement came only after an astonishing reversal in Beowulf's life and must be followed by equally unforeseen reversals. Thus, however abrupt the shift from prosperity to doom may appear, the sudden reversal is basic to the thematic development of the fitt.

The final paragraph of the fitt begins abruptly with a prophecy of the deaths of Higelac and his son, Heardred; but the death of the former is implicit in Beowulf's gift to Hygd of the necklet, because when it was given to him Higelac's death was foretold. In turn, because Hrethel's sword has association with the feud between the Geats and the Swedes, it is an omen of the renewal of this feud in which Heardred will lose his life. The future accession of Beowulf to the throne is next announced, a regal succession implicit in the transfer to him of the patrimonial sword of Hrethel. The paragraph concludes with the coming of the dragon. As Beowulf's reign is implicit in the gift of the sword, in his reign, long as Hrothgar's, future disaster is also implicit, for as the coming of Grendel is implicit in Hrothgar's success, so the coming of the dragon is in Beowulf's. To conclude the paragraph, the dragon is aroused because a treasure has been stolen from his hoard; appropriately the fitt has dealt with Beowulf's gift of the treasure he has brought from Denmark, which culminates in his being given the treasured and portentous sword of Hrethel; in turn the treasure stolen from the dragon portends the disaster that will ensue. Thus, far from being unmotivated, the abrupt shift to the future introduced at line 2200 is an integral part of the structure of the fitt, organized on the theme of reversal.

It seems likely, then, that fitt *31* cannot be divided without destroying its rhetorical and thematic unity. Every element in it plays its part in deepening the sense of doomed present through evocation of the past and premonition of the future. In the heroic world presented by the poet, disaster must follow prosperity, "the dead succeed the dying." The exchange of gifts carries with it the memory of a bloody past and a portent of the future, as with the gifts of the necklet to Hygd and of Hrethel's sword to Beowulf. Even the loyal amity of Beowulf and Higelac is shadowed by the overtly-stated fact that they are the last survivors of Hrethel's line, a condition resulting from the blood feud which began in the past and will continue in a future, and which will eventuate in the death of Heardred and the coming to the throne of Beowulf, now, indeed, the last survivor. In turn the future long and glorious reign of Beowulf is merely a prelude to the coming of the dragon, the culmination of a premonitory series, not the beginning of a new series of events.

Although detailed support will not be given until later in this chapter, even this overview of the structure of fitt *31* suggests its complex organization and structural integrity and appears to preclude Klaeber's division of it as well as his assumption that "the poem of *Beowulf* consists of two distinct parts joined in a very loose manner and held together only by the person of the hero." The evidence of the unity of fitt *31* involves precisely the opposite assumption that the poem is, in fact, structurally unified.

The structural design of *Beowulf* is evidenced objectively in the fitt beginnings and endings. These would seem to support the hypothesis that the fitts are organized into larger units, or episodes, as with the first three which appear to provide a thematic prologue in which the fatal course of the earthly city is presented. The beginning of the hero's adventures, fitt *4*, is signalled by the recapitulatory *Swa þa* retrospectively introducing his enterprise by giving the cause for it. The division of his adventures is suggested by the fitt ending to *27* and by the distinctive differences in deployment of the *maþelode* between *1–27* and *28–43*. Such considerations must suffice for the present to suggest a hypothetical structuring of the poem to consist of Prologue, *1-3*, the Earthly City; Part One, *4-27*, the Hero in Youth; Part Two, *28-43*, the Hero in Age.

Part One, *4-27*, the Hero in Youth: Narrative considerations and the rhetorical deployment of fitts suggest that Part One contains three episodes, each of eight fitts. Episode A, *4-11*, is governed by a pattern of challenge and response.[16] In the first four fitts, *4-7*, Beowulf comes to Denmark and is challenged by the coastguard, *4*; responds effectively and is permitted to approach Heorot, *5*; at the door of the hall is again challenged, *6*, and then is permitted to enter and make his offer to Hrothgar, *7*. In fitts *8-11* his offer is gladly accepted by Hrothgar, *8*, but Beowulf is again, abruptly and violently, challenged by Unferth, *9*, to whom he makes response, a response, divided for emphasis at *10* where it is concluded, leading to his formal acceptance as champion and being left to guard the hall, *11*. In Episode B, *12-19*, the battle with Grendel is narrated in the first two fitts, *12-13*; in *14-15* the ensuing morning of celebration; in *16-19*, the evening feast, which centers on the Finnsburh tale. In Episode C, *20-27*, the attack of Grendel's dam is narrated in *20*; fitts *21-26* center on the battle in the tarn, *23-24*, with fitts *21-22* being preparatory to it and *25-26* concluding it in ensuing festal celebration. The battle is further framed, with the first fitt, *20*, providing its cause and the final fitt, *27*, concluding it with the departure of Beowulf, the feud having been brought to a conclusion.

Part Two also consists of three episodes, but in distinction from One, comprised of four, eight and four fitts respectively. Episode A, *28-31*, begins with Beowulf's return home, *28*. The episode centers on the narrative of his adventures, *29-30*, and concludes in *31* with the present of Beowulf's glory reversed by the prophecy of future disaster with which the fitt ends. Episode B, *32-39*, begins directly from the end of *31* with a continuing account of the robbing of the hoard and of the dragon's reprisal at night, into which is interwoven the past history of the barrow, *32*. In *33* the account of the dragon's reprisal is concluded, followed by Beowulf's heroic determination to seek revenge, counterpointed against his inner feeling of doubt and need of assurance through remembrance of the past; in *34* and *35* this remembrance is divided and concluded as he gives his formal boast, which introduces the onset of battle, culminating in Beowulf's deadly peril, interrupted by a shift to the absent retainers, in particular, Wiglaf. This shift leads directly to *36*, which extends the break in the narrative of battle by an account of Wiglaf's patrimonial armor and by his challenge to the retainers and his speech to Beowulf as he enters the fray. The battle itself resumes at the end of the fitt, with the second attack of the dragon that leaves Beowulf defenseless. This second moment of peril is divided at fitt *37*, which begins with the killing of the dragon and concludes with the dying Beowulf gazing on the barrow as Wiglaf attends him. Fitts *38-39* are concerned with the death of Beowulf; in *38* Wiglaf fetches from the barrow the treasure that Beowulf had longed to see and upon which he gazes before giving his final speech and dying. In *39* Wiglaf looks upon the dead adversaries, then is joined by the recreant retainers whom he berates. In the final episode C, *40–43*, the dismal consequences of Beowulf's death are presented. Fitt *40* begins with the messenger's prophecy of doom, continued in *41* and followed by a viewing of the dead adversaries. Fitt *41* is concluded with auctorial comment on the curse of the treasure, which is divided and and concluded in *42.* Fitt *42* continues with Wiglaf's lament and concludes with the emptying of the battlefield. In *43*, Beowulf's funeral pyre is erected, and his ashes and the treasure are entombed.

This proposed structure would appear in outline as shown on the facing page, with fitt-divided actions indicated by connecting lines. Although it would serve only the purpose of tedium to retrace the long path of trial and error which led to the proposed two-part, episodic structure, the hypothesis itself must be tested, and an overview of the structure in some detail seems best suited to such a test. This survey, in particular, will concentrate on the pattern of deployment of fitt introductions and conclusions and on the verse paragraph organization of the individual fitts.

Prologue, *1–3*, the Earthly City: The following analysis of fitts *1–3* provides an example of the detailed analysis through which the proposed structure was reached, and thus deals not only with verse paragraph, but with periodic structure as well. It is intended as a paradigm, obviating the need for such exhaustive treatment of ensuing fitts, except for fitt *31* which requires such analysis.

Fitt *1* consists of two paragraphs. The first, *1–25*, which deals with Scyld and his son, Beowulf the Dane, is governed by backward-forward movement and is framed by the motif of glory, *ellen*, 3, and *lofdædum*, 24. In the first period, 1–3, the poet looks back to the legendary past of the Danish kings, with Scyld, period 2, 4–11 serving as example of Danish royal glory. In this period his triumph in battle is first noted; then backward reference is made to his mysterious and humble beginnings as a foundling; finally the period returns to his victorious glory through war. Period 3, 12–19, looks forward, a[1], 12–14, to the birth of Scyld's heir, the Danish Beowulf; then, *b*, 14–16, returns to the time of trouble from which the Danes were rescued by Scyld in God's design; a[2], 16–19, continues from *a* with the prophecy of Beowulf's glorious reign, further evidence of God's mercy.[17] In effect, the backward reference in the period reveals, in counterpoint, that glory is not the result of heroic prowess, but of God's design. Period 4, 20–25, consists of a description of Beowulf the Dane's pragmatic plans to ensure peaceful dominion, an effort which is commended in a generalization, rhetorically signalling the conclusion to the paragraph, and thematically calling attention, through its misguided approval, to the limitation placed on all human efforts to main-

Prologue: The Earthly City

1 Scyld: earthly peace
2 Heorot: glory
3 Grendel: doom

Part One: Youth

Episode A Prelude to Battle	Episode B Grendel	Episode C Grendel's dam
4 Arrival and challenge	12 Attack	20 Attack
5 Response and entry	13 Victory	21 Hrothgar
6 Challenge and response	14 Celebration	22 Beowulf
7 Entrance and presentation	15 Hrothgar	23 Battle
8 Hrothgar's welcome	16 Feast	24 Victory
9 Challenge and response	17 Finnsburh	25 Hrothgar's homily
10 Response and acceptance	18 Finnsburh	26 Homily
11 Awaiting battle	19 Wealhtheow	27 Departure

Part Two: Age

Episode A Homecoming	Episode B Battle	Episode C Aftermath
28 Return	32 Dragon	40 Forebodings
29 Beowulf's narrative	33 Recall	41 Treasure
30 Beowulf's narrative	34 Recall	42 Treasure
31 Reversals	35 Battle	43 Funeral
	36 Wiglaf	
	37 Battle	
	38 Death	
	39 The dead	

Time Sequences

Part One

Episode A: Travel time plus day 1
Episode B: Night 1 and day 2
Episode C: Night 2, day and night 3, day 4

Part Two

Episode A: Travel time, day 1 plus fifty years
Episode B: After the fifty years day and night 1, a second day
Episode C: Second day and a third, after ten days of preparation

tain order without an understanding of God's design which Faith alone can provide.

Paragraph ii, 26–52, deals with a single subject, the burial of Scyld. Period 1, 26–27, from an implicit Christian point of view, asserts that Scyld had departed into the protection of the Lord. The final period 6, 50–52, reveals through Scyld's mourners the pagan ignorance of eternity, thus counterpointing the Christian understanding implied in period 1 and providing an envelope pattern of introduction and conclusion for the paragraph.

In turn, the body of the paragraph is sequentially developed: 2, 28–33, procession to the shore; 3, 34–42, the placing of Scyld on the ship; 4, 43–45, the provision of treasure; 5, 46–50 final commitment to the sea. Each of these four periods is rhetorically governed by verbs in the third person plural with repetitive pattern (homoeoteleuton): *ætbæron, aledon, teodan, asetton, leton, geafon.* Additionally, the four periods are governed by a balanced pattern of forward-backward reference. In period 2, Scyld's men carried him to where (*þær*) the ship waited, an action modified by backward reference to the immediate past when Scyld ruled. In period 3, they placed him in the ship where (*þær*) it is laden with treasure of "weapons and trophies of war," which looks both back to Scyld's years of triumph, and forward to the time when it will go "with him afar in the sea's holding," 42. In the parenthetical period 4, the treasure with which his retainers had supplied him is given backward reference to the distant past of Scyld's destitute arrival in Denmark. Thus, the present loading of treasure on the ship preparatory to launching it into the mysterious future is intertwined with the memory of the launching of the infant Scyld upon a future which is now past. Two final actions, period 5, complete the burial, and each reflects an aspect of the past. First, the setting up of the standard (*setton segen*) completes the action of placing the war treasure amidships; concomitantly it reflects the period of Scyld's triumphs in battle because the standard marks the king's place in the forefront of battle. (For example, Higelac dies *under segne*, 1204, and his standard leads the way into the Swedish stronghold, 2958.) Second, the launching of the ship, which, for emphasis is marked by compound verbal variation, *letton, geafon*, not only completes the action begun in bearing Scyld to the ship, period 2, but also looks back, as in period 4, to the time before Scyld's glory when as a lonely infant he was launched upon the waters into an unknown future. With equal significance the launching looks forward to a future even more mysterious. The period ends with the mourning of Scyld's men. Finally, period 6, their mourning is darkened because they lack assured knowledge or external life. The narrative present of the burial is not only placed in the dwarfing context of the pagan ignorance of the future, but also counterpointed against the Christian assurance of a known future for Scyld, expressed in the introductory first period.[18]

Fitt *1* thus sets the limits of heroic glory which lacks the eternal reference made possible through Christian faith. Scyld's glorious peace, as faulty emblem of God's peace, is subject to the same withering criticism that Augustine made of the *pax Romana*: "But since these Romans were in an earthly city, and had before them, as the end of all offices undertaken in its behalf, its safety, and a kingdom, not in heaven, but in earth — not in the sphere of eternal life, but in the sphere of demise and succession, where the dead are succeeded by the dying — what else but glory should they love, by which they wished even after death to live in the mouths of their admirers" (*City of God*, v, 14). The noble and self-sacrificing heroes to whom God grants dominion (although their goal is glory and not salvation), for Augustine have the function of serving as pagan exemplars of the love of the Heavenly Jerusalem which they do not know (v. 16). Augustine here provides the only commentary needed on the meaning of the triumphant, war-like reign of Scyld, of his glory and the absence of any understanding of its true Author on the part of those who mourn him.

In fitt *2*, the first paragraph, 53-63, narrates the reign of Scyld's son, Beowulf, but with reference back to the death of Scyld and reference forward to the birth and reign of Beowulf's son, Healfdane, period 1, 53-58. In period 2, 59-63, the three sons and daughter of Healfdane are named. In paragraph ii, 64-85, however, this orderly succession is interrupted by the sudden introduction of the reign of the second son, Hrothgar, no mention being made of the reign of the oldest son, Heorogar, and no explanation given of how Hrothgar succeeded. It is only later that we learn that Heorogar had reigned and died, 467, and that he had a son Heoroweard who, though loyal, had been passed over in the succession which went to his uncle, Hrothgar. In the sudden introduction of the latter, then, a pattern of expectation appears to be deliberately broken. The succession, Scyld, Beowulf, Healfdane, should lead to Heorogar and his son; instead it leads to Hrothgar in the fullness of conquest, paragraph ii, period 1, 64-67, and the evidence of Hrothgar's glory in the building of Heorot, period 2, 67-74. The building of Heorot represents the culmination of the earthly prosperity established by Scyld, but this glory has implicit temporal limits. That is why at its building it suggests the tower of Babel, period 3, 75-81; why at its completion, a premonition of its doom by fire is introduced, period 4, 82-85, and why the destructive "glory-demon", *ellengæst*, will come.

The first paragraph of fitt *2* pictured an orderly succession that in paragraph ii is interrupted by the abrupt introduction of Hrothgar, whose rise to glory culminates in the building of Heorot. The earthly prosperity thus symbolized is, equally abruptly, shattered by the announcement of a new reign of disorder, paragraph iii, 86-114, with the coming of Grendel who is aroused by the song of the scop within the hall, period 1, 87-90. The scop sings of Creation, period 2, 91-102, and it is not until period 3, 103-11, that Grendel is named and his mysterious dwelling and descent from Cain are noted.[19] In the final period

4, 112–15, a concluding generalization on the race of Cain reveals the monstrosity and inevitable doom of the enemies of God. This conclusion provides, with period 1, an envelope for the paragraph, which begins with Grendel's being "wracked in torment," *earfoðlice / þrage* , because of the Creation song, and ends *lange þrage*, 114, the "enduring time" that the descendents of Cain, like Grendel, have suffered because they contended with God, a generalization which serves to place Grendel in the context of biblical history. In addition the conclusion to iii where the verb *onwocon* precedes *lange þrage*, "from [Cain] arose ... / [the evil] who contended against God / for enduring time," provides a chiastic envelope pattern with paragraph i, 54–60, where the verb follows, *longe þrage ... onwoc ... wocun*, "Beowulf was long / ... Healfdane / was born ... to Healfdane / were born." The effect of this envelope in fitt *2*, on the one hand, is to underscore the contrast between the order represented by the succession of Beowulf and Healfdane and the disorder represented by Grendel as the descendent of Cain, the archetypal foe of familial order. On the other hand, the envelope serves to link the two successions, both being outside God's scheme of salvation, whether as neutral, non-participants or as active enemies. Within this frame of reference stands Hrothgar's reign, which culminates in the building of Heorot, a symbol of fallen man's reliance on possession and worldly glory. The significance of Heorot is made clear by being placed within the two generations, that of Cain and that of earthly man.

The analysis of the periodic structures of fitts *1* and *2* was necessary and will serve as a paradigm. The periodic structure of fitt *3*, 115–88, however, is fairly straightforward and does not demand such analysis, so that only echoic framing patterns and verse paragraph structure will be taken into consideration for fitt *3*, and in the remainder of this survey, except for fitt *31* with its special importance. Fitt *3* counterpoints Grendel's domination, paragraph i, 115–63, against Hrothgar's prostration, paragraph ii, 164–88. The two paragraphs are framed by ironic echoic pattern: i begins with Grendel's evil-intentioned approach to the hall; ii with his lawless approach to Hrothgar's throne, an action which by metaphorical extension has deprived him of the possibility of approaching God's throne.[20] Concomitantly, in the second paragraph, period 3, 171–83, the Danes in desperation approach the altars of their gods who are, in fact, demons at one with Grendel as enemies of God, the approach to Whom would be their only true recourse. This is made clear in the conclusion to the fitt, period 4, 183–88, in which a Christian *sententia* establishes the ultimate end of those who live for the earthly city. The anagogical frame of reference, in addition, makes clear the meaning of the cyclical movement in fitts *1–3* from disaster through Scyld to prosperity and back to disaster in the coming of the glory-demon.

Part One: Youth

EPISODE A: PRELUDE TO BATTLE (*4–11*)

Fitts 4–7, to Heorot. Fitt *4* begins with the unique variant *Swa þa,* announcing the opening of the hero's adventures by recapitulating Hrothgar's plight. His need of help, in effect, provides the cause for Beowulf's enterprise. In the first paragraph, 189–228, the retrospective transition is followed by a swift account of Beowulf's heroic resolve and of his voyage to Denmark. In paragraph ii, 229–57, having arrived in Denmark Beowulf is challenged by the coast warden. This challenge leads directly to Beowulf's response, fitt *5, Andswarode* introducing paragraph i, 258–85. This is echoed in *Weard maþelode,* opening paragraph ii, 286–300, which gives the warden's affirmative reply, and is again echoed in the conclusion to paragraph iii, 301–19, *word æfter cwæð,* 315, where the warden takes his farewell, having conducted the Geats to where they can see Heorot. In fitt *6,* 320–70, the *stanfah* street (see above, page 65) directs Beowulf to Heorot to which he comes, i, 320–31, and is again challenged by Wulfgar, ii, 331–55. He responds, *andswarode,* 340, echoing the introduction to fitt *5,* with the verb, found only in these two instances in the poem, serving to link the first two sets of challenge and response. Because Beowulf's response is effective, Wulfgar gives an affirmative report to Hrothgar inside the hall, iii, 356–70, his report ending *wisade,* which with *wisode,* 320, provides a frame for the fitt. In fitt *7* the first section of the episode is concluded. Paragraph i, 371–404, introduced with the *maþelode* formula, begins with Hrothgar's welcoming response and concludes with Beowulf's entrance into the hall. In paragraph ii, 405–46, Beowulf responds, *maþelode,* presenting his credentials and, iii, 426–55, concluding with his offer of championship and his vow. The fitt appears to be framed, if faintly, by the repetition in variation, *Hreðel,* 374, *Hrædlan,* 454.

Fitts 8–11, Acceptance. In this section the pattern of challenge-response is completed and culminates in Beowulf's being left to guard the hall. Fitt *8* is again introduced with *maþelode* as Hrothgar expresses his delight in Beowulf's offer, i, 456–90; it is concluded in a brief paragraph, ii, 491–98, descriptive of the joyful amity that now appears to exist in the hall. Immediately in Fitt *9* the show of amity is rudely interrupted by Unferth's challenge, paragraph i, 499–528, again introduced by *maþelode.* Beowulf begins his response, *maþelode,* in the second paragraph, 529–58, a response, in accordance with the poet's rhetorical strategy, given emphasis by division at Fitt *10,* 559–681. This fitt is introduced by the *Swa* formula, as was fitt *4,* opening the episode, both serving to introduce recapitulations of perils: the first that of Grendel which overcame Hrothgar; the second that of the sea monsters which Beowulf overcame. The implied promise of Beowulf's response, i, 559–610, serves to convince Hrothgar who at the conclusion of the paragraph expresses joy in having found a champion. In paragraph ii, 611–41, Wealhtheow enters and also expresses her joy. In paragraph iii, 642-61, Hrothgar formally appoints Beowulf to guard the hall.

The entire scene of challenge, response, and final acceptance is framed by an elaborate echoic pattern. Fitt *8* ends, *Þær wæs hæleða dream*, 497, expressing the general joyful response to Beowulf's offer, which is, however, interrupted by Unferth's challenge, fitt *9*. To this challenge Beowulf makes a triumphant response which leads to Hrothgar's grateful joy, *Þa wæs on sælum sinces brytta*, 607, and that of the entire court, *Þær wæs hæleþa hleahtor*, 611. Finally, Hrothgar's formal appointment of Beowulf, paragraph iii, 642-61, is echoically introduced, *Þa wæs eft ... þeod on sælum / sigefolca sweg.*

Episode A is concluded in fitt *11*, 662-709, which is marked by ironic, contrastive envelope: paragraph i, 662-90, is introduced, *Ða him Hroðgar gewat*, signalling Hrothgar's departure from the hall in the face of Grendel's nightly approach; the final paragraph, iii, 702-9, is introduced in counterpoint, *Com on wanre niht*, signalling Grendel's actual approach. This pattern of counterpoint is maintained throughout the fitt: in paragraph i the fear betokened by Hrothgar's departure stands in contrast to Beowulf's self-confidence as he remains in the hall; in ii, 691-702, the fear of the Geats is counterpointed against their actual safety in God's protection; in iii, the menace of Grendel's approach is counterpointed by their symbolic sleep, as in turn their sleep stands in contrast to the watchful waiting of Beowulf, God's agent. Finally, a narrative frame is provided for the entire Episode A which opens (fitt *1*) with Hrothgar's despair because of Grendel; now in fitt *11* because of Beowulf, hope replaces despair. To mark this narrative frame, only fitts *4* and *11* are introduced with the *Þa* formula.

EPISODE B: GRENDEL (12-19)

In this episode the *Ða* formula replaces the prevalent *maþelode* of A which in B introduces only fitt *15*.

Fitts 12-13, Battle. Fitt *12*, 710-90, begins *Ða com of more* in echo of the beginning of the final paragraph iii of the preceding fitt, *Com on wanre niht*, 702. The echoic pattern functions not only to provide a suspenseful transition, but also to provide a thematic frame of reference. Because the threat implied by Grendel's coming, *com*, was mitigated, *11*, iii, by the auctorial observation that "the sinful oppressor... / could draw no one / into the night if God wished it not," 705-7, the ensuing action of fitt *12*, echoically introduced, by *Com*, is given a foregone conclusion by being placed in the hands of God. The echo also functions to establish a verbal pattern for paragraph i, 710-36, of fitt *12*: Grendel came, *com*, 710, advanced toward, *wod*, 714, sought the hall, *ham gesohte*, 717, as he had in the past; came to it, *Com þa to recede*, 720, burst in, *dura sona onarn*, 721, and prowled within, *treddode*, 725. At this point the verbal pattern is altered: Grendel gazed at the men, *Geseah*, 728, and gleefully anticipated a feast, *Mynte... wistfylle wen*, 731-34.

His expectations were to be frustrated, for, paragraph ii, 736-57, his anticipatory gaze was met by Beowulf's as he observed the monster, *beheold*, 736. Grendel did feast on one warrior, but then advanced on Beowulf, *ætstop*, 745, and, with evil intention, seized him, *ræhte ongean*, 747, to be countered by Beowulf who with hostile purpose grappled with him, *onfeng hraþe / inwitþancum*, 748-49. Grendel now discovered that he had met his match, *onfunde*, so that terrified, *on mode ... / forht*, 750-54, he altered his former intention to one of flight, *Hyge wæs him hinfus*, 755. In paragraph iii, 758-90, periods 1 and 2, Beowulf who kept in mind, *Gemunde*, 758, his evening boast, was equally determined to prevent Grendel's escape. In ironic contrast to his first gleeful intention, *mynte*, 731, the monster was now solely intent, *mynte*, 762, upon flight. In the next three periods of paragraph ii, the scene shifts cinematically to the outside of the hall, where the Danes listened fearfully to the strife within, the third period being framed by *Dryhtsele dynede*, 767 — *reced hlynsode*, 770. This pattern is echoed at the beginning of the fifth period, *Sweg up astah*, 782, the sound being that of Grendel screaming in despair as he found himself gripped by Beowulf, period 6, *Heold him fæste*. The battle in paragraph ii is framed by repetition of the motif of Grendel's discovery that he had met the strongest of men to end paragraph i, *mette middangeardes / ... on elran men / mundgripe maran*, 751-53, and to conclude paragraph ii, *se þe manna wæs mægene strengest / on þæm dæge þysses lifes*, 789-90.

Fitt *13* divides the battle; paragraph i, 791-818, continues with Grendel's escape and ii, 818-36, announces Beowulf's victory. The uniquely employed *Nolde* introducing the fitt provides a transition from *12* by emphasizing Beowulf's determination as expressed in *11*, and also introduces a pattern of contrast between verbs of intention and discovery: Beowulf was determined, *Nolde*; his men wished to aid him, *wolde*, 796; they intended, *þohton*, 800, to kill the monster with their swords, not having discovered, *ne wiston*, 785, that Grendel was impervious to them. In turn Grendel discovered *onfunde*, 804, that he was in the grip of one much stronger than he had ever expected. Paragraph ii begins with the announcement of Beowulf's victory and concludes with the evidence of his victory, *Þæt wæs tacen sweotol / ...Grendles grape*, 833-36.

Fitts 14-15, Morning Celebration. The motif of Grendel's claw provides the transition to fitt *14*, 837-942, which begins with the men gathering at the hall to gaze at the wonder, *Pa wæs on morgen ... / ymb þa gifhalle guðrinc monig / ... wundor sceawian*. The first paragraph, 837-63, continues with their following Grendel's traces to the tarn and concludes with their return home, racing their mares and praising Beowulf, *Panon eft gewiton / ... fram mere ... mearum ridan / ... Ðær wæs Beowulfes / mærðo mænad*, 852-57. This is repeated to introduce paragraph ii, 864-917, *Hwilum heaþorof ... / on geflit faran fealwe mearas / ... eft ongan / sið Beowulfes ... styrian*, and is echoed, 916-17, *Hwilum flitende fealwe stræte / mearum mæton*, to provide an envelope for the praise of Beowulf by comparison with Sigemund and by contrast to Heremod. The fitt concludes in paragraph iii, 917-24; the morning having passed, *Đa wæs morgenleoht / ... scynded*, the men again gather at that hall to marvel at the claw, *searowundor seon*, and are joined by Hrothgar and Wealhtheow. The fitt is framed by the repetition of the index of time and of the motif of gazing at the claw. As the motif of gazing at the claw served to conclude fitt *13* and to frame fitt *14*, it is similarly employed in fitt *15*, 925-90, which begins with Hrothgar's speaking, *mapelode*, as he gazes at the claw, *geseah / ... Grendles hond*, and concludes with the assembled company once again so occupied, *hand sceawedon / ... blodge beadufolme*, 983-90. The envelope has a further complication. The fitt is introduced by *mapelode*, uniquely in the episode, and is developed on the pattern of statement and response: paragraph i, 925-56, begins *Hroðgar mapelode* with his statement on the claw. To this, paragraph ii, 957-79, Beowulf responds, *mapelode*; in eloquent contrast iii, 980-90, opens with Unferth's silence and concludes with the assemblage commenting on the claw, *æghwylc gecwæð*, 985.

Fitts 16-19, the Feast. Fitt *16*, 991-1049, introducing the feast, is governed by an elaborate counterpoint between concealment and revelation developed from the motif of the visible evidence, *tacen*, of Beowulf's victory, Grendel's claw. The fitt begins, i, 991-1009, with a mildly humorous picture of the Danes being summoned, *Đa wæs haten*, to repair with their hands, *folmum*, the damages within the hall, *Heorot innanweard*, caused at the hands of Grendel and Beowulf. The damage is quickly hidden by hangings, but in counterpoint the futility of attempting to conceal the ultimate truth of man's mortality is stated in a maxim which concludes the paragraph. In paragraph ii, 1009-19, the feast begins in Heorot, *Heorot innan*, with an outward show of amity between Hrothgar and his nephew, Hrothulf, which hides, however, an implied future of treacherous deeds, *Nalles facenstafas / þenden fremedon.*[21] The ominous counterpoint of the first two paragraphs serves as cautionary preface to paragraph iii, 1020-49, which details Beowulf's reward, the outward token, like the claw, of his victory.

Fitts *17* and *18* center on the divided Finnsburh tale. Fitt *17*, 1050-1124, is introduced by the transitional *Đa*, with its first paragraph, 1050-62, continuing from *16* an account of Hrothgar's gift-giving and concluding with an introduction to the Finnsburh tale, which begins in paragraph ii, 1063-1124, and is divided at fitt *18*, 1125-91. The first part of the tale, paragraph ii, concludes with a thematically significant generalization on the insecurity of the human estate where glory is consumed in the funeral ashes. The second part is introduced, *18, Gewiton þa*, with an irony implicit in the Frisians returning home in security which will be shattered by the impending awakening of the feud. The tale itself is framed by its introduction in paragraph i of *17, Đær wæs sang and sweg / ... gid oft wrecen / ...healgamen*, 1063-66, and its echoic conclusion at the end of the first paragraph of *18, Leoð wæs asungen / gleomannes gyd; gamen eft astah / ... bencsweg*, 1159-61. The conclusion serves to introduce the entrance of Wealhtheow in ii, 1162-91. The irony of her appearance immediately after the tragic tale of an earlier Danish peace-weaver is reinforced by echoic intimation of ensuing doom; she enters the hall where Hrothgar and Hrothulf, with Unferth at their feet, sit together in an amity which still prevails, *Þa gyt wæs hiera sib ætgædere*, 1164, an amity like that in the Finnsburh tale which hides the future treachery intimated earlier in fitt *16, nalles facenstafas / ... þenden fremedon*, 1017-18.[22]

The action of the ensuing fitt *19*, 1192-1250, concluding the episode, is continuous from *18*, at the end of which Wealhtheow approaches Beowulf, and at the beginning of *19* has the cup brought to him, *Him wæs ful boren*. Fitt *19* centers on Wealhtheow and the theme of dubious future. In i, 1192-1215, she presents the ill-fated necklet, a gift which foreshadows the death of Higelac; in ii, 1215-31, she places upon Beowulf the burden of securing the future succession of her son, and at the end of the paragraph further indicates her distrust of the future loyalty of Hrothulf and the Danes by protesting too much her confidence in them. Finally, in paragraph iii, 1231-50, the overshadowing of present security by future disaster is suggested by the Dane's joyful return to their custom of guarding the hall at night. Ironically, in the light of what is to follow, the paragraph concludes with a generalization on their habitual armed preparedness.

EPISODE C: GRENDEL'S DAM (20-27)

The discontinuous action of challenge and response in Episode A was marked by repetition of the *maþelode* formula as introduction and speech ending as conclusion. In Episode B the continuity of action from the battle through the ceremonies of celebration was marked by the passage of time; the use of transitional introductions and conclusions, and only a single use of the *maþelode* formula (*15*). In Episode C, returning to the pattern of A with six of the eight fitts being introduced with *maþelode*, the action advances in steps: first, the retaliatory attack of the dam, *20*; second, the approach to the tarn, *21-22*; third, the battle, *23-24*; fourth, the festal thanksgiving, *25-26*; finally, Beowulf's departure, *27*. This final fitt, along with the introductory fitt *20*, serves to frame the episode, the first introducing the central action by providing its cause, the last concluding to the final adventure in Denmark.

Fitt 20, Attack. As fitt *20*, 1251-1320, begins the Danes feel so secure that they go to sleep. Their sense of security arises not because they feel prepared, but because they think they have no reason for fear. They sleep, unlike the Geats earlier, oblivious to lurking and inescapable menace. The irony is enforced by the formula introducing their sleep in *20, Sigon þa*, a proximate echo of the introductory formula to *18, Gewiton þa*: there the Frisians went home, secure in the promised peace; here the Danes go to sleep, secure in their feeling that no further menace exists. Their oblivion, paragraph i, 1251-78, is shattered by the final act of vengeance of the diabolical race of Cain, ii,

1279-1311, which begins echoically, *Com þa to Heorot*, and swiftly narrates the attack of the dam and the discovery of the horror of her vengeance. In iii, 1311-20, when Beowulf comes to Hrothgar, the paragraph is introduced by the coming of day, *ærdæge*, an index of time which throughout the episode will mark the steps of the action.

Fitts 21-22, Approach to the Tarn. In fitt *21*, 1321-82, introduced *Hrothðgar maþelode*, the king announces the death of Æschere to Beowulf, i, 1321-44, and in ii, 1345-82, gives his account of the monsters and requests Beowulf to accept the duty of vengeance. Fitt *22*, 1383-1472, opens with Beowulf's response given in paragraph i, 1383-98, which begins, *Beowulf maþelode*. Paragraph ii, 1399-1441, continues with the ominous account of the approach to the tarn. In paragraph iii, 1441-72, framed by *Gyrede*, 1441 and *gegyrede*, 1472, Beowulf arms himself. The entire fitt *22* appears to be framed by *domes*, 1387 and *dome*, 1470, glory.

Fitts 23-24, Battle. In fitt *23*, 1473-95, Beowulf gives his farewell speech, introduced by *maþelode*, and plunges into the tarn, paragraph i, 1473-95. Paragraph ii, 1495-1528, narrating his descent, begins with the second index of time, "daytime," *dæges hwile*.[23] Paragraph iii, 1529-56, gives the onset of Beowulf's battle with the mother and is governed by repetition of a verb of discovery: *ongytan*, 1496, *onfunde*, 1497, *ongeat*, 1512 and 1518, *onfand*, 1522. To begin fitt *24*, 1557-1650, Beowulf saw, *Geseah*, a providential giant sword, the variation from the *maþelode* formula marking the division of the battle. *Geseah*, in turn, introduces a verbal pattern of seeing which governs the action of paragraph i, 1557-99: *Geseah*, 1557, *wlat*, 1573, *geseah*, 1585. In the second paragraph, 1600-22, the scene shifts (as in the battle with Grendel) to the watchers on the shore and is introduced by a third index of time, *non dæges*, "midafternoon." The third paragraph, 1623-50, narrates Beowulf's triumphant return with Grendel's head. It concludes with the Danes gazing on the head in awe, the action, along with the introductory *Geseah*, serving as envelope frame for the fitt and also as echo of the motif of gazing on the claw, framing fitts *14-16*.

Fitts 25-26, the Feast. These fitts center on Hrothgar's divided homily, which comprises paragraphs ii and iii of *25* and i and ii of *26*. Fitt *25*, 1651-1739, begins with a pattern of report and response: in i, 1651-86, *Beowulf maþelode* introduces Beowulf's report; in ii, 1687-1724, *Hroðgar maþelode* introduces Hrothgar's response. In ii, framed by *eald eþelweard*, 1702, and *wintrum frod*, emphasizing Hrothgar's age, Hrothgar predicts Beowulf's rising future as against Heremod's decline. In counterpoint, iii, 1724-39, he warns him against pride, the spiritual pitfall of the heroic. He continues his warning with a picture of the necessary consequences of pride in the hero, paragraph i, 1740-68 of fitt *26*, 1740-1816. The division is marked by the second variation from the *maþelode* pattern, *Oðþæt*, which serves as in the later Ingeld prophecy, as an index of ensuing disaster. He concludes his homily in paragraph ii, 1769–89, with the lesson to be drawn from his own life, and the company prepares to feast. The third paragraph, 1789–1816, begins with the next index of time, *Nihthelm geswearc*, which brings the feast and the day of battle to a close. The paragraph concludes with the final index of time, the announcement of the ensuing day by the unlikely raven, 1801–06; this conclusion becomes a transitional introduction to the next fitt, *27*, which brings the episode to its close with Beowulf's departure.

Fitt 27, Departure. The fitt, 1817–87, begins *Beowulf maþelode*, introducing Beowulf's leave-taking, i, 1817–39, to which Hrothgar replies, *maþelode*, ii, 1840–65. The third paragraph, 1866–78, framed by the motif of reward, begins with Hrothgar's final gifts and ends with the praise of his magnanimity, tempered by a concluding generalization on the ravages of time. The intertwined motifs of treasure and age provide a suitable conclusion to the adventures in Denmark, as well as a transition to Part Two in suggesting the themes which will dominate it.

Part Two: Age

The absence of *maþelode* as fitt introduction and the sparing use of concluding generalizations are rhetorical features distinguishing Part Two from Part One. The narrative of Part Two is continuous and is interrupted only by the passing mention of an interval of fifty years at the end of fitt *31*. The continuity of action, however, is obscured by a narrative movement in which the past and future are interwoven into the present. This temporal interweave governs the narrative strategy of the three episodes of Part Two.

EPISODE A: HOMECOMING (28–31).

The action here is so continuous as to form a single unit.

Fitt 28, Return. This begins with the Geats leaving Denmark and arriving home, i, 1888–1919. The paragraph is framed by envelope pattern: in period 1 the Geats return to the Danish shore where they are greeted by the coast warden, *landweard*, 1890; in the final period 6, they land on the home shore and are greeted by the Geatish coast warden, *hyðweard*, 1914. In paragraph ii, 1920–62, the continuity of action is interrupted by the introduction of Higelac's queen, Hygd, through contrast with another queen, Thryth. This contrast appears to demand recollection of other peace-weaving queens: the tragic Hild of the past of the Finnsburh tale; Wealhtheow whose tragic future has beem implied in fitts *18* and *19*; her daughter, Freawaru, who will not succeed through love in securing a lasting peace, as Beowulf will prophesy, *29–30*. This thematic interplay is enforced by the envelope provided by its opening and closing periods, which take note of two kingly husbands, Higelac,

period 1, 1920-25, and Offa, period 6, 1957-62: Thryth was evil as Hygd
is good, but Thryth was transformed by her marriage to a truly great king,
Offa; conversely, Hygd, for all her goodness, will not be able to dissuade
Higelac from a reckless adventure in which he will lose his life, wearing the
necklet that came to him from Wealhtheow through Hygd. The intermezzo,
with its interweaving of past, present and future and its suggestion of the theme
of the helplessness of the peace-weaver in a society based on war, thus sets
the pattern of thematic and structural interlace of Part Two.

   Fitts 29-30, Beowulf's narrative. In fitt *29*, 1963-2038, continuity of present
action is marked by the introductory formula, *Gewat* and index of time, *woruld-
candel scan.* In i, 1963-76, Beowulf's arrival is completed; in ii, 1977-98, Higelac
asks for an account of Beowulf's adventures that leads to the beginning of
Beowulf's narrative, iii, 1999-2038. This narrative of the immediate past is
interrupted by the future of his Ingeld prophecy, which is divided at fitt *30*,
2039-2143, and introduced by *Oðþæt*, as was the division of Hrothgar's homily. The Ingeld prophecy is concluded in i, 2039-69. In ii, 2069-2117, Beowulf
resumes his narrative of adventure with an account of his battle with Grendel,
and in iii, 2117-43, with the account of his battle with the dam, which completes his feud with the monsters. His account in iii is concluded with mention of the great reward he has won.

   Fitt 31, Reversals, lines 2144-2200, is introduced by the recapitulatory *Swa*,
as was the beginning of his adventures, fitt *4*; in it Beowulf concludes his narrative of the immediate past, continuing from the end of *30* the mention of
his reward, period 1, 2144-47 of paragraph i, 2144-76. In period 2, 2148-51,
he returns to the narrative present in offering the treasure he has gained to
Higelac, his last kinsman of the royal line to whom, he declares, he owes
everything. This moving declaration serves to evoke the past in requiring an
explanation of why Higelac and Beowulf are the sole survivors, the as yet unexplained result of the past loss of Higelac's brothers, which Beowulf will recall,
2437-46 and 2468-83. At the same time, the theme of the last survivor
foreshadows the deaths of Higelac and his son, Heardred, that will leave
Beowulf, indeed, the last survivor, as will be foretold at the end of the fitt.
Further, the theme of the "last survivor" is premonitory of a theme which will
feature prominently in what ensues in the poem. [24]

   In period 3, 2152-62, Beowulf gives Higelac the patrimonial war gear which
Hrothgar had presented to him, declaring that Hrothgar had required that
he report that the armor once belonged to Heorogar, his older brother, who
had refused to leave it to his only son, Heoroweard. An obvious reason for
Heorogar's symbolic witholding of the patrimonial armor would be the son's
treachery; however, this is specifically denied, but without particulars. Although
Beowulf's report in fact clarifies nothing, it does serve to evoke the prologue
theme of succession and to remind that the question of Hrothgar's accession

to the throne has not been answered, except that it wokuld appear, from Hrothgar's view, that it resulted from Heorogar's own wish. That the sword, in particular, is Healfdane's is known from line 1020, *Forgeaf þa Beowulfe brand Healfdenes*.[25] The history of the armor thus recurs to the distant past of Hrothgar's unexplained succession, with its suggestion that the order of God's dispensation to Scyld and his successors had been broken. Beyond this allusive, thematic evocation of the past, the history of the transfer of the sword looks forward to Higelac's returning gift to Beowulf of Hrethel's sword, an action of climactic importance, as will be seen, leading directly to the dire events foretold at the end of the fitt.

In period 4, 2163–69, Beowulf completes his gifts to Higelac, and in its conclusion is commended for loyalty as against those who "weave the web of malice." This theme of loyalty is given narrative expression in the ensuing picture of the mutual accord between Beowulf and his responsive uncle, period 5, 2169–71. In the context of Beowulf's just-completed description of the brittle situation in Denmark, however, the sententious emphasis upon loyalty provides a reminder that the appearance of festal unity in the world is itself ominous, as when Hrothgar and Hrothulf, uncle and nephew in apparent amity "were still at peace / and each true to the other."[26] In turn, the happy present of loyal relationship between Higelac and Beowulf casts the shadow of a future revealed at the end of the fitt. For Beowulf's loyalty will not keep Higelac or his son from death in battle. Indeed, his loyalty to the latter, attested by his refusing Hygd's offer of the throne in place of Heardred, is itself the occasion for Beowulf to commit an act of treachery. For Beowulf, in accepting the throne offered to him by the Swedish king Onela, after the latter had slain Heardred, secretly plotted treacherous revenge which resulted in the bloody renewal of the feud with the Swedes, 2389–96. Yet Beowulf, in dying, will affirm, "I never contrived treacherous quarrel with many false oaths," 2738–40, an apparent contradiction that, in fact, reveals the falsity of the heroic code. Because Beowulf, like Hengest, lived by a code in which treachery may be demanded by the imperative of absolute loyalty, he is unable to perceive the ethical dilemma in which he is involved.[27] Finally, at the end of the poem, to complete the thematic pattern of the inadequacy of the heroic ideal of loyalty, the loyal Wiglaf will not be able to prevent the death of Beowulf, 2077–81. In turn, Wiglaf's loyalty, like Beowulf's, will be rewarded by the gift of dominion over a kingdom, the future of which is dubious battle, "where the dead are succeeded by the dying."

In period 6, 2172–76, the gift-giving is concluded with the account of Beowulf's gifts to Hygd, in particular of the necklet given to him by Wealhtheow. The emphasis placed on this gift evokes the theme of reversal in the past and the future. On the occasion of its presentation to Beowulf, the necklet was described by analogy with the legendary ring of the Brosings which Hama took from Ermanric and brought with him when his fortune was finally reversed as he "chose eternal good," 1197–1201. At the same time is prophesied the death of Higelac, to be foretold again at the end of fitt *31*. The necklet which will adorn Hygd's breast thus glitters with an heroic past and a bloody future.

Indeed, the whole first paragraph glitters with present glory and bloody past and future. The gift of Beowulf's reward to Higelac occurs in a present where loyalty and trust abound, but in the context of bloody, heroic feuding, past and future. His final gift to Hygd of the necklet presents in epitome a picture of doomed and disastrous glory, seen in the mirror of Augustine's question, "in the sphere of demise and succession, where the dead are succeeded by the dying, what else but glory should they love?"

As with paragraph i, the second, 2177–99, is introduced by *Swa* and begins, period 1, 2177–83, with a recapitulatory affirmation of Beowulf's magnanimity, which has led him to seek glory for the sake of glory, not of possession, a magnanimity revealed positively by his generosity and negatively by the absence in him of savage blood-lust and vainglory. This negative attribution of magnanimity because he is *not* bloody-minded is like the attribution to him in paragraph i of loyalty because he does *not* "weave the web of malice," 2167. His lack of vainglory is the result of his recognizing that his strength is a gift from God, a recognition which juxtaposes the concept of spiritual against that of temporal treasure, the leading theme of i. Beowulf nurtures his strength as a spiritual gift that he directs to the end of glory, not of self; therefore he dispenses liberally, for the sake of honor, the temporal treasure he has won through God's gift to him.

Beowulf's recognition that his strength is a spiritual treasure serves to introduce an overview of his life, period 2, 2183–88, beginning with an account of events which occurred before Beowulf's rise to fame, before his adventure with Breca, whenever that was, and when Hrethel still lived.[28] Because, in contrast to his present glory, his early life was humble, even abject, it illustrates the law of reversal, *edwenden*, period 3, 2188–89. This theme was first introduced at the very beginning of the poem in the picture of the destitute foundling, Scyld, rising to bring to the suffering Danes peaceful prosperity through war, which in turn brings him glory. Such prosperity cannot last, however, and embodies its own doom, represented by Grendel lurking in the moor. Thus the unlikeliness of the *lumpenkind*, Beowulf, by the law of reversal, portends his future greatness. Conversely, because Beowulf, like Scyld, does not know God, the prosperity and glory he achieved cannot last and is, indeed, an omen of future disaster which must come sooner or later.

The theme of reversal is thus of critical importance.[29] It provides the key both to the backward-forward movement of fitt *31*, with its depiction of present prosperity in the context of past and future disaster, and to an understanding of Beowulf's role as hero. As Heremod began with promise and thus with a self-assurance which led to his downfall through self-seeking pride, the inauspiciousness of Beowulf's beginings led to his recognition of spiritual indebtedness and thus kept him pure in his self-sacrificing search for glory for its own sake. However, dimly aware as he is of indebtedness, Beowulf cannot, in fact, know the true Author of his heroic success and thus cannot comprehend his role as hero. Great as his virtues are, Beowulf remains subject to the iron law of reversal.

Period 4, 2190–99, returns to the action of gift-giving, with Higelac repaying Beowulf, in particular, with the gift of the patrimonial sword of Hrethel. The transfer functions as the climax to Beowulf's moment of glory.[30] It is climactic also because it leads directly to the foretelling of the deaths of Higelac and of his son and of Beowulf's succession, which, however, abruptly introduced in paragraph iii, are actually implicit in the transfer of Hrethel's sword, carrying with it the burden of the bloody past and future of the feud with the Swedes. Specifically, the sword completes the earlier gift to Beowulf of Hrethel's armor. This he already possesses, as is established early, 452–55, by his request to Hrothgar that if he is slain his armor "once worn by Hrethel" be returned to Higelac. Although the occasion of the gift of armor is not given, it may be inferred from Beowulf's speech before the battle with the dragon, 2484–94, and from the messenger's foreboding reminiscences, 2985–98. Together these passages give an account of the aftermath of Higelac's revenge for his brother through the slaying of Ongentheow, the Swedish king, by Higelac's retainer, Eofor, who stripped Ongentheow of his armor and gave it to his lord. Since Higelac later rewarded Eofor with land and the hand of his daughter, he must himself have kept the armor, which he then wore as the visible evidence that he was, indeed, "the slayer of Ongentheow," as he is called, 1968. Since after the slaying he also rewarded Beowulf, as Beowulf himself declares, 2490–91, his gifts must have included Hrethel's armor, except for the sword which Higelac would have retained as symbolic of his patrimonial succession. Now in giving the sword to Beowulf he appears to acknowledge the truth of what Hrothgar had declared, that the Geats could find "no man more fit / to be their king" should Higelac die without heir, 1845–53. The transfer of the sword is the climactic act in the celebration of Beowulf's glory, but a glory that bears with it a burden of bloody past and future strife.

Implicit in the transfer of the patrimonial sword is a foreboding symbolism, whether of the disruption of order, as in Beowulf's account of how Healfdane's sword came to Hrothgar, or of impending violence as in his recent, prophetic tale of Ingeld, where the young Dane's wearing of a patrimonial sword is the direct cause of the bloody rupture of a love-gained peace. More strikingly the wording of Higelac's gift of the sword, *bearm alegde*, "laid on his bosom,"

2094, is echoic of the ominous action in the Finnsburh tale where Hunlafing laid the sword upon Hengest's bosom, *bearm dyde*," 1144, there signalling ensuing slaughter as it does here where it is immediately followed, paragraph iii, by the foretelling of the deaths of Higelac and Heardred.[31] As the death of Higelac is implicit in the gift of the necklet, the death of Heardred is implicit in the gift of Hrethel's sword, which carries with it not only the burden of the past feud with the Swedes, but also the foreboding of its renewal when Heardred will be killed. The occasion for this will be Onela's attack upon the Geats because they had allied themselves with his rebellious nephews, Eanmund and Eadgils. In turn this will lead to Beowulf's renewal of the feud to revenge upon Onela the death of Heardred. Beyond this, the transfer of the sword implies a continuation of the feud even after Beowulf's death when it becomes Wiglaf's burden through the transfer to him by the dying Beowulf of Hrethel's sword and armor. For, in accepting this patrimony, Wiglaf will lay aside his own patrimonial sword which once belonged to the Swedish prince, Eanmund, the ally of the Geats, slain by Wihstan, Wiglaf's father, who had stripped it from the dead prince and had offered it to his lord, Onela. Unlike Higelac, Onela chose not to keep the armor, but gave it instead as reward to Wihstan, the slayer of his nephew, 2610-19. Thus Eadgils, who, as a result of Beowulf's revenge has become the Swedish king and will remain so at the time of Beowulf's death, must surely seek to avenge his brother by renewing the feud against the son of his slayer, Wiglaf, son of Wihstan.

The transfer of Hrethel's sword is the culminating recognition of Beowulf's heroic glory, but by the law of reversal, through its implications it leads simultaneously to paragraph iii, 2200-20, where with deliberate abruptness, the deaths of Higelac and Heardred are summarily foretold, period 1, 2200-6, as is the succession of the last survivor, Beowulf, who will reign for fifty years, 2, 2207-10. but this glorious reign will end, as it must, with the coming of the dragon, 3, 2210-14. The fitt is concluded, period 4, 2214-20, with the ominous recurrence to the theme of treasure, this time the dragon's, the robbing of which leads to the dragon's attack.

EPISODE B: BATTLE (32-39).

In Episode A the fitts serve to divide a continuous present narrative into which is woven a counterpoint of past and future narrative. Such division and interweave also characterize Episode B.

Fitt 32, Dragon, continues the story of the robbing of the hoard, i, 2221-31. Into this is interwoven, ii, 2231-70, the history of the hoard, which continues in iii, 2271-2311, from the occupation of the barrow by the dragon to the present narrative time of the robbing of the hoard and the dragon's retaliation. The fitt ends with a prophecy of Beowulf's death and is framed by *sare*, 2222, and 2311.

Fitt 33, Recall, divides and continues the account of the dragon's retaliation, followed by its return to the barrow in false security, i, 2312–23. In the second paragraph, 2324–54, Beowulf, receiving the news, is filled with an unaccustomed sense of doubt and an uneasy feeling that he has transgressed against the old law. Nonetheless, he comes to the inevitable heroic decision for revenge and makes his preparations, seeking assurance in his memory of his victory over Grendel's race. In iii, 2354–99, Beowulf continues his search for reassurance in a mournful third-person recall of the heroic past: first of the adventure in Frisia where Higelac lost his life, then of his loyal service to Heardred. His loyalty, however, has not kept Heardred from death in the renewal of the feud with the Swedes.

Fitt 34, Recall, divides and continues the bloody remembrance, with Beowulf plotting revenge against Onela at the very moment that he secures from him his accession to the throne, the result, it must be assumed, of his having given Onela assurances of loyalty. He intends treachery, but considers himself to be guiltless because such treachery is demanded by the imperative of familial loyalty in the heroic code to which he subscribes. This critical revelation is given emphasis by its use to mark the division of the recall to introduce fitt *34*, where the formula used is that of the nominative clause, a formula used only here and at fitt *32* to introduce the coming of the dragon. In paragraph ii, 2399–424, Beowulf's recall of the past is brought up to the present as he approaches the dragon's barrow, which he observes as he prepares to give his farewell address, still with "grieving heart ... restless with death." The paragraph is concluded with auctorial prophecy of Beowulf's impending doom. In iii, 2425–59, Beowulf begins his backward-looking farewell address, which ends with his reflections on Hrethel's death by analogy with the death wish of the father whose son has died on the gallows.

Fitt 35, Battle, completes the analogue at the beginning of paragraph i, 2460–509, which continues with a recall of the feud with the Swedes when it is renewed at the death of Hrethel; it concludes with his recall of his deeds in the raid on Frisia where Higelac lost his life. In ii, 2510–37, Beowulf makes his formal boast and gives his last commands, and in iii, 2538–601, the battle with the dragon begins and Beowulf is brought to a moment of deadly peril. Here the action is suspended by a shift to the watching retainers, in particular, the faithful Wiglaf, the fitt ending with a sententia on kinship. This conclusion and that of fitt *39* serve to frame the final action of the battle. A faint chiastic envelope may be perceived for the fitt: *sorhleoð ... anum*, 2461–62, and *anum / ... sorgum*, 2599–600.

Fitt 36, Wiglaf, continues with an account of Wiglaf's lineage, i, 2602–30, and in ii, 2631–68, with his appeal to the craven followers and his determination to come to Beowulf's aid. In paragraph iii, 2669–93, the battle is resumed and again suspended, as Beowulf falls into even more imminent danger. A faint chiastic envelope is provided in the fitt by *heregriman hat*, 2605, and *hat ond heaðogrim*, 2691.

Fitts 37 and 38, Battle. In fitt *37*, 2694–751, the battle is divided and concluded, i, 2694–723, with the death of the dragon and with Beowulf, mortally wounded, gazing on the barrow as Wiglaf attempts to revive him. In ii, 2724–51, Beowulf asks Wiglaf to fetch treasure from the barrow so that he may look upon it. Then in fitt *38*, 2752–820, Wiglaf enters the barrow, i, 2752–82 and in ii, 2783–820, returns with the treasure, upon which Beowulf gratefully looks before he gives his final farewell and dies. Both *37* and *38* are introduced with the *Đa ic gefrægn* formula, found only here in the poem, an exceptional pattern in variation of the introductory formula of fitt *1*, which serves to mark the climax of the poem in the death of the hero.

Fitt 39, The dead. The final fitt of the episode begins with Wiglaf gazing on the dead adversaries, i, 2821–45, introduced by the transitional *Đa wæs gegongen*, echoic of the transition introducing the assault of the dragon, *33*, where the final adventure finds its beginning. In ii, 2846–91, Beowulf's men return to be berated by Wiglaf. His condemnation, with a note of rhetorical finality, ends with a formal sententia, the last to be employed as fitt conclusion. It echoes the penultimate sententia concluding *35*, and thus serves as frame to the final action of the battle.

Episode C: Aftermath (40–43)

The action of the final episode continues directly from B and is itself continuous, although with shift of locale.

Fitt 40, Forebodings, begins *Heht þa*, with Wiglaf's command that the fatal message be brought to the waiting Geats, and the messenger's announcement of Beowulf's death, i, 2892–910. In paragraph ii, 2911, 21, the messenger begins a foreboding prophecy of a bitter future for the Geats because the Franks may well find in Beowulf's death an opportunity to avenge Higelac's raid. In paragraph iii, 2922–45, he predicts that the Swedes will certainly find in his death an opportunity to renew the ancient feud.

Fitt *41*, 2946–3057, divides and continues the messenger's warning of what may be expected from the Swedes as a result of a long and bloody history, paragraph i, 2946–98, which is introduced, *Wæs sio swatswaðu*, a significant echo of the introduction to fitt *6*, which serves to interlace the beginning of Higelac's heroic adventures with the beginning of Beowulf's in Denmark (see above, p. 65). The gloomy message is concluded, paragraph ii, 2999–3027, with a metaphoric picture of impending doom, and in iii, 3029–57, the dead adversaries are again viewed. The paragraph ends with auctorial comment on the fatal curse placed upon the treasure within the frame of God's destinal purpose. Fitt *42*, 3057–136, divides and concludes the thematic statement, paragraph i, 3057–75.[32] In ii, 3076–119, Wiglaf comments on Beowulf's heroic recklessness and reports his dying wish that he be remembered by the building of a barrow to hold his ashes. In iii, 3120–36, the treasure is taken from the barrow and the dragon tumbled into the waves in parody of the sea-burial of Scyld. Finally the treasure and the dead hero are brought home.

Fitt *43*, 3137–82, begins (paragraph i, 3137–55), with Beowulf being placed upon the pyre and consumed to ashes as his people lament, an effective echo of the Finnsburh tale where the dead are also cremated. In paragraph ii, 3156–82, the barrow is built in ten days and Beowulf and the treasure are placed within; his people lament, echoing the mystified mourning of Scyld's retainers lamenting his past glory. Both paragraphs are organized in a complex deployment of *Pa* and third person, plural verbs in homoeoteleutic pattern, also echoic of that employed in the paragraph depicting the burial of Scyld,[33] in i, *þa gegiredan*, 3137, *alegdon*, 3141, *Ongunnon þa*, 3143, *mændon*, 3148; in ii, *Geoworhton ða, betimbredon, beworhton, mihton*, 3156–62, *dydon, hæfdon, forleton*, 3163–66, *Pa ... riodan, eahton, demdon*, 3169–74, *begnornodon, cwædon*, 3178–80.

The proposed design of the poem has been supported in sufficient detail to make clear its ordered complexity, and to amass further corroborating detail would serve little purpose. However, in conclusion attention may be drawn to the mathematical structure of the poem, based on the counterpointing of two and three.[34] There are three fitts in the Prologue, corresponding to the number of Beowulf's three battles, and there are three episodes in each of the two parts of the poem; in turn, each episode is constructed on multiples of two, comprising as they do, either eight or four fitts. Further, each fitt contains either two or three paragraphs, which themselves comprise two, four, or six periods, except for the sixteen of fitt *35*, where the climax of the poem, the final battle, is recounted. Thus the complexity of the rhetorical interlace of narrative design and verbal ambiguity is supported by a clear, mathematically-ordered structure which governs the poem, as the table of contents that precedes the translation suggests.

Notes

1. Daniel Calder, "Setting and Ethos: Patterns of Measure and Limit in *Beowulf*," *Studies in Philology* 69 (1972): 21–37, ably defends the two-part structure of *Beowulf*. He sees a contrast between the "bleakness of the view at the end of *Beowulf*" and the "nearly Christian optimism of Part I." See also Martin Stevens, *Modern Language Quarterly* 39 (1978): 219–38.

2. The frequently perceptive comments of Pamela Gradon, *Form and Style in Early English Literature* (London: Methuen, 1971), pp. 128–30, leave an impression of vagueness about structure, symptomatic of the present general uncertainty. She considers that "the fundamental pattern of the poem can be seen in the Scyld Prologue.... Then Hrothgar and Beowulf are seen in success and reversal of fortune; and finally we have a picture of Beowulf himself, whose rise and fall straddles and links the last two parts of the poem, and whose life presents us with a mirror image of the life of Scyld. For Scyld's death presaged the rise [return?] to glory of his people, whereas that of Beowulf presaged the downfall of his nation." If by this she would imply that the poem has two parts, plus prologue, she opts for an interesting variation of the two-part structure; if, however, she implies that the first part of the poem consists of Hrothgar's reversal of fortune, with Beowulf's three battles comprising the last two parts, she would suggest an unusual tripartite structure with Prologue. See also Joan Blomfield, "The Style and Structure of *Beowulf*," *Review of English Studies* 14 (1938): 396–403.

John Gardner, recapitulating his observations in "Fulgentius' 'Expositio,' " (Chapter Two, note 18), *Construction of Christian Poetry in Old English* (Carbondale: Southern Illinois University Press, 1975), pp. 55–60, makes a persuasive argument for a tripartite scheme, based on Fulgentius' interpretation of *arma* — valor, *virum* — wisdom, *primus* — glory. "In *Beowulf*, the basic Fulgentian scheme of the *Aeneid* appears intact, with the important exception that the ending of *Beowulf* is tragic," p. 56. John Nist, *The Structure and Texture of Beowulf* (Sao Paulo, Brazil, 1959) p. 55, and Barbara Raw, *The Art and Background of Old English Poetry* (Chapter Two, note 2), p. 89, both opt for a tripartite structure, but supply only subjective reasons for their views.

On stylistic grounds John Niles makes an interesting variation on the tripartite structure, "Ring Composition and the Structure of *Beowulf*," *Publications of the Modern Language Association* 94 (1979): pp. 924–35. He sees the poem as based on "ring" composition: A, consisting of a Prologue ending with Hrothgar's order to build Heorot; B, of the first and third fights; C, of two interludes of celebration which frame the second fight. His conclusions are undermined, however, by his apparent uncertainty, suggested by the elusiveness of his line numberings (where does A end, for example?). His statement, 925, is puzzling in the extreme, "All the preliminary action of the poem (lines 1–702a) leads up to a single event: the hero's hand-to-hand struggle against ... Grendel," which appears at variance with his having A end with Hrothgar's order to build Heorot. He continues with an equally contradictory statement: "Apart from certain transitional lines that summarize some of the chief events of the preceding years (lines 2200–10a, 2354b–96) this story [the fight with the dragon] occupies the whole of Part II of the poem up to [through?] the final fitt (lines 2200–3182)," which appears to impose a duality upon his tripartite "ring" scheme. Frequently perceptive, his essay appears to me to illustrate the impossibility of establishing the structure of the poem on purely narrative considerations, which remain inherently subjective. Such difficulty is also evident in H. W. Tonsfeldt, "Ring Structure in *Beowulf*," *Neophilologus* 61 (1977): 443–52. He is able correctly to identify chiastic patterns in set speeches (see notes to Chapter Five, lines 237–85), but is quite unconvincing in his narrative ordering, for example, of lines 129–149, 2355–72, and particularly in his entirely subjective patterning of the Finn episode, except for his observation that lines 1017-19—1164-67 provide a frame, where he finds support in rhetorical pattern (see note 22 below).

Finally, H. L. Rogers, "Beowulf's Three Great Fights," *Review of English Studies*, New Series 6 (1955): 339-55, found it significant that "the three fights form a progression," but not significant enough to make him believe "that *Beowulf* can be regarded as an artistic unity in the modern sense [why should it?], or that the poem has a higher theme than the life and death of its hero." This "failure" of structure he blames on the poet who "found as he went on that the material he was obliged to use [?] would not conform to his design." Such a view of the poet of *Beowulf* reduces his to a caricature of one of Chaucer's comic and helpless narrators and is at variance with both common sense and literary sensibility.

3. Klaeber, ix-xii, subdivides the two Parts. I, Denmark, contains three episodes: A, Grendel, consisting of four scenes; B, Grendel's Mother, four scenes; C, Beowulf's Homecoming, three scenes, concluding at 2199. II, Beowulf's Death, contains seven scenes, not divided into episodes. The fitts he does not view as structurally functional.

4. *Beowulf*, edited and translated by Howell Chickering, Jr. (Garden City, N. Y.: Anchor Books, 1977), pp. 19-23; *Beowulf*, edited by C. L. Wrenn, revised by W. F. Bolton (New York: St. Martin's Press, 1973), pp. 74-82.

5. For example, Burton Raffel, *Beowulf* (New York: New American Library, 1963) and David Wright, *Beowulf* (Baltimore, Md.: Penguin Books, 1957), follow the fitt numeration of the MS without headings, the former adjusting the discrepancy in numbers by inserting a thirtieth fitt, 2093-2143. Constance Hieatt, *Beowulf* (New York: Odyssey, 1967), does not give fitt numbers, but supplies headings which divide the poem into Prologue, 1-85; Part I, The Cleansing of Heorot, consisting of eleven episodes, concluding at 2199; Part II, Beowulf and the Dragon, of five episodes; E. Talbot Donaldson in *Beowulf*, edited by Joseph Tuso (New York: W. W. Norton, 1975), gives fitt numbers, which are generally disregarded in the headings supplied; these apparently provide for a Prologue, 1-36; Part I, 37-1816; Beowulf and Grendel, consisting of eight episodes; Part II, 1817-2149, Beowulf's Return, without subdivisions; Part III, Beowulf and the Dragon, 2220-end, with three episodes.

6. The starting point for an understanding of these rhetorical signals and divisions is Adeline Bartlett, *The Larger Rhetorical Patterns in Anglo-Saxon Poetry* (New York: Columbia University Press, 1935). My *Web of Words* (see Chapter Two, note 7) provides a study of the organization of poetic units. In making this study I overlooked the importance of the Ms. fitt numeration, a defect which I would now rectify. A fruitful example of rhetorical analysis is found in André Crépin, "Wealhtheow's Offering of the Cup to Beowulf: a Study in Literary Structure," *Saints, Scholars and Heroes* (Chapter One, note 2), pp. 45-58.

7. If two scribes copied a single exemplar of the poem, the misnumbering would have occurred when the second scribe, B, took over. He began his portion of the text in the middle of A's fitt xxvii and followed A in numbering the next fitt, line 1963, xxviii. When he reached the beginning of the next fitt, however, he capitalized and spaced to indicate a fitt beginning, but he omitted numeration; then at line 2144 he numbered the next fitt xxxi, instead of xxx as demanded by A's numeration.

B's divergence can be explained simply by the assumption that the exemplar from which they both copied began, line 1, with i, but that Scribe A chose to begin his numeration at line 53, the second fitt, his line numbering in consequence one less than that of the exemplar. When B took over in the middle of a fitt, he simply followed A in his numbering of the next fitt, but in coming to the one after he may have noticed a discrepancy in numbering. In uncertainty, he may have marked the fitt division but without numbering it, perhaps with a view to later correction. Then when he came to the next fitt he decided to follow the numeration of the hypothetical exemplar, which he did faithfully, except for one lapse where he again omitted the number although he spaced and capitalized. He did not alter the ensuing sequence of numbers.

8. Benno Timmer, "Sectional Divisions of Poems," *Modern Language Review* 47 (1952): pp. 319-22, made an early appeal for attention to the fitt segments. However, his very tentative suggestion that they represent "psychological units because they agree with the duration of the momentary inspiration of the poet," 322, seems implausible and, in any event, not very helpful.

David Howlett, "Form and Genre in *Beowulf*," *Studia Neophilologica* 46 (1974): 304-25, attempts by an analysis of narrative genre to establish a scheme based on "the number of fitts in each section," p. 323, but the difficulty is that his "sections" turn out to be based on purely subjective narrative criteria. The same reservation must be made for Eamon O'Carrigan's earlier attempt at structuring by narrative ordering of fitts, "Structure and Thematic Development in *Beowulf*," *Proceedings of the Royal Irish Academy* 66, Section C, No. 1 (1971): 1-51.

Thomas Hart, however, has provided objective, tectonic criteria for examining the fitt structure in "Ellen: Some Tectonic Relationships in *Beowulf* and their Formal Resemblance to Anglo-Saxon Art," *Papers on Language and Literature* 6 (1970): 263-290; "Tectonic Design, Formulaic Craft and Literary Execution: the Episodes of Finn and Ingeld in *Beowulf*," *Amsterdamer Beiträge zur älteren Germanistik* 2 (1972): 1-61, and most recently in "Tectonic Methodology and an Application to *Beowulf*," *Essays in Numerical Criticiam of Medieval Literature*, edited by Caroline Eckhardt (Cranberry, N. J.: Associated University Presses, 1980), pp. 185-210.

Constance Hieatt, "Envelope Patterns and the Structure of *Beowulf*," *English Studies in Canada* 1 (1975): pp. 249-65. examines the fitt structure in the light of Adeline Bartlett's "envelope pattern." This promising effort returns uncertain results because in spite of her assertion that the fitts are "circumscribed by such remarkable, self-containing envelope patterns" as to rule out coincidence, 251, she is able to establish this with certainty for only a limited number. Indeed, she is able to show that the envelope pattern serves to circumscribe larger groupings than fitts, although the design she draws appears too complex to carry conviction. It must be borne in mind that the envelope pattern is a rhetorical device chiefly limited to circumscribing verse paragraphs, not fitts, and thus is not *per se* a determinant of larger units than the verse paragraph.

Brian Shaw, "The Speeches in *Beowulf*, a Structural Study," *Chaucer Review* 13 (1978-79): pp. 86-92, explores briefly the objective evidence provided by the patterning of Beowulf's speeches, in which he finds "two thematic series of seven with a transition." The attempt is too brief to be anything but inconclusive and hinges on making the speeches the basic pivot of structure.

Finally, Sylvia Horowitz, "The Interrupted Battles in *Beowulf*," *Neuphilologische Mitteilungen*, forthcoming, has given significant evidence of an objective relation between fitt structure and thematic design.

9. These are as follows: *2, lange þrage ... onwoc*, 53-56, and *onwocon ... lange þrage*, 111-12; *5, andswarode*, 258, and *word æfter cwæð*, 315; *6, wisode*, 320, and *wisade*, 370; *7, Hreðel*, 374, and *Hrædlan*, 454; *11, gewat*, 662, *com*, 704, and *com*, 710, introducing *12; 14, Pa wæs on morgen ... wundor sceawian*, 837-40, and *Pa wæs morgenleoht ... searowundor ... seon*, 917-20; a pattern continued in *15, geseah ... Grendles hond*, 926-27, and *hond sceawedon*, 938; *21, domes*, 1388, and *dome*, 1470; *24, Geseah*, 1557, and *sawon*, 1650; *33, sare*, 2222 and 2311; *35, sorhleoð ... anum*, 2461-62, and *anum ... sorgum*, 2599-600; *36, heregriman hat*, 2605, and *hat ond headogrim*, 2691. See Constance Hieatt (note 8), 251-53. To her list I have added my observation of envelope pattern in *5* and *11*.

10. This evidence is presented in diagrammatic analysis in the table following. (In the diagram the functions of both introductions and conclusions are given. For the introduc-

tions the verbal patterns are also provided since they appear part of a pattern; only the gist of the conclusions is given since they do not appear to me to give evidence of verbal patterning, except for the envelope instances given in note 9.)

		Introductions			Conclusions	
Fitt	*Lines*	*Verbal formulas*	*Functions*	*Lines*	*Gist*	*Functions*
1	1	Hwæt we ... gefrunon	Epic introduction	50–52	Pagan ignorance of eternity	Sententious transition
2	53	Ða wæs ...	Transitional announcement	111–12	Doom of the enemies of God	Sententious transition
3	115	Gewat ða	Transitional announcement	186–88	God's mercy and justice	Concluding sententia
4	189	Swa ða ... seað	Introductory recapitulation	251–57	Challenge	Speech ending generalization
5	258	... yldesta andswarode	Speech beginning	316–19	Farewell	Speech ending
6	320	Stræt wæs	Transition	366–70	Worth of Beowulf	Speech ending
7	371	Hroðgar maþelode ...	Speech beginning	455	Beowulf's faith in Fate	Speech ending sententia
8	456	Hroðgar maþelode	Speech beginning	496–98	Sounds of revelry	Transition
9	499	Unferð maþelode	Speech beginning	557–58	Beowulf's victory over sea monsters	Speech division
10	559	Swa mec ge-lome	Division of speech	660–61	Hrothgar's promise	Speech ending
11	662	Ða ... gewat	Echoic transition	705–9	Watchfulness of God and Beowulf	Transition
12	710	Ða com	Echoic abrupt transition	789–90	Beowulf's might	Generalization, dividing action
13	791	Nolde	Division of action	835–36	Evidence of victory	Transition
14	837	Ða wæs on morgen ...	Transition	920–24	Court assemblage	Transition
15	925	Hroðgar maþelode ...	Speech beginning	987–90	Wonder at the claw	Transition
16	991	Ða wæs haten	Preparatory transition	1046–49	Greatness of Hrothgar's gifts	Transition
17	1050	Ða gyt ... gesealde	Transition	1122–24	Glory and consuming flame	Generalization dividing speech
18	1125	Gewiton ... ða	Echoic speech division	1189–92	Wealhtheow comes to Beowulf	Preparatory transition
19	1192	Him wæs ful boren	Transition	1246–50	Danish custom of armed preparation	Transitional generalization
20	1251	Sigon þa to slæpe	Echoic transition	1319–20	Beowulf speaks to Hrothgar	Preparatory transition
21	1321	Hroðgar maþelode	Speech beginning	1380–82	Promise of reward	Transitional speech ending
22	1383	Beowulf maþelode	Speech beginning	1471–72	Comparison of Beowulf-Hunferth	Transitional generalization

#	Line			Line		
23	1477	Beowulf maþelode	Speech beginning	1554-56	God's judgement	Generalization dividing action
24	1557	Geseah ða	Division of action	1648-50	Grendel's head	Preparatory transition
25	1651	Beowulf maþelode	Speech beginning	1738-39	Sententious analogue of proud man	Analogue dividing speech
26	1740	Oð þæt ... weaxeð	Division of speech	1816	Beowulf greets Hrothgar	Preparatory transition
27	1817	Beowulf maþelode	Speech beginning	1885-87	Hrothgar's age and magnanimity	Concluding generalization
28	1888	Cwom þa	Echoic transition	1960-62	Analogue of Offa	Division of action
29	1963	Gewat him ða	Echoic transition	2036-38	Sword as incitement to vengeance	Division of speech
30	2039	Oð þæt ... forlæddan	Division of speech	2141-43	The treasure of Beowulf's reward	Division of speech
31	2144	Swa. lyfde	Division of speech	2214-20	Robbing of the hoard	Preparatory transition
32	2221	Nælles ... se ðe ... gesceod	Transition	2309-11	Fury of dragon's onset	Preparatory transition
33	2312	Ða se gæst ongan	Echoic transition	2390	He was a good king	Generalization dividing recall
34	2391	Se ðæs ... gemunde	Division of recall	2458-59	Death and the end of joyful sound	Division of analogue
35	2460	Gewiteð þonne	Echoic division of speech	2600-1	Imperative of kinship	Sententia dividing action
36	2602	Wiglaf wæs haten	Division of action	2691-93	Dragon seizes Beowulf	Preparatory transition
37	2694	Ða ic ... [gefrægn]	Division of action	2749-51	Beowulf's faith in power of gold	Transitional speech ending
38	2752	Ða ic ... gefrægn	Echoic transition	2819-20	Journey of Beowulf's soul	Conclusion of action
39	2821	Ða wæs gegongen	Echoic transition	2890-91	Death better than ignominy	Transitional speech ending
40	2892	Heht ða ... biodan	Transition	2943-45	Higelac rescues the Geats	Preparatory transition
41	2946	Wæs sio swatswaðu	Echoic division	3054-57	God's design	Division of the tic generalizati
42	3058	Þa wæs gesyne	Division of generalization	3134-6	Gold and hero brought home	Preparatory transition
43	3137	Him ða gegirdan	Transition	3178-82	Mourning	Conclusion of poem

11. The deployment of introductory verbal formula is as follows:

Þa plus durative: *2, 14, 36*
  plus inchoative: *3, 11, 18, 20, 33, 35, 39*
  plus inceptive: *12, 16, 17, 24, 28, 37, 38, 40, 42, 43*
Maþelode: 5 (*andswarode*), *7,8,9 − 15 − 21,22,23,25,27*
Swa: 4 (with *þa*), *10, 31, Oþ þæt: 26, 30*

Wæs as simplex: *6, 41*
  as auxiliary: *19, 36*
Nominative clauses: *32, 34*

12. The deployment of introductory function is as follows:

Introduction to action: *1, 4*
  to speech: *5,7,8,9, −15−21,22,23,25,27*
Divisions: *10,13,18,24,26, −30,31− 34,35,36,37, −41,42*
Transitions: *2,3, −6−11,12−14,16,17,19,20, −28,29, −32,33, −38,39,40,43*

13. The deployment of conclusions by type is as follows:

Formal sententia: *3, 7, 35, 39*
Thematic statement: *1,2, 6, 9,10,11,12, 15,16,17, 19,21,22,23, 27, 30,33, 37,38, 41,43*
Analogue: *25, 28, 34*
Narrative: *4,5, 8, 13,14, 18,20, 24,26, 29,31,32, 36,37,40,42*

The deployment of conclusions by function is as follows:

Division: *9, 12, 17, 23,25, 28,29,30, 33,34,35,41*
Conclusion of speech: *4,5,6,7, 10, 21, 37,39*
  of action: *3, 27, 43*
Transitions: *1,2, 8, 11,13,14,15,16,18,19,20,22,24,26, 31,32, 36,38,40,42*

14. Further support is provided by the fact that of the twelve examples of fitts framed by envelope pattern, nine are found in fitts *1-24* (see note 9).

15. Robert Hanning, "Beowulf as Heroic History," (See Chapter Two, note 20) has independently placed "the first two hundred lines of *Beowulf* as a prologue to the hero's appearance," p. 90. I assume he is here giving a round number, not a specific one.

16. Charles McNally, "First-Person Speeches in Beowulf" (Ph.D. dissertation, State University of New York at Binghamton, 1975), in his semantic study provides a convincing description of the pattern of challenge and response.

17. John Niles (note 2, above) finds in the period, which he terms without explanation a paragraph, an example of Adeline Bartlett's envelope (or "ring") pattern, which she overlooked. In fact it does not conform to her criteria, not being a paragraph and lacking any verbal or other rhetorical signal. His elaborate dissection is beside the point; what is involved is simply the a^1-b-a^2 backward-forward movement of cause and effect, a^1 and a^2 giving the effect, Beowulf's rise to glory, b, the cause, God's mercy. The lettering a,b, disignates clausules, as explained in *Web of Words*, pp. xvi-xx.

18. Robert Hanning (note 15 above) has independently observed that "the contrast between the Dane's ignorance about Scyld and the poet's (and audiences') awareness of God's hand at work is thematic," p. 90.

19. For the punctuation of period 2, see Chapter Five, note to lines 90–101.

20. See Chapter 5, note to lines 168–69.

21. Gerald Morgan, "The Treachery of Hrothulf," *English Studies* 53 (1972): pp. 23–39, has attempted to rehabilitate Hrothulf's reputation and to deny the imputation of treachery. His argument, however, is based largely on what is not in the poem, and he ignores the implicit evidence of lines 1018-19 and 1164-65. His assumption that it was natural for the king's son to be superseded is belied by the refusal of Beowulf to take the crown from Heardred though it was offered him by Hygd with the consent of the Geats. If Beowulf's action is noble, it follows that Hrothulf's action would be, at the least, less than noble.

22. Donald Fry, *Finnsburh* (London: Methuen, 1974), 13, has observed the close rela-

tion to the Finnsburh tale of Wealhtheow's tragic role. The echoic pattern (1017–18 and 1164–67) was noted by Arthur Brodeur, *The Art of Beowulf* (Berkeley: University of California Press, 1960), p. 139. See also H. W. Tonsfeldt, "Ring Structure" (note 2, above).

23. See Chapter Five, note to line 1495.

24. Compare the history of the burial of the treasure in the barrow, 2236–70, and Beowulf's dying speech where he laments his lack of an heir and turns to Wiglaf as the last survivor of his father's race, 2729–32, 2813–16.

25. See Chapter Five, note to line 1020.

26. See note 21, above.

27. Compare with Hengest's betrayal of Finn, a treachery apparently considered noble by the singer of the tale; see Chapter Five, note to line 1129.

28. See Chapter Five, note to lines 2183–88.

29. Theodore Andersson, "Tradition and Design in *Beowulf*," *Old English Literature in Context*, edited by John Niles (Totowa, New Jersey: Rowan and Littlefield, 1980), pp. 90–106, who makes an inconclusive attempt to get at the design of the poem by reference to "a pre-established narrative framework" [?]; perceptively observes that "the organizing principle in operation throughout the poem is 'mutability,' " pp. 97–104.

30. James Rosier, "The Two Closings of *Beowulf*," *English Studies* 54 (1973): 1–2, notes the significance of the bestowing of the sword "as dramatic climax to Beowulf's earlier career," in completing the gift of armor.

31. Lewis Nicholson, "Hunlafing and the Point of the Sword," *Anglo-Saxon Poetry* (Chapter Two, note 23), p. 59, has also observed the echoic function of the two phrases as prelude to disaster.

32. See Chapter Five, note to lines 3074–75.

33. James Rosier, "The Two Closings," (see note 30), p. 3, without elaboration has called attention to the verb pattern in paragraph i.

34. Number symbolism, a significant element in the Augustinian conception of typological correspondences, was part of the Old English poet's scheme, the counterpointing of the dualism of the two cities and the unity of the Trinity being of primary importance. See *Doctrine and Poetry* (Chapter Two, note 8), pp. 21, 107–10, 162, 197–200, 215, note 74. W. F. Bolton, *Alcuin and Beowulf* (Chapter Two, note 2), without reference to my earlier study, comments on the number symbolism employed by Alcuin as perhaps parallel to that in *Beowulf*, pp. 75–76. See also the studies by Thomas Hart cited in note 8 above.

Chapter five
translation

Since the translation aims to present the shape and form of my reading of *Beowulf*, it makes no attempt at poetic recreation, only at following the text, as I understand it, with minimal deviation from line by line congruence. An attempt is made, however, at suggesting the alliterative metrical system of the original in its simplest form. Thus each long line is divided by caesura, and each half-line is connected to the other by alliteration; that is, each half-line contains two stressed and two or more unstressed syllables, and at least one of the stressed syllables in the first half-line alliterates with at least one in the second. The pattern may be illustrated by lines 43–46:

> They Léft with hïm   a nátion's Légacy,
> tréasure as Gréat   as iń the beGïnning
> théy had Fúrnished   who sént him Fórth
> aLóne upon the wáters   a Lónely chïld.

Although the translation aims at readability, clumsiness in diction and structure is permitted where it is demanded by the overriding need to translate echoic pattern and deliberate verbal ambiguity.

Punctuation of a translation of Old English poetry presents difficulties. The problem is not in paragraphing which requires chiefly a sensitivity to rhetorical signals, largely the envelope patterns of repetition and variation. In turn, the periodic (sentence) structure is usually made clear once the shape of the verse paragraph is determined. The problem rests with the units (clausules) which are clustered in phrases and clauses to make up the period. Modern punctuation with its demand that commas separate appositive phrases and non-restrictive clauses can obscure the relation of elements within the period. In the *Web of Words* I attempted to solve this problem by breaking from modern usage in the handling of commas and semi-colons. However, my attempt to apply this system with Orm-like thoroughness to the translation of *Beowulf* tended, I found, to conflict with modern habits of reading to no real advantage; in consequence, except rarely, the punctuation is in accord with modern usage. The reader must be aware, nonetheless, that the period of Old English poetry is not linear, but is, instead, developed by clustering, frequently incremental, and it is the totality of the period that must be addressed. The attempt to read the poem in this way is well worth the effort.

Beowulf

The Argument

B — *Victory Over Grendel*

Beowulf
a translation

PROLOGUE

The Earthly City

1 · Scyld: Earthly Peace

i *Rise and succession*

   Hear the ancient tale   that we are told
of heroic deeds   of Danish kings,
of how these lords   lived for glory!
Oft Scyld Scefing   in shock of battle
5 took the meadhalls   of many nations
from the terrified foe;   a poor foundling
he appeared in Denmark   and there prospered,
growing to greatness,   gaining much honor,
until every nation   neighboring his
10 paid him tribute   over the seapaths,
gave him obedience   —he was a good king.
Then to him in season   a son was born,
a child in the house   sent by Heaven
as solace to the people;   for pitying
15 their sore distress   and long suffering
while they were lordless   the Lord of Life,
the Master gave him   mortal prosperity;
Beowulf was famous   —his glory spread far—
the son of Scyld   in the Scylding land.
20 Thus a young prince   should practice magnificence,
giving bounteously   from his father's bosom
that when he becomes old   an endeared company
will remain by his side   to serve the people
at the onset of war   —whoever in this world
25 works to earn praise   will everywhere prosper.

1 Danish glory

2 Scyld's triumph

3 The succession

4 Sententia:
worldly
prosperity

ii *The burial of Scyld*

Then in fullness of strength   at the fated hour   *1 Scyld's death*
Scyld took his way   into God's protection.
Then his dear comrades   were dutiful to commands   *2 Procession*
given before death   by the Danish king,
30 and carried their beloved   after his long reign,
as he had said they should,   to the shore of the sea
where the prince's ship   with its ringed prow
icily rested,   ready in the harbor.
Then they laid down   their beloved lord   *3 Ship burial*
35 and bountiful master   in the ship's bosom,
hard by the mast   where were heaped
precious treasures   from far-off places
—I've heard of no ship   more nobly furnished
with battle weapons   and trappings of war,
40 with blade and mail—   upon his bosom was laid
the precious wealth   which was to go
with him afar   in the sea's holding.
(They left with him   a nation's legacy,   *4 (The treasure)*
treasure as great   as in the beginning
45 they had furnished   who sent him forth
alone upon the waters,   a lonely child.)
Then above his head   they set on high   *5 Commitment*
the golden standard,   gave him to the ocean,   *to the sea*
let the sea take him;   their souls were saddened,
50 their hearts mournful.   Here under the heavens   *6 Ignorance*
no warrior or counselor   had the wisdom to say   *of eternity*
into whose keeping   that cargo would come.

2 · Earthly Prosperity

i *Order of succession*

Then the son of Scyld   ruled in the stronghold,   *1 Orderly*
—his lordly father   had left this world—   *succession*
55 the beloved Beowulf,   long their ruler,
famed among nations;   the noble Healfdane
in turn was born,   brave and venerable
he ruled the Danes   until his death.
As I have heard   to Healfdane were born   *2 Healfdane's*
60 Heorogar and Hrothgar   and Halga the good,   *children*

and besides these sons   a single daughter,
Yrse who became   the consort of Onela,
the beloved queen   of the Swedish king.

ii *Hrothgar and Heorot*

  Then Hrothgar gained   honor by battle
65 and conquest by war   so that comrades eagerly
hastened to obey him   until a host of youths
swelled his might.   It came to his mind
that he command   the building of a meadhall
more magnificent   in its mighty height
70 than any that humans   had ever heard of,
therein to offer gifts   to old and young
of all that God   had given him
except for common land   and the lives of men.
75 Then widely I've heard   from the world's people
many were summoned   to make the hall
a work of beauty;   in a brief time,
as men reckon,   the mightiest of buildings
was ready for use;   the ruler whose word
held nations in check   named it Heorot;
80 true to his promise   he shared his treasure,
gave gifts at the feast.   The gabled hall
towered on high   and awaited the torch,
the rush of fire;   but festering hatred
had not yet driven   the daughter's husband
85 to fierce hostility   against her father.

*1 Hrothgar's
unexplained
succession*

*2 His plans
for Heorot*

*3 Building
of Heorot*

*4 Omens of
disaster*

iii *Grendel's response*

  The glory-demon   glowered in the darkness
where he waited   wracked in torment
as he listened each day   to the loud music
resounding in the hall   where notes of the harp
90 joined the song of the scop.   (He spoke who knew
the ancient account   of the creation of man;
he declared that God   created the earth,
the shining shore   surrounded by the sea,
in victory set   the sun and the moon
95 as lamps to light   those living in the world,
and made beautiful   with leaves and branches
the regions of land,   and also gave life
to every kind   of animate creature;

1 Grendel aroused

*2 (The song
of creation)*

thus lordly men   lived blessedly
100 in happiness   until the fiend in hell
began to do   his wicked deed.)
Grendel was the name   of the grim demon   *3 Grendel's descent from Cain*
famed as a wanderer   of wasteland and fen,
the moor his stronghold;   the miserable wretch
105 had inhabited for long   the land of the giants
after Cain's race   had the Creator's curse
laid upon it   — the Lord avenged
the slaying of Abel,   his savage murder;
Cain's feud was joyless   as far from men
110 God sent him into exile   because of his sin.
From him arose   all monstrous races,   *4 Cain's descendants*
elves and ogres   and evil spirits,
the giants too   who contended with God
for enduring time   — their toil He repaid,

3 · Grendel's Domination

i *Grendel's victory*

115   After night had fallen   he went to find   *1 Attack*
what warriors remained   in the mighty hall,
and the doing of the Danes   after their drinking;
he discovered therein   a noble company
asleep after the feast   who felt no threat
120 of sorrow or grief;   grim and greedy,
cruel and savage,   the evil creature
soon was ready   and took from their rest
thirty warriors;   after this he went
to seek his house,   returning home
125 exulting in the booty   of slaughtered bodies.
At break of day   with the coming of dawn   *2 Discovery*
Grendel's power   was made apparent;
after merriment   the morning brought
loud lamentation.   Illustrious Hrothgar,   *3 Hrothgar's grief*
130 once glorious,   now seated in gloom,
suffered terribly   an intense grief
after the discovery   of the accursed traces
of the hated fiend   — the strife was too fierce,
too long and savage.   Time did not linger,   *4 Renewed attack*
135 for the very next night   Grendel visited upon them

murder more fell   and lawless feud
—he felt no remorse,   evil held him fast.
After the hatred   of the hall retainer   *5 Surrender of*
was seen and known   by no doubtful sign,   *the hall*
140 easy to find   in the Danish fellowship
was he who chose   to bed in chamber
away from the hall;   only he kept safe,
escaped the foe,   who stayed afar.
Thus Grendel ruled   and fought against right,   *6 Grendel's*
145 one against many,   until the mightiest of halls   *domination*
stood desolate;   the lord of the Danes
for the long time   of twelve winters
suffered misery,   every sadness
and wretched sorrow;   in songs of grief
150 it was made known   to the sons of men
and widely revealed   that for many winters
Grendel had waged   war against Hrothgar,
venting his fury   in lawless feud
and relentless foray;   he would not listen
155 to talk of peace   or petition to end
the deadly war   with Danish wergild;
nor did the council   expect compensation
or handsome repayment   from the slayer's hands,
for the dark adversary   and deadly shadow
160 kept up his pursuit,   setting his snares
for human kind,   and in darkness holding
the misty moors;   it was a mystery to men
where the demons went   in their wanderings.

ii *Hrothgar's prostration*

Thus the savage enemy   and solitary wanderer   *1 Grendel's*
165 visited upon mankind   much violence   *triumph*
and lawless hate;   he occupied Heorot's
dearly encrusted hall   in the dark of night
—no gift or greeting   could he give before God
at the lord's throne   or know his love.
170 The lord of the Danes   was left broken-hearted   *2 Hrothgar's grief*
in great sadness.   Many nobles sat
in secret deliberation;   they considered   *3 The blind lead*
what counsel to offer   men of courage   *the blind*
for surest countering   of sudden affliction;
175 in their pagan temples   at times they offered

idolatrous service,   sought from the devil
and slayer of souls   succor for their people,
comfort in adversity,   such being their custom
and heathen hope;   to hell was given
180 reign over their souls   —they knew not the Ruler
and Judge of the living,   the Lord their God,
nor knew how to praise   the Protector
and Heavenly King.   Woe is to him   *4 Christian*
who through deadly sin   shall cast his soul   *sententia*
185 into the fire's bosom   —never to find solace
or hope for release;   joy is to him
who may dwell with the Lord   after his death day
—there to find peace   in the Father's embrace.

Part One

the hero in youth

A — *Prelude to Battle*

4 · The First Challenge

i *The journey*

1 *Recapitulation*

    Thus Healfdane's son   grievously suffered
190 the ravages   without respite
of the cruel,   crushing tyranny
nightly inflicted   upon his followers,
 —a strife too fierce,   too long and savage.

In his distant home   a retainer of Higelac,   2 *Beowulf's decision*
195 honored by the Geats,   heard of Grendel's deeds;
this mighty noble   surpassed all men
in the great strength   he had been given
in this mortal life;   he commanded that a ship
be made ready to sail   and said he would seek
200 across the sea   the illustrious king
and warlike lord   who lacked warriors.

The lords of council,   though they loved him much,   3 *Consent*
were easily persuaded   to consent to his venture
and gave him encourgement,   the omens being good.
205 The worthy selected   from the Geatish warriors   4 *Boarding*
the men he found   most of courage;
with his fellowship   of fourteen men
he sought the seawood,   a skillful sailor,
he showed the way   that led to the shore.
210 The time had come   — on the sea under the cliff
the ship waited;   vigilant warriors
climbed the prow   —the sea currents
merged with the shore;   the men carried
on the bosom of the ship   the bright treasure
215 of polished wargear;   men with a will

launched on the journey   the well-locked wood.
Over the sea ways   the wind-driven ship   *5 Journey*
floated swanlike   with foamy neck;
on the due hour   of the second day
220   the curve-prowed craft   had come so far
that the seafarers   could see the land,
the shining cliffs   and steep mountains,
the wide headlands   — the water was crossed
and harbor come.   Then hastily the Geats   *6 Landing*
225   beached their ship   up on the shore,
moored the seawood   — their coats of mail
and gear clattered;   they gave thanks to God
that they had sailed   the sea in comfort.

ii *First challenge*

Watching from the wall,   the Danish warden   *1 The warden*
230   appointed to guard   the sea approaches
saw bright shields   and battle-ready armor
borne across the plank;   his calm was broken
by his wish to know   who these warriors were.
Hrothgar's lieutenant,   turning his horse,   *2 "Who are you?*
235   rode to the harbor;   brandishing in his hands
his mighty spear   he made enquiry:
"Who are you warriors   bearing weapons,
covered in armor,   who have crossed the sea
in your high ship   and have come here
240   over the waters?   For many winters   *3 "I guard the shore*
as warden of the coast   I have held watch
that none of our foes   with force of ships
could raise havoc   in the homeland.
No men more openly   have made their way here   *4 "You come*
245   with shields in hand,   though heedless of password   *unannounced"*
or other sign   of the court's consent
to your warlike passage.   In this world I have seen   *5 "I note the*
no noble more mighty   than one man in armor   *nobility of one*
who is part of your company;   he is no commoner
250   fitted with weapons   —his features could never
belie their appearance.   Now I must learn   *6 "I must know*
your lineage,   lest with deceit,   *who you are."*
coming as spies   upon Danish soil
you venture further;   now voyagers
255   from distant land   listen to my plain

and simple advice;   your surest course
is quickly to tell   whence you have come."

5 · Beowulf is Admitted to Denmark

i *Beowulf's first reply*

    The lord of the troop,   the leader replied,   *1 "We are Geats*
for him unlocked   his hoard of words:
260 "We come of the race   and kindred of the Geats,
and are Higelac's   hearth companions;
my noble father   was named Ecgtheow,
among men a name   of honorable renown,
he lived many winters   until with age he went
265 his way from life,   remembered well
by men of wisdom   throughout the world.
In friendly sincerity   we have come to seek   *2 "We seek Hrothgar*
the son of Healfdane,   your high protector
and ruler of his people   — tell us what is right;
270 we bear a message   of import to his majesty
the king of the Danes   which I propose to declare
when I come before him.   You know clearly   *3 "Is the tale of*
if there is truth   in the tale we've heard   *Grendel true?*
that a criminal enemy   of a kind I do not know,
275 a mysterious demon,   manifests to the Danes
in the dark nights   a dreadful menace
and murderous hate.   With fullness of heart   *4 "I come to help."*
I may give to Hrothgar   in his aged goodness
counsel to help   conquer his enemy;
280 either chance will bring   change for the better
and his grievous sorrow   will find surcease,
the surges of care   be quieted,
or else he must endure   day without end
harrowing misfortunc   while the greatest of halls
285 still holds its place   on the high hill."

ii *Favorable response*

    The fearless soldier   upon his steed,   *1 "I grant you passage*
the warden spoke: "A sensible warrior
who uses his mind   must distinguish
and know the difference   between word and deed;
290 from what I have learned   the lord of the Danes

may trust this company;   you may come with me
in your war gear.   I will guide you,   *2 "I will guide you and*
and I will see   that my soldiers   *guard your ship."*
attend and guard,   properly protect
295 your goodly ship   against every foe
while on the shore   new-tarred it waits
with its curved prow   to cross the sea again
to the land of the Geats   with the loved man
who through great deeds   and the grant of grace
300 will safely survive   the savagery of battle."

iii *Leavetaking*

Then they moved on   — moored to its anchor,   *1 The Geats leave*
bound to its rope,   the broad-beamed ship   *the shore*
quietly abided.   The boar heads gleamed   *2 Their golden*
over the cheek guards   encrusted with gold,   *helmets gleam*
305 hardened by fire   — a hardy warrior
held the boatwatch.   Together the men hastened   *3 They see the*
until they could see   the stately timbered,   *golden hall*
gold-encrusted   home of the king;
the hall where he lived   was under heaven
310 the most renowned   among living men,
the gleam of its light   illumining many lands.
The warden showed them   the shining hall,   *4 "God grant*
the home of proud men,   so that they could hasten   *you success."*
directly to it;   after turning his horse
315 the bold warrior   uttered these words:
"It is time to go   — by decree of grace
may the Almighty Father   afford to you
a safe venture —   I must return to the sea
to hold the watch   against hostile bands."

6 · Second Challenge

i *To Heorot*

320 Encrusted with stone   the street directed   *1 Approach*
the band of men;   the byrnies shone,
and the hard meshing   of gleaming mail
sang as they advanced   in soldierly gear
and came at last   to the lofty hall.
325 Weary of the sea   they set their shields,   *2 Arrival*

hardened in war,   along the wall;
they rested on the bench;   the men's byrnies
and armor clanged   as the company
grounded together   their gray-tipped spears
330 of trusty ash   — the iron troop
was honored in its weapons.

ii *Challenge and response*

                              Then brave Wulfgar   *1 Challenge*
asked the warriors   what their lineage was:
'Whence do you bring   your bright shields,
your coats of mail,   your helmet masks
335 and host of spears?   I am the herald   *2 Identification*
and servant of Hrothgar;   though I've never seen
so many strangers   come in such strength,
I believe you are driven   by your daring,
not by exile's necessity,   to seek Hrothgar."
340 Masked by helmet   the brave hero   *3 Reply*
who led the Geats   gave this answer,
replied in these words: "We are partakers
of Higelac's bounty;   Beowulf is my name;
I wish to make   my message known
345 to your illustrious   lordly ruler,
the son of Healfdane,   if his highness
permits us to give   our greeting to him."
Wulfgar replied   —he was of Wendel race   *4 Response*
and known by many   for his manly soul,
his wisdom and fortitude: "What you are seeking
I will make known   to my noble master
who rules the Danes   in regal bounty
and ask his view   of your venture;
I will return speedily   to tell you the answer
which his goodness   sees fit to give."

iii *Wulfgar's announcement*

    Hastily he returned   to where Hrothgar sat   *1 He returns*
with his company of nobles;   the proud man came   *to Hrothgar*
to Denmark's great king,   old and gray-bearded,
and knowing stately custom   stood at his shoulder.
360 Wulfgar addressed   his well-disposed Lord: *2 "Beowulf has come*
"Here from afar   certain hardy Geats   *with his men*
have made their way   across the waters,

a soldierly company   who call their leader
Beowulf by name;   they ask this boon,
365 that you my lord   will listen and reply
to their spoken words.   May it be your will   *3 "I advise consent."*
to grant them audience,   gracious Hrothgar.
In their war gear   they appear worthy   *4 They appear*
of lordly welcome,   and the leader   *worthy.*
370 who directed them here   is a right good man.

7 · Second Response

i *Reception*

Hrothgar the protector   spoke his intent: *1 "I knew him*
"When I knew him   he was a child,   *as a child*
and famed Ecgtheow   was his father
to whom Hrethel of the Geats   gave in marriage
375 his only daughter;   now his doughty son
comes here and finds   a friendly king.
Sea travellers   who took to the Geats   *2 "Sailors speak*
the treasure gifts   of their tribute   *of his strength*
on returning have said   that he is battle-tried,
380 and has the might   of thirty men
in his hand grip.   By decree of grace,   *3 "God has sent him;*
as I believe,   the Holy Lord   *I shall reward him"*
has sent him here   to save the Danes
from Grendel's terror;   in return for his daring
385 I shall offer gifts   to this good warrior.
Go back quickly   to say I request   *4 "Bid them enter."*
that all the company   should come to me
and warmly make known   that they are welcome
to the Danish people."   Going to the door   *5 "Hrothgar*
390 Wulfgar from within   spoke in these words: *welcomes you."*
"My valorous lord   and victorious king
bids me announce   he knows you are noble
who have crossed the sea   to come to him,
and makes you welcome   as courageous men;
395 you may come within   clothed in armor
and with helmets   to have audience with Hrothgar,
but leave your shields   and spear shafts here
as you await   his decision on your words."
The mighty one arose,   around him gathered   *6 The Geats enter*

400 a valorous band;   obedient to their leader
      some waited outside   to guard the weapons
      while the rest hastened   under Heorot's roof;
      guided by Wulfgar,   Beowulf made his way
      bravely helmeted   until he stood by the hearth.

ii *Beowulf presents himself*

405   Beowulf gave greeting,   —his battle mail gleamed,   *1 "Hail Hrothgar*
      artfully linked   by the armorer's skill:
      'Hail, great Hrothgar!   I am Higelac's   *2 "I am Higelac's*
      kinsman and champion;   in youth I have accomplished   *kinsman*
      many famed deeds.   The Grendel affair   *3 "I have heard*
410 became known to me   in my native land;   *of Grendel*
      sailors in their visits   have said this hall
      in great stateliness   stands desolate
      and empty of life   after the light at dusk
      becomes hidden   in the bright heaven.
415 Then the best men   and the most wise   *4 "My people*
      among my people   persuaded me   *have sent me*
      to come to you,   kingly Hrothgar,
      being mindful   of my mighty strength;
      they saw it tested   when I returned from battles
420 encrusted in blood;   I killed five giants
      and destroyed their race,   and in the sea I crushed
      demonic monsters   in the perilous dark,
      avenging in the sea   their violence to the Geats
      —they asked for trouble;   now is the time
425 when I must myself   hold a meeting
      with the giant Grendel.

iii *Request and promise*

              "Now of your grace,   *1 "I ask permission*
      princely protector   of the Danish realm,   *to cleanse Heorot*
      I ask you to grant   a single gift,
      friend of the people,   now I have come this far;
430 guardian of warriors,   do not gainsay
      that I alone   with my lordly band
      and brave company   may cleanse Heorot.
      I have also heard   that the adversary,   *2 "I shall fight to*
      wanting in prudence,   cares nothing for weapons;   *death without*
435 so that the heart   of my lord Higelac   *weapons*
      may rejoice in me   I reject with scorn

carrying my sword   or covering myself
with shield in battle,   for I shall seize
my foe with my hands,   and hating and hated
440 will battle for life   —he will believe
the doom of God   whom death captures.
If he should win   he will, I expect,   *3 "If he wins*
feast as before   without trace of fear   *I will perish*
in this battle hall   upon this glorious band
445 of noble Geats;   nor will you have need
to entomb my head,   for he will take me away,
encrusted in blood,   captured by death,
to make his meal   without remorse,
in solitude   smearing his fen retreat
450 with my bloody corpse   —you will have no cause
for long concern   over my body's sustenance.
Have borne to Higelac,   if battle takes me,   *4 "Return my coat*
the coat of armor   that covers my breast,   *of mail to Higelac."*
the splendid mail   of Weyland's making
455 once worn by Hrethel   —Fate goes as it will."

8 · Welcome

i *Hrothgar's Welcome*

The great Hrothgar   graciously replied:
"My friend Beowulf,   bound by honor   *1 "You have come*
and by decree of grace   you have come to us.   *here honorably."*
Once your father   incited violent feud   *2 "I gave refuge*
460 with the Wilfings,   fatally wounding   *to your father*
Heathlaf in combat;   his Geatish kinsmen
for fear of reprisal   could afford him no refuge,
and across the water   he came to us,
to the Danish people,   the proud Scyldings,
465 when first in youth   it fell to me
to rule the Danes,   govern their realm
and treasure house;   Heorogar had died,
Healfdane's eldest son,   inheritor of his throne
—he was my brother   and better than I.
470 To settle the feud   I sent over the sea   *3 "I settled*
a wealth of treasure   as the Wilfing's wergild,   *the feud*
and your father   swore his faith to me.

I suffer in mind   when I must speak

to any man   of Grendel's malice,

475 his infliction upon Heorot   with fearful suddenness

of his baneful presence;   my band of warriors

is fewer in number,   for fate has swept them

into the grasp of Grendel   —God may readily

make powerless   the maddened fiend.

480 Often my captains   over the ale cups,

drunken with beer,   have solemnly boasted

that they would await   in the wine hall

with greedy swords   Grendel's onslaught;

then in the morning   this lordly meadhall

485 was encrusted with gore,   and when day came

hall and benches   were steeped in blood

and gore of battle;   my goodly company

was reduced by those   whom death had taken.

Welcome to the feast,   and when you wish

490 reveal to these men   your famous victories.

4 "Now I suffer from a desperate feud"

5 "All have failed against Grendel

6 "Join the feast."

ii *Amity*

Then a place was made   in the meadhall

for the close knit   company of the Geats;

the stout-hearted men,   proud in their strength,

seated themselves.   An attentive servant

495 poured the bright drink   from the bright cup

he carried in his hand.   At times the scop sang

clear-voiced in Heorot.   The goodly company

of Geats and Danes   were happy together.

1 The Geats are seated

2 And served

3 The scop sings

4 Amity

9 · Third Challenge and Response

i *Unferth's challenge*

Unferth, son of Ecglaf,   from where he sat

500 below Hrothgar's throne   unlocked his thoughts,

spoke in challenge;   he was much vexed

by the bold daring   of the seafarer Beowulf

because he begrudged   any man's gaining

greater honor   here upon earth

505 and under heaven   than he himself:

'Are you the Beowulf   who vied with Breca

in water contest   on the wide sea

1 "Are you the Beowulf who vied with Breca?

where the two of you   tempted the waves,
ventured your lives   through vanity
510 and foolish pride?   Neither friend nor foe   *2 "You could not*
succeeded in attempts   to keep you two   *be dissuaded*
from the sorry venture   of rowing on the sea
where with pull of hands   and pressure of arms
both of you measured   the might of the deep
515 and rode the currents;   the ocean was rough
with winter storms;   together in the water's grip
you labored seven nights.   He left you in his wake,   *3 "Breca won*
having more strength;   then in the morning
the sea carried him   to the Norwegian coast;
520 from there he came back   to the Bronding land,
his dear native soil   and his fair stronghold
where as beloved ruler   he reigned over his people,
their city and treasure;   truly Breca
made good his boast   against you there.
525 Even if success had attended   your every strife   *4 "You will fail*
I warrant you   a worse issue   *against Grendel."*
in deadlier battle   if you dare abide
the nearness of Grendel   all of the night."

ii *Beowulf's response*

The son of Ecgtheow,   Beowulf spoke: *1 "You speak of Breca*
530 "My friend Unferth,   you have spoken freely
after your beer drinking   about Breca
and his triumph.   I say in truth   *2 "The truth is*
that I possess   greater strength at sea,   *different*
might upon the waves,   than any other man.
535 We were only boys   with youthful bodies   *3 "Youthful folly*
when both of us   boastfully vowed   *led us*
that we dared lay   our lives on venture
out upon the sea   —and so we did;
to give us protection   against the whales
540 we had naked swords   next to our hands
as we rowed the waves.   In the water   *4 "We were parted*
he could not sail   swiftly enough   *by a storm*
to speed away   —and I would not;
for five long nights   we were never parted,
545 until the surging sea   drove us asunder
when the waves were stirred   by savage storm
of northern wind   in the darkening night

and rasping cold;   the waves were rough.
The sea monsters   were roused to madness;
550 my covering of armor   and coat of mail
with links of steel   enlaced with gold
guarded my breast   and gave me protection
against my foes.   A foully encrusted,
fiendish monster   forced me to the bottom,
555 fast in its grasp;   yet it was granted me
that I should pierce   with point of sword
my adversary of the sea;   savage battle destroyed
the mighty beast   by means of my hand.

*5 "I battled with
   sea monsters*

*6 "I was dragged
   to the bottom"*

10 · Response and Acceptance

i *Response (II) and acceptance*

"So without respite   the loathly ravagers
560 pressed me sorely;   with my dear sword.
I waited upon them   as was their due;
seated at the board   at the bottom of the sea
looking forward   to their fill of me,
the evil fiends   had no joy in the feast,
565 for in the dawn   cut down by my sword
in the sleep of death   they lay on the surface
beside the shore;   thereafter sailors
held their courses   upon the high seas
without any let;   the light came in the East,
570 God's bright beacon;   the storm abated
so that I might see   the wind-swept shore
and the headlands   —Fate often helps
an undoomed warrior   if his valor is of worth.
Somehow it befell me   to slay with sword
575 nine of the monsters;   no battle by night
of which I've heard   was harder under heaven,
no man more wretched   upon the ocean waters;
somehow, though exhausted,   I withstood in strife
the clutch of the foe;   then sea currents
580 and waves of the sea   washed me ashore
upon Finnish land.   Unferth, I lack
knowledge of your doing   any such deeds
of sword terror;   neither of you two,
Breca or you,   in trial of battle

*1 "My venture led to
   victory over monsters*

*2 "Nine monsters
   were slain*

*3 "You have done
   no such deed*

585 has done any deed   so daringly
with encrusted blade   —I do not boast of it—
though you did kill   your nearest kin,
your two brothers;   for this the torment
of hell awaits you   however worthy your wit.
590 I say to you truly,   son of Ecglaf,

4 "You dare not face Grendel

that if your account   of your courage
and stout-heartedness   did not stray from truth
the dread adversary   would never have done
so much harm and injury   to your lord and Heorot,
595 but he has found   little need to fear
the deadly feud,   the dire response
of your people,   the proud Scyldings;
he takes unsparingly   his terrible toll
of the Danish race,   for he does as he wants,
600 he kills and feasts,   counts upon the Danes
not to fight back.   But now I'll reveal,

5 "I will face Grendel."

make clear to him,   the might and courage
of the Geats in battle;   he who will may go
proudly to the mead   when tomorrow comes,
605 and the radiant sun   shining in the South
brings morning light   to the sons of men."
Then gray and valorous   the giver of treasure,

6 Hrothgar accepts Beowulf as champion

the Danish lord,   protector of his land,
became happy;   he counted on help
610 for he had found Beowulf   firm of purpose.

ii *Joy returns to the feast*

    There men's laughter   made merry sound;

1 Joy resumes

the words were fair.   Wealhtheow appeared,

2 Wealhtheow enters

Hrothgar's consort,   mindful of kinsmen,
gave her greeting   to the gold-adorned men.
615 The gentle lady   gave the cup first

3 Hrothgar begins the feast

to Denmark's lord,   his land's protector,
bidding the prince,   beloved by his people,
joy at the revels;   the victorious ruler
gladly partook   of feast and goblet.
620 Wealhtheow the Helming   then went about

4 Ceremonial pouring

among courtiers and warriors,   gave costly cups
to each in turn,   until the time came
for the bejeweled queen,   versed in courtesy,
to bear the beaker   for Beowulf to drink;

625 she greeted the prince,   gave thanks to God
for granting her   her greatest wish,
the coming of a hero   upon whose help
she could rely.   He drank from the cup   *5 "I vow to do or die."*
Wealhtheow had poured;   prepared for battle
630 the valiant warrior   made vow upon the cup;
the son of Ecgtheow,   Beowulf spoke:
'When I boarded ship   with my band of men
to traverse the sea   I was determined
either to do   what needs be done
635 for your people   or to perish
in the clutch of the foe;   I shall accomplish
this heroic deed   or in this meadhall
will meet my death   my final day."
The Geat's promise   was most pleasing   *6 Wealhtheow is*
640 to the noble lady;   in golden loveliness   *pleased*
the queen went to be seated   beside her lord.

iii *The hall is left to Beowulf*

Then as before   the hall was filled
with noble speech,   the sound of rejoicing   *1 Joy continues*
by happy men.   But the son of Healfdane   *2 Hrothgar ends*
645 suddenly signified   his wish to seek   *the feast*
his night's repose;   he knew that by day
while they could see   the light of the sun
the adversary schemed   his siege of the hall
after the dusk   with encroaching dark
650 and shape of night   with covering shadows
came across the sky.   The court arose.   *3 The court rises*
Hrothgar then bade   goodnight to Beowulf,
gave over to him   his banquet hall;   *4 "I entrust the*
wishing him well   he said these words: *hall to you."*
655 "While I could hold   my shield in hand
until this time   I have never entrusted
this mighty hall   to any man;
have now and hold   this best of houses,
remember honor,   show heroic strength,
660 be alert for the foe;   you will lack for little
if unscathed you do   this deed of glory."

11 · Awaiting Battle

i *Hrothgar's fear: Beowulf's confidence*

Then with his attendants   the Dane's protector,   *1 Hrothgar leaves*
Hrothgar proceeded   out of the hall;
the war leader   wished to be bedded
665 with Wealhtheow his queen.   Heaven's King placed   *2 God had*
a guard in the hall   against Grendel   *appointed a guardian*
as men have heard;   seeing Hrothgar's plight
He gave protection   against the giant.
In truth the Geat   trusted firmly   *3 Beowulf's trust is in*
670 his own great strength   and the Ruler's grace.   *himself and God*
He then unclasped   his coat of mail,
doffed his helmet,   handed to his attendant   *4 He discards armor*
his adorned sword,   dearest of weapons,   *and sword*
and bade him keep   the battle gear.
675 The worthy Beowulf   uttered the words   *5 "I will fight*
of solemn boast   before he lay on his bed: *to the death*
"Because I value my worth   in deeds of war   *without weapons."*
no less highly   than Grendel does his,
I shall not slay him   by means of sword,
680 thus cut him down   as I could easily do;
he is ignorant of good usage,   how to give blows
or to slash shield   though he has the strength
for violent deeds;   but we will do without swords
the two of us this night   if he dare attempt
685 battle without weapons;   the Lord of Wisdom,
God of holiness,   will apportion glory
to him or me   as He thinks fit."
The warrior lord   laid himself down,   *6 The company rests*
leaning cheek on bolster;   about him his band
690 of bold seamen   were bedded in the hall.

ii *Anticipation*

None expected   to leave that place   *1 Foreboding*
and return to their beloved   land and people,
the noble city   of their nurturing,
because they knew   of the countless number
695 of Danish people   death had taken
in the great hall.   But the Lord granted   *2 God protected them*
His aid and favor   and fortune of victory
to the Geatish men   so that they might

conquer their foe   through the skilled force
700 of one alone   — that the mighty Lord
everywhere rules   the races of men
is known as truth.

iii *Grendel's Approach*

He came in the dark night   *1 Approach*
stalking the shadows.   The warriors slept   *2 All but*
who were to guard   the gabled hall,   *Beowulf sleep*
705 except for one   — the sinful oppressor
as was known to men   could draw no one
into the night   if God wished it not —
for he lay waking   with wrathful heart,
in anger awaiting   settlement by war.

B — *Victory Over Grendel*

12 · The Battle

i *Approach*

710 Bearing God's anger   Grendel then came   *1 Grendel comes*
from out the moor   in the cover of mist;   *from the moor*
the sinful oppressor   planned to ensnare
some human being   in the high hall.
He advanced in the shadows   until he viewed   *2 He approaches*
715 the gold encrusted walls   of the wine hall   *the hall*
where men had feasted;   it was not the first time
that he had sought   the home of Hrothgar,
but had never met   such men in the hall
or ever found   a worse fortune.
720 The warrior journeying   in joyless doom   *3 He opens the door*
came to the hall;   at the touch of his hands
the well-secured door   gave way at once,
and inflamed by hate   he flung open
the mouth of the hall.   Hastily then   *4 He enters*
725 in mad fury   the fiend prowled
the encrusted floor;   a fearful light
most like to fire   flared from his eyes.

He saw in the hall   soundly sleeping   *5 He sees the*
a company of warriors,   a band of kinsmen   *sleeping men*
730 gathered together.   The grisly adversary
was gleeful of mind;   before morning   *6 He anticipates*
he intended   to tear apart   *a feast*
each life and body,   to sate his lust
with his fill of feast   — he was fated
735 after this night   not to partake
again of mankind.

ii *Battle*

                 Higelac's mighty kinsman   *1 Beowulf*
waited to see   how the sinful oppressor   *watchfully waits*
intended to strike   in swift suddenness.
The adversary   did not consider delay,   *2 Grendel rushes*
740 but in his first rush   he fastened upon   *to feast*
a sleeping man,   rent him savagely,
bit into his body,   drank the blood from his veins,
swallowed him in gobbets;   soon he had gobbled
the lifeless body,   leaving nothing
745 from feet to hands.   The foe advanced,   *3 He seizes*
seized in his claws   the strong-hearted warrior.   *Beowulf*
The resting man   reached for his foe
with opposing hand;   in hostile purpose   *4 Beowulf*
hastily grappling   he heaved himself up.   *retaliates*
750 The keeper of crimes   quickly discovered   *5 Grendel discovers*
he had never found   in the far reaches   *Beowulf's strength*
of the middle earth   another man
with so mighty a grip;   in mind and spirit
he grew afraid   — but fear did not free him.
755 His soul yearned for flight   and sought darkness   *6 He tries to flee*
in the company of devils;   his encounter now
was different from those   of former days.

iii *Grendel's defeat (I)*

    The kinsman of Higelac   keenly remembered   *1 Beowulf holds*
his evening speech   and stood erect,   *him fast*
760 gripping him fast;   his fingers burst;
the giant pulled away,   the earl kept pace.
The infamous one wanted   to get away   *2 Grendel tries*
as far as he could,   to flee from there   *to escape*
to his fen haven;   his fingers felt the grip

765 of hostile might   —it was a miserable time
for the vile oppressor   to venture into Heorot.
The great hall boomed   —to the brave Danes   *3 The Danes listen*
living in the city   it seemed that death   *in terror*
was pouring its cup;   both keepers of the hall
770 raged in anger   —the building roared.
There was much wonder   how the wine hall   *4 They wonder that*
withstood the battlers,   why the fair building   *the hall can stand*
did not fall to earth,   but it was made fast
on both its sides   with iron bands
775 through the smith's skill;   in their mad strife
the mead benches   embellished with gold
were torn from the floor   as I was told;
the Danish seers   had ever been sure
that the hall could fall   only in the fiery bosom
780 of devouring flame,   that no murderous foe
could ever rend it   or rip it apart
by force of cunning.   With fearful strangeness   *5 They hear*
the noise rose higher;   horrifying terror   *Grendel's screams*
held all the Danes   who from their houses
785 heard the desperate,   clamorous howling,
the fearful lament,   the song of defeat
and grievous sorrow   sung by God's foe,
the captive of hell.   He held him fast   *6 Beowulf holds*
who was mightiest   of any man   *him fast*
790 living his day   here in this life.

13 · Victory

i *Grendel's defeat (II)*

The will of the defender   was fully fixed   *1 Beowulf's*
on keeping death's visitor   from escaping alive;   *determination*
he did not think   that the days of his life
benefitted anyone.   In loyalty to Beowulf   *2 His men come*
795 his men swiftly drew   their ancestral swords,   *to his aid*
wishing to defend   so far as they might
the life of their prince   and beloved lord.
When his fearless men   entered the fight   *3 They did not know*
and slashed at the foe   from every side,   *Grendel's magic*
800 fiercely seeking   his soul's dwelling,
they were not aware   that in this world

even the best   of battle swords
could do no harm   to the hostile oppressor,
for by magic   he had made useless
805 the power of the sword.   The space of time   *4 Grendel's doom*
for living his day   here in this life
would end sorely,   and the alien spirit
would voyage far   to the realm of the fiend.
He had often before   done many foul deeds,   *5 Grendel is*
810 afflicted in mind   against mankind,   *now powerless*
— he feuded with God —   but this time he found
that the cover of his body   gave no security,
for the high-spirited   kinsman of Higelac
held him in his grip.   Each begrudged the other   *6 His arm*
815 continuance of life;   the terrible adversary   *is torn off*
felt tearing pain;   upon his shoulder appeared
a savage wound   — sinews and joints
were torn asunder.

ii *Beowulf's victory*

                         Triumph in battle   *1 He flees*
was granted to Beowulf;   the dying Grendel
820 journeyed in flight   to his joyless home
under the fenland cliffs;   he felt certain
that death was near,   the days of his life
wholly numbered.   What the Danes hoped for   *2 The Danes*
had been fulfilled   through the deadly fight;   *rejoice*
825 the wise visitor   voyaging from afar
had valiantly held   Hrothgar's hall
and cleansed it of horror.   He rejoiced in his claim   *3 Beowulf is*
to the night's glory;   the heroic Geat   *triumphant*
in keeping his promise   to the Danish people
830 had made an end   of the misery
they had endured   and of the deep grief
they had suffered   because of the savagery
visited upon them.   This was revealed   *4 Grendel's arm*
under the broad roof   by the bold warrior   *gives proof*
835 when he showed the arm,   the hand and shoulder,
the grasping whole   of Grendel's claw.

14 · The Day's Celebration

i *Morning*

In the morning   as was told me   *1 Before the hall*
many warriors   were at the hall;
from everywhere   the elders came   *2 The viewing*
840 over the wide ways   to witness in wonder
the path of the foe.   His parting from ,life   *3 The tracks*
was not lamented   by any of the men   *to the tarn*
who viewed the tracks   of the vanquished,
the desperate path   pointing the way
845 to the monstrous tarn   with bloody traces
of fated flight   after violent defeat.
There the water   bloodily welled   *4 The tarn covers*
with the boiling surge   of battle gore   *the traces*
flung up in clots;   the drear waves closed
850 over the melancholy   death-doomed monster
who surrendered   his body and soul
in his fen haven   —there hell received him.
Then from the tarn   the old retainers   *5 Return*
and the many youths   returned merrily
855 mounted on horseback   riding their mares
in high spirits.   Much was spoken   *6 Praise*
about Beowulf's fame;   many affirmed
that South or North   under heaven's span
on the spacious earth   between the seas
860 there was no warrior   who was worthier,
nor any man   more fit for command
—though they found no fault   with their friendly lord,
the kindly Hrothgar,   for he was a good king.

ii *Ceremonies of rejoicing*

First the young lords   let their bay mares   *1 Horse racing*
865 try their mettle   in sprinting matches
where they knew the going   was fair and good
and best for coursing.   Next the king's retainer   *2 Story telling*
interlaced words,   interlocked truly;
he remembered   many old songs,
870 heroic tales   and timeless legends
stored in his memory;   then he started
to fashion a tale   of fitting comparison
which would aptly serve   to celebrate

Beowulf's heroism;   what he had heard
875 of the wide voyaging   of Sigemund Walsing
he remembered much   not known to many men,
and told the story,   the mysterious tale
of the hero's deeds,   his hard struggles
and lawless feuds   which alone his nephew
880 Fitela had heard   because his uncle saw fit
to relate them to him   after they were linked
in battle-fellowship   when in fierce strife
they engaged with swords   the race of the giants
and slew full many.   Sigemund's fame   *3 Sigemund's fame*
885 endured long   after he died
because he had killed the dragon,   the treasure keeper;
noble of birth,   hardy in battle,
he had fared alone   without Fitela
upon the grim foray   under the gray stone,
890 yet it came to pass   that his sword pierced
the glittering dragon,   and its great blade
cut deep into the wall   — the dragon suffered death;
the bravery of its adversary   brought it to pass
that he might enjoy   the jeweled hoard
895 at his own will;   Sigemund Walsing
loaded his boat   bore to its bosom
the dear treasure   — the dragon melted in its heat;
of all wanderers   this protector of warriors,
through heroic deeds   which brought him honor,
900 was most celebrated   by the world of men
after the fall   of Heremod's fame
for heroic virtue.   Heremod was betrayed   *4 Heremod's fall*
into the hands of the foe   by whom he was held
and swiftly slain   — sorrow too long
905 had overwhelmed him;   many wise men
had frequent doubts   in earlier days
about his stubborn deeds,   yet dared to hope
that in succeeding   to his sire's throne
and kingly rule   of the Danish realm,
910 the native land   and nation's stronghold,
he would end its sorrow   and ensure prosperity;
instead he rested   a ruinous burden
upon his country.   Beowulf would become   *5 Beowulf's rise*
dearer by far   not only to friends
915 but to all mankind   — Heremod was seized by crime.

On the sandy road   they again raced   *6 Horse racing resumed*
their coursing mares.

iii *Afternoon*

As the light of morning   *1 At the hall*
hastened on its way   many warriors went
resolute of heart   to the high hall
920 to see the wonder.   From his wife's chamber   *2 Enter Hrothgar*
the protector of treasure   approached with his troop,
the king himself,   famed for his heroic
and courteous deeds,   his queen joining him
with her train of women   on the way to the hall.

15 · Hrothgar and Beowulf

i *Hrothgar's thanksgiving*

925   Hrothgar spoke   —having come to the hall   *1 "I thank God*
he stood on its threshold   and saw on high
the gold-encrusted roof   and Grendel's hand:
'Swift thanks be given   to God Almighty
for this great sight;   I was grievously afflicted
930 by Grendel's hate,   yet the Keeper of heaven
may ever work   wonder upon wonder.
Not long ago   I was left without hope   *2 "Succor has come*
that while I lived   relief would come
from the heavy sorrow   of seeing this hall
935 covered with blood,   encrusted with gore;
all my counselors   were crushed by grief
and helplessly   abandoned all hope
of ever protecting   the people's treasure
from the demons;   what none could do
940 when we tried before   to trap and take
the monstrous foe   this man has done
through God's might.   Who gave him birth   *3 "I praise your*
may surely say   if she yet lives   *mother*
that she was favored   by the God of our fathers
945 above all women   in bearing into the world
a child like this.   I cherish you Beowulf,   *4 "I adopt you as son*
sovereign among men,   and as my own son
I take you to my heart;   henceforth hold well

this new kinship.   You will never lack   5 "I promise you
deserved gifts
950 what you wish in this world   while I wield power;
many times for less   I have lavished treasure,
the reward of merit,   upon men less worthy,
less daring in war.   You have won by deeds   6 "You have won
fame."
such lasting fame   that it will live
955 into eternity;   may the Almighty continue
to endow you with goodness   as He has done till now."

ii *Beowulf's reply*

The son of Ecgtheow,   Beowulf spoke:
"Very willingly we did   this heroic deed,   1 "The Geats triumphed
made good the fight,   faced the ghastly
960 might of the unknown.   I would be more pleased   2 "I wish I had
held him
if the foe himself   in all his finery
and death sickness   could be seen by you.
I intended quickly   to tie him fast   3 "I meant to
hold him
with binding grip   upon the bed of death
965 so that breathing his last   in my arm's embrace
he would lie dead,   but his body eluded me.
Because the Lord willed it not   I lacked the power   4 "God did not
will it
to prevent his going   however hard I gripped him,
for the deadly foe   was too fiendishly strong
970 to be kept from leaving.   Yet to cover his tracks   5 "Yet he
is doomed
and save his life   he left his shoulder,
his arm and hand;   but help will not come
to the hapless wretch   by any such wrench.
The loathly tormentor   will not live longer   6 "His death and
doom are near."
975 in the misery of sin,   for a mortal wound
has bound him fast   in the baneful fetters
of its merciless clutch;   encrusted in sin
the demon must await   the day of doom
when the radiant Ruler   will render his judgment."

iii *Awed Viewing*

980   Then the son of Ecglaf,   Unferth was more silent   1 Unferth's
silence and the
awe of the court
made fewer boasts   of his battle deeds
after the lords   looked toward the roof
where the hero's might   had placed the hand
and fiend's fingers.   Facing everyone   2 The claw
985 were the stark nails   most like to steel
of the hideous   heathen claw

of the adversary;   everyone said
that the sturdiest blade   of ancient sword
could not harm him,   and that the bloody hold
of this warrior   would not weaken.

16 · The Evening Feast

i *Preparations*

When hands were summoned   hastily to bedeck *1 Concealment*
Heorot within   there appeared a host
of men and women   to prepare the winehall,
the house for guests;   gold encrusted hangings
995 gleamed on the walls,   wondrous spectacles
for all the guests   to gaze upon;
within the bright building,   banded with iron,
all the interior   was torn to pieces,
the doors unhinged;   only the roof endured
1000 entirely sound   after the sin-encrusted
doomed adversary   sought to flee death,
despairing of life.   There is little hope *2 Death cannot*
of escaping death   —do what one may; *be concealed*
for every human   inhabiting the earth,
1005 each living soul   by force of necessity
must seek the place   prepared for him
where his bodily robe   upon the bed of rest
will sleep after the feast.

ii *Evening feast*

At the festal hour *1 Hrothgar begins*
the son of Healfdane,   the king himself, *the feast*
1010 wishing to feast,   went to the hall;
I have never heard   of a better behaved
or greater host   gathered around their king;
famed for their deeds   they sat to the feast,
partook their full;   firmly resolute,
1015 Hrothgar and Hrothulf,   their high kinsmen,
in courtesy shared   many cups of mead
in the high hall.   Heorot within *2 Ominous foreboding*
was filled with friends   —still in the fated future
were the treacherous deeds   the Danes were to do.

iii *Gifts to Beowulf*

1020   Hrothgar gave Beowulf   the sword of Healfdane   *1 The first four gifts*
as reward for his victory   and a war standard
heavy with gold,   helmet and armor—
many men saw   the magnificent sword
borne to the hero.   Beowulf in the hall   *2 Beowulf drinks;*
1025 drank from the cup;   no cause for shame   *accepts the gifts*
was given him before men   because of these gifts;
to my knowledge   not many have given
to another man   upon the meadbench
four golden gifts   with greater friendliness.
1030 Around the helmet top   protecting the head   *3 Helmet described*
there stood a rim   strengthened by bands
so that no blade,   sharp and battle-hard,
could savagely wound   the warrior
whenever he faced   the hostile foe.
1035 Then the protector of men   commanded eight mares   *4 Further gifts*
with golden bridles   be brought upon the floor
inside the hall;   upon one was a saddle
skillfully encrusted   with covering of gems,
the battle seat   of Healfdane's son
1040 when the mighty king   was minded to engage
in the play of swords   —his famed prowess
never failed in the van   where bodies fall.
The protector of the Danes   pressed upon Beowulf   *5 The formal grant*
horses and arms   to have and to keep,
1045 bade him enjoy   both the gifts well.
The illustrious king,   keeper of the treasure,   *6 Hrothgar's gift*
so generously repaid him   with gold and horses   *was noble*
for his fierce strife   that none could find fault
who wished to tell   only the simple truth.

17 · Gifts to the Geats and Finnsburh I

i *Gifts to the Geats*

1050   Then the great lord   rewarded each Geat   *1 Gifts to the Geats*
seated on the meadbench;   to each of the men
who had come with Beowulf   across the sea
he gave an heirloom   and commanded that gold
be given in repayment   for the one whom Grendel

1055 had sinfully murdered   — and would have slain more
     if the wisdom of God   and the courage of the Geat
     had not prevented him.   (The Lord prevailed   *2 (The might of God*
     in the doings of men   as still He does;   *and the uncertainty*
     therefore understanding   and the spirit of prudence   *of man's life)*
1060 are best for all men;   who long abides
     in the world's day   of wine and affliction
     will experience fully   both fair and foul.)

ii *Finnsburh I*

     Then music and lay   were interlaced   *1 The story introduced*
     before the commander   of Healfdane's men;
1065 the harp was struck   and the story retold
     when Hrothgar's minstrel   beside the meadbench
     to entertain the company   recited his tale
     of Finn's followers;   when disaster befell them
     the Scylding hero,   the Danish Hnaef,
1070 was lost in death   in Frisian land.
     Hildeburh was given   no grounds for trust   *2 Hildeburh's grief*
     in the enemies' faith;   through no fault of hers
     she suffered the loss   of son and brother
     in the dash of shields;   they died as was fated,
1075 wounded by spears   — she was a mourning woman;
     not without cause   did the queen bewail
     the decree of destiny   after day had come
     and she could behold   under the heavens
     her murdered kinsmen   in whom she most placed
1080 her worldly bliss.   Because battle had taken   *3 The offer of truce*
     all of Finn's men   except for a few,
     he could no way manage   at place of meeting
     to press the fight   upon the prince's thane,
     nor was he able   in battle with Hengest
1085 to expel the survivors;   but the Danes proposed
     having the benches   in the lower hall
     and the high-seat cleared,   the Danes in their half
     to have the same power   the enemy people had,
     and Finn each day   to honor the Danes,
1090 to entertain   the troop of Hengest,
     at the gift-sharing   give them treasure,
     provide them with riches   of such value
     as to equal the gifts   he would give the Frisians
     to cheer their hearts   in the feasting hall.

1095   Then both parties   agreed on peace   *4 Agreement on truce*
        by firm treaty;   Finn upon oath
        without reservation   vowed to Hengest
        that guided by custom   he would govern honorably
        the Danish survivors,   that by word or deed
1100   none of his company   would break the covenant,
        nor through malice   would ever mention
        that necessity had forced them   leaderless to follow
        the murderer of their prince   who had given them much;
        if any Frisian,   fearless of consequences,
1105   gave voice to the memory   of murderous hatred
        then the blade of the sword   would repay his blunder;
        with the addition of gold   drawn from the hoard
        the oath was completed.   The Danish prince,   *5 The funeral*
        first among warriors,   was prepared for the fire;
1110   armor encrusted with gore   and golden boars
        of iron helmets   were heaped in plenty
        upon the funeral pyre   with the many fallen heroes
        wounded to death,   — many had died in the battle;
        then Hildeburh commanded   that her son be committed,
1115   given to the flames   upon the funeral pyre,
        his flesh to be burned   in the fire with Hnaef;
        beside the pyre   in sorrowful song
        the woman lamented   — the warrior was laid on the pyre.
        The funeral fire   flared before the mound   *6 Consummation*
1120   and mounted to heaven;   the headbones melted,
        gaping wounds burst   as the blood gushed
        from gashes in the bodies;   that greediest of spirits,
        the fire swallowed   all whom death had destroyed
        of both people   — their glory had passed.

18 · Finnsburh (II): Wealhtheow

i *Finnsburh II*

1125   Then Frisian warriors   bereft of friends   *1 Frisian warriors*
        took leave to return   to their land and dwellings.   *return home*
        While Hengest still,   though he remembered home,   *2 The winter of*
        stayed in the houses   of Finn's stronghold   *Hengest's*
        of his own will   that slaughter-encrusted winter   *discontent*
1130   though free to sail   across the sea
        in ring-prowed boat;   in battle with the wind

the stormy water surged   and winter locked the waves
in bonds of ice   until the better time
made its stay on earth   —as it still does—
1135 when sunbright weather   observes its season
in perpetual renewal.   Now with the passing of winter   *3 Spring unlocks*
earth's bosom was fair;   the exile was bent   *his anger*
upon leaving the guesthall,   but his mind lingered
less on voyage   than upon revenge
1140 and upon the hope   he held in his mind
of hostile meeting   with the enemy men.
So he did not reject   what the world judged right   *4 The stirring*
when Hunlafing placed   the precious sword,   *of strife*
the flame of battle,   upon his bosom
1145 whose edges became feared   among the Frisians
as when later there fell   upon courageous Finn
the hour of death   in his own home
after Guthlaf and Oslaf   openly mentioned
and grievously complained   of the grim attack
1150 which followed the sea voyage.   All restraint fell   *5 Revenge*
from the restless heart;   the hall was adorned
with the bodies of the foe;   Finn with his bodyguard
was also killed   and the queen taken;
the Scylding warriors   bore to their ships
1155 all the household property,   such precious jewels
as they could find   in the home of Finn,
the king of the land;   across the sea
they took to the Danes,   returned to her people,
the noble lady.   The lay was sung,   *6 The end of*
1160 the minstrel's song;   mirth and laughter   *the lay*
arose from the benches;   from rich beakers
the cup-bearers poured wine.

ii *Wealhtheow*

Wealhtheow appeared   *1 Approach*
wearing her crown of gold   and went to where the goodly two,
uncle and nephew sat together   —they were then still at peace
1165 and each was true to the other,   and at the feet of the Danish king
Unferth, the spokesman, was seated;   all were sure of his courage
and of the greatness of his daring   though he had not dealt honorably
with his kinsmen at the play of swords.   The Scyldings' lady spoke:
"Partake of this cup,   giver of treasure   *2 "Be of good cheer*
1170 and my cherished lord;   be of good cheer,   *and greet the Geats*

generous king,   and with cordial words
address the Geats   as is right and good.
Favor the Geats   both near and far;   *3 "Favor them*
attentive to reward   now you intend,
1175   as I've been told,   to take this warrior
to be your son   —the bright gifthall
Heorot is cleansed;   take happiness while you may   *4 "Attend to*
in liberal rewards   and leave to your heirs   *the future*
your land and power   when elsewhere you will learn
1180   the decree of destiny.   I know my dear   *5 "I trust*
and gracious Hrothulf   will hold the children   *in Hrothulf."*
honorably as guardian   if you should go from the world,
friendly king of the Danes,   before he does;
I believe he will return   to our two sons
1185   repayment of kindness   if he keep in mind
how we cherished him   when he was a child,
attentive to his pleasure   and honorable estate."
She then bent her way   to the bench where her boys,   *6 She comes*
Hrethric and Hrothmund, sat   among the sons of nobility,   *to Beowulf*
1190   the young warriors,   and where the worthy
Beowulf of the Geats   sat beside the two brothers.

19 · Wealhtheow's Gifts

i *Wealhtheow's Gifts*

The flagon was brought   and friendship offered   *1 The gifts*
with the giving   of inlaid gold
in great bounty   —two arm bracelets,
1195   garment and rings,   and the richest collar
that I have heard of   here on this earth.
I've never been told   of a mortal treasure   *2 Comparison*
more precious under heaven   since Hama carried off   *with Hama's*
the Brosing collar   in its costly setting   *stolen treasure*
1200   to the gleaming stronghold   —fleeing the stark
terror of Ermanric   he chose eternal good.
The golden collar   Higelac the Geat   *3 The ominous fate*
of Swerting's lineage   took on his last adventure   *of the collar*
when under his standard   he stood to protect
1205   and defend his booty   —fate destroyed him;
he asked for trouble   when in pride he attempted
feud with the Frisians;   across the flood

the mighty king   carried the necklet
with its precious stones   — he died under his shield.
1210 To Frankish bosom   came the king's body,   *4 Geatish*
his coat of mail   and the collar too;   *disaster*
after the carnage   the corpses were plundered
by lesser warriors,   and the field was left
to the Geatish slain.

ii *Wealhtheow's speech*

                      Applause greeted the gift.   *1 Applause*
1215 Queen Wealhtheow spoke   before the company:
"Beloved young Beowulf,   good luck attend you;   *2 Wealhtheow*
enjoy this collar,   rejoice in the robe   *presents*
and ancestral treasures;   prosper truly   *the gifts*
in the fame of your courage,   and be of good counsel
1220 to my boys   — I will remember reward.
You have done such feats   and performed such deeds   *3 He has won*
that men will extol you   in all times and places   *fame*
even to the walls   of the windy home
of the encircling flood.   Prince, may you flourish   *4 Her hope*
1225 the while you live   — I wish for you   *for Beowulf*
abundance of fortune   — may you be to my sons
a friend in deed   while your joy endures.
Here every peer   is peaceful in spirit,   *5 Her trust*
trusts his fellow,   protects his king;   *in the Danes*
1230 the men who drink here   obey my commands."
She went to her seat.   *6 She takes her place*

iii *The watch over the hall*

                      There men drank wine   *1 The feast ends*
at the best of feasts;   they were unaware of fate   *in unawareness*
and fearful destiny   that was to befall   *of fate*
1235 the company of lords   after evening came
and princely Hrothgar   repaired to his dwelling
to take his rest.   A troop of lords   *2 The watch*
held watch in the hall   as had been their wont.   *is readied*
They cleared the benches;   beside them bedding   *3 Their arms*
1240 and bolsters were spread   — death was speeding   *are handy*
toward one doomed feaster   as he lay down to rest;
beside their heads   they set their shining
wooden battleshields,   and upon the bench
above each lord   his lofty helmet,

1245 his coat of mail   and mighty spear
    were in clear sight.   Their custom was   *4 Such was*
    to be alert   and battle-ready   *their custom*
    in defending their homes   or in fighting abroad
    as royal necessity   required them to serve
1250 the king's bidding   — the company was worthy.

C — *Vengeance Avenged: Grendel's Dam*

20 · Vengeance

i *The monsters' lineage*

    Then they fell asleep.   It befell as before   *1 They sleep*
    while Grendel held   the golden hall   *2 One will die*
    until he ended in death   his lawless deeds
    and sinful course   that it came to one
1255 to pay sorely   for his slumber.
    Thus it became evident   that an avenger   *3 The avenger*
    was still alive.   For a long time   *4 The avenger's*
    after the murder   Grendel's mother,   *history*
    the womanlike adversary,   brooded on the woe
1260 of her dwelling   in the dread waters
    of frozen streams   enforced by fratricide
    when Cain murdered   his closest kin,
    his father's son;   sin-encrusted he fled
    from the joys of men,   marked for his murder,
1265 to inhabit the wasteland;   from him awoke
    the demonic race   of the ravaging Grendel,
    the accursed foe.   He found in Heorot   *5 Grendel's death*
    awaiting battle   a wakeful man
    who in the hard grasp   of his adversary's hold
1270 yet remembered   his mighty strength,
    the precious gift   God had given him,
    and trusted in the Almighty,   in His mercy,
    His aid and comfort   — thus he conquered
    the hellish fiend.   The foe of mankind,   *6 Grendel died*
1275 deprived of happiness,   sought the place of death   *but his mother*
    in abject misery,   but now his mother,   *lived to avenge him*
    gallows-minded,   was greedy to undertake
    dismal vengeance   for her son's death.

ii *The attack and discovery*

She came to Heorot where in the hall	*1 A woman comes to*
1280 the Danes lay sleeping; there was swift alteration	*attack the men*

She came to Heorot   where in the hall

1 A woman comes to attack the men

1280 the Danes lay sleeping;   there was swift alteration
of their good luck   after Grendel's dam
forced an entry;   she was less to be feared
than a warrior   because as a woman
she lacked the might   of a man who wars
1285 with inlaid sword   of the smith's forging
and cuts with edges   encrusted in blood,
hewing the boar crest   above the helmet.
Then in the hall   the hard-edged swords,

2 The Danes are aroused to battle

snatched from the benches,   and the broad shields
1290 were held firmly   —he took no heed
of helmet or armor   whom the horror seized.
Once her presence was known   she was pressed by desire

3 Grendel's dam hastens her vengeance

to save her life   by leaving quickly,
yet before returning   in haste to the tarn
1295 with savage clutch   she seized a man
as he lay sleeping   and slaughtered him
whom Hrothgar held   for his heroic virtue
as the worthiest   in the sea-girt world
to be his companion   —Beowulf was not there,
1300 for after the gift-giving   the famous Geat
was appointed   to a dwelling apart.
Cries filled Heorot   —she took the famed claw

4 Discovery and escape

covered with blood   —there came to the dwellings
renewal of sorrow.   It was for both sides

5 Vengeance is a bad bargain

1305 a poor exchange   paid at the price
of precious lives.   The prudent heart

6 Hrothgar's grief

of the gray-haired king   was filled with grief
after he learned   of the loss of the man
who was his friend   and first of his lords—
1310 hastily Beowulf   blessed in victory
was called to his chamber.

iii *Dawn*

At coming of day

1 Beowulf attends

the noble warrior   went with his men
to where the wiseman   waited and wondered
if the Almighty   would ever make
1315 some turn for the better   in his tale of grief.

Tried in combat   the hero crossed   *2 He speaks*
the floor with his troop   —the timbers thundered—   *to Hrothgar*
and addressing his words   to the wise king
he sought to know   because of the urgent summons
1320 if he had passed   the night pleasantly.

21 · Hrothgar's Charge to Beowulf

i *The murder of Æschere*

The lord of the Danes   Hrothgar lamented;   *1 "Grief has returned*
"Ask not of pleasure,   for painful grief
has returned to the Danes.   Æschere is dead,   *2 "I lament*
born Yrmenlaf's   older brother,   *Asher*
1325 my confidant   and counsellor
who stood at my shoulder   when in the strife
we slashed helmets   and protected our own heads
in the clash of war: if ever there were a worthy
of proven merit   such was princely Æschere.
1330 A dire, murderous,   restless demon   *3 "He was slain*
slew him in Heorot   and slipped away   *by a demon*
to an unknown place,   gloating in pleasure
in her carrion feast.   She came as avenger   *4 "His death resulted*
in the feud with Grendel   in which you engaged   *from your feud*
1335 the night you killed him   in your crushing grip   *with Grendel*
because too long   he had lessened
the number of my people   —in battle he left
his life as payment;   another sinful oppressor,
plotting revenge,   has now appeared
1340 and has gone far   to avenge the feud,
as must appear   to many of the men
who in grief lament   their gift-giver
with breaking hearts   now that the hand lies still
which once could grant   what gift was wished.

ii *Beowulf's perilous duty*

1345   I have heard tales   told by my people,   *1 "The monsters*
counsellors of my court   and country folk;
they tell of seeing   two such enormous
haunters of the moor,   monstrous creatures
keeping the fenland;   so far as they
1350 could get at the truth   one of the two

was womanlike;   the other wretched creature
on the path of exile   appeared to be male,
except he was more giant   than he was man
and named Grendel   in days long gone
1355 by the land folk   who knew of no father
or of mysterious demons   that might have been
begotten before him.   They inhabit a hidden   *2 "Their dwelling*
land of wolf dens,   windswept headlands,
a hideous fenland   where from the heights
1360 a cataract falls   and flows within
the headland mists;   not far from here   *3 "The mere*
measured in miles   does the mere stand;
over it hangs   hoar-frosted trees,
and fast-rooted woods   shadow the water;
1365 on its surface each night   fire can be seen
in menacing portent;   no living person,
no son of man   may sound its depth;
if the antlered hart   crossing the heath,
harried for long   by pursuing hounds,
1370 should seek the wood,   at the water's edge
it would stand and die   rather than dare
to plunge within;   it is not a pleasant place;
in wild surges   its waters blackly
strive toward the skies   when the wind stirs
1375 menacing weather,   and the heavens weep
from rain-dark clouds.   Now help must come   *4 "Help can come*
from you alone;   you do not know the land,   *only from you."*
the fearful place   where you may find
the sinful creature   — seek it if you dare;
1380 I shall repay   your part in the feud
the way I did before   with ancient wealth
of twisted gold   if you return.

22 · Preparations

i *Beowulf accepts the duty*

     The son of Ecgtheow,   Beowulf spoke: *1 "Revenge is better*
"Revered one, do not grieve;   to revenge a friend   *than grief*
1385 is better for a man   than to mourn much;
to each must come   the close of his life
here in this world;   let each warrior

gain fame before death,   for he will find it
enduringly best   after his day is done.
1390 Arise, great king,   let us go quickly   *2 "Arise*
to mark the traces   of Grendel's mother.
I take my oath   that turn where she may   *3 "She will*
on the bosom of earth,   the broad ocean deep   *not escape."*
or mountain forest,   she will find no escape;
1395 let this day pass   in patient endurance
of painful woe   as I expect you will.
Joyously the old king   jumped to his feet,   *4 Hrothgar overjoyed*
thanking mighty God   for what the man had said.

ii *The mere*

Then was a horse   with braided hair   *1 Hrothgar mounts*
1400 prepared for Hrothgar;   the revered prince
set forth in state,   the foot soldiers
marching in his train.   The traces she left   *2 Her tracks*
crossing the fields   to the forest trails
were widely seen   as straight she went
1405 over the fen,   fleeing with the soulless
body of a lord   and best of warriors
whose duty under Hrothgar   was to rule the Danes.
Then a noble youth   by way unknown   *3 The way*
through narrow passes   and lonely paths
1410 climbed the steep   and stony cliffs,
the looming headlands   where sea-monsters lived;
with a few experienced men   he went before
to have a look   at the lay of the land,
when he suddenly chanced   on a cheerless wood
1415 of mountain trees   with trunks which bent
over gray rocks.   A grisly pool   *4 The mere*
bloodily churned below   —the Scylding lords
and Danish retainers   with difficulty
tried to endure   the dire grief
1420 each of them felt   after they found
the head of Æschere   on the high sea-cliff—
as the people gazed   the steaming pool
bloodily surged.   The battle-horn sounded   *5 The spectacle*
its song of death   and the troop was seated;
1425 they looked about them   at the teeming lake
where the monstrous serpents,   the sea dragons, swam
or other times lay   along the slope;

then that morning   they watched the monsters,
seeing the serpents   venture on the sea
1430 in joyless voyage   —in violent anger
they headed away   when they heard the trumpet
loudly resound.   The lord of the Geats   *6 The killing*
took aim at one   and killed it with an arrow
as it swam in the water   so that the war shaft
1435 pierced its body   —in coursing the pool
it was more sluggish   when it was slain;
through speedy engagement   and spirited attack
with the barbed hooks   of the boar spears
it was grappled in the water,   and the strange wave-goer
1440 was pulled to the shore;   the people gazed
at the baleful visitor.

iii *The arming of Beowulf*

           Beowulf armed himself   *1 Protective armor*
in his rich armor,   reckless of life;
his dearly encrusted   coat of chain-mail,
skilfully woven,   would in the waters
1445 be sorely tried   by its attempt to protect
his body from the clutch   of murderous claws
and keep from harm   the heart within;
the shining helmet   would protect his head
as he made his way   through the waters of the mere
1450 to stir its depths;   its splendid strength
was anciently forged   with fabled skill
and bound by the smith   in encircling bands
with the boar emblem   set above them
to prevent the bite   of battle sword.
1455 The hilted sword   which Hrothgar's spokesman   *2 Unferth's sword*
lent for the venture   was not the least   *of proven worth*
in giving him help;   called Hrunting by name
it was prized from antiquity   for priceless worth;
its encrusted iron blade   was hardened in blood
1460 of furious strife;   it never failed
when borne into battle   by a brave man
perilously daring   to press the attack
upon the home of the foe   —not for the first time
it was summoned to do   heroic deeds.
1465 In lending the blade   to a better swordsman   *3 Unferth's reputation*
Unferth, Ecglaf's son,   indeed did not seek   *is diminished*

to stir recollection   of what he had said
when he was drunk,   for he dared not
venture his life   in valorous act
1470 under the heaving waves;   there he became unworthy
of heroic fame.   This did not befall the other   *4 Beowulf's is not*
after he armed himself   for arduous battle

23 · Battle

i *Beowulf's Farewell*

The son of Ecgtheow,   Beowulf spoke: *1 Reminder*
"Illustrious Hrothgar,   son of Healfdane,   *of promise*
1475 generous king,   now that I go
upon your mission   remember well
what you said before   that if I should fall
in the attempt   you will take the place
of a dear father   to a dead son.
1480 I ask you to protect   the young retainers   *2 Request*
of my fellowship   if I fall in battle,
and send the gold   which you gave me,
beloved Hrothgar,   to the lord of the Geats
so that Higelac,   the son of Hrethel,
1485 seeing the treasure,   will understand
that here I found   the full munificence
of a princely provider   and prospered the while.
Permit Unferth   the well-known man   *3 Bequest to*
to wield my ancestral   wave-patterned   *Hunferth*
1490 hard-edged sword;   I with Hrunting
shall attain glory,   or death will take me."
After these words   the Geatish warrior   *4 Entry into*
heroically hastened,   having no wish   *the mere*
to await a reply   —the surging waters
1495 received the warrior.

ii *Descent by day*

Then it was day   *1 Descent*
before he saw   the bottom of the sea.
Grim and greedy   the ravenous guard   *2 The monster attacks*
of the waters   for fifty winters
soon discovered   that some human
1500 was exploring from above   the monster's abode;

she clutched at him   and with dread claws
gripped the warrior,   but could not wound
the body inside,   for the links kept him safe
from her fiendish talons   trying to tear
1505 into the coat   of covering mail.
The sea-wolf bore him   to the bottom   *3 She carries him*
and so carried the prince   into her cave   *to the cave*
that despite his courage   he could not lift
his sword to strike;   in his descent
1510 many sea monsters,   pursuing their adversary
with their fierce tusks,   tearing his mail,
had sorely wounded him.   Then the lord saw   *4 Beowulf observes*
he was in a hall   hostile in its mystery   *the cave*
where no water   in any way troubled him
1515 because the roof   kept the rushing flood
from penetrating;   it was pallidly lit
by the flaming   of a bright fire.
The worthy saw   the monstrous witch   *5 He observes*
of the sea's depth   and struck at her   *the monster*
1520 with baneful sword   whose hilted blade,
slashing unchecked,   sang upon her head
its violent song.   Then the visitor found   *6 The sword fails*
that the battle flame   had lost the force
of fatal bite   —now the edge failed
1525 to serve its lord;   in single combat
it had long hewed   through helmet and armor
of the doomed foe   —now the dear treasure
for the first time   became less in fame.

iii *Dubious battle (I)*

   Yet Higelac's kinsman   was no laggard hero;   *1 Beowulf relies upon*
1530 the warrior remained   mindful of glory   *main strength*
and in stern resolution   threw down his sword,
the steel-edged blade   in ornamented strength
striking the ground;   he trusted in the great
might of his hands   as a man must
1535 in doing battle   —when he seeks to buy
a lasting fame   he cannot worry about life.
The prince of the Geats   seized Grendel's mother   *2 He throws her*
by the shoulder   —he did not shrink from the feud—
and hardened in battle   with bursting anger
1540 he flung his deadly foe   down upon the floor.

In turn swiftly   she retaliated   *3 She retaliates*
by grappling him   grimly to her,
and the strongest of men   in battle-strength,
faltering in weariness,   was given a fall;
1545 she sought to avenge   her only son
and bestriding her guest   grasped her dagger
with sharpened edge.   Upon his shoulder   *4 Beowulf survives*
the links of mail   guarded his life
by withstanding the passage   of point or edge;
1550 if the battle mail   of his byrnie
had not saved him   the son of Ecgtheow,
the daring Geat,   would have gone in death
into the wide earth   —but the wise Ruler,
the Holy Lord,   God of Heaven,
1555 after he rose   justly ruled
and easily provided   victory for him.

24 · Victory and Return

i *The sword: victory through Grace (II)*

He saw amidst the gear   a victorious sword;   *1 Beowulf sees*
given its hardness   in the age of giants,   *a giant sword.*
the glory of warriors   excelled among weapons
1560 except that this goodly   work of giants
was too heavy   for any other human
to carry with him   into combat.
The champion of the Danes   fiercely daring   *2 He strikes her dead*
then seized the hilt,   drew the sword,
1565 in fury struck   with final desperation;
grimly the blade   gashed her neck,
broke the ring bones   and bit right through
the fated coat of flesh;   she crumpled to the floor
—the weapon was bloody,   the man joyful in his work.
1570 The light glowed within,   brightly gleaming   *3 The light guides*
even as heaven's candle   in clear radiance   *him to Grendel*
shines from on high;   Higelac's retainer,
enraged and resolute,   looked about the room,
turned along the wall,   lifted the weapon
1575 boldly by the hilt;   its blade was not useless
to the warrior,   who wished speedily
to repay Grendel   for the repeated violence

which he had done   to the Danish people
in the many raids   he had made after the one
1580 when he slew and swallowed   as they slumbered
in the depth of sleep   fifteen Danish men,
hearth companions   of King Hrothgar,
and carried away   an equal count
as foul booty.   The furious warrior   *4 He strikes off*
1585 made full repayment   when he found Grendel,   *Grendel's head*
deprived of life,   lying in rest,
weary of battle   with the wounds inflicted
in the fight at Heorot;   the corpse leaped high
when after death   it endured the savage
1590 blow of the sword   and the severing of its head.
At once the councillors   of Hrothgar's company   *5 The Danes*
staring at the sea   saw that on the surface   *see blood on*
the waters were troubled,   welled and were encrusted   *the surface*
with a surge of gore.   Gathered about their lord   *6 They lose hope*
1595 the gray-haired veterans   gave vent to misgivings,
for they did not expect   that the prince in victory
would ever return   to attend upon
their illustrious king;   many concluded
that the sea-wolf   had destroyed him.

ii *Mid-afternoon*

1600   At mid-afternoon   the noble Danes   *1 The Danes depart*
and their friendly lord   left the headland
to proceed home.   With saddened hearts   *2 The Geats*
the visitors stayed   and stared at the mere;   *despairingly hope*
they hoped but did not think   that they would see
1605 their beloved lord.   Then wondrously below   *3 Melting of*
the blade of the sword   began in the blood   *the sword*
to melt away   in murderous icicles
until nothing remained,   much as does ice
when the deadly fetters   of the binding frost
1610 are freed by the Lord,   the true Father,
Who holds in His sway   time and season.
Of the great treasure   the lord of the Geats   *4 Beowulf takes*
saw in the cave   he seized on nothing   *no booty*
except for the head   and the sword hilt,
1615 preciously encrusted;   the patterned blade
had burned and melted   in the poisoned blood
of the alien spirit   whose life was spent.

Having endured in battle   till his foes were dead   *5 Beowulf ascends*
he soon began   his upward swim.
1620 After the alien spirit   had spent his days   *6 The mere is purified*
in this fleeting world   the surging waters
in their mighty expanse   were purified.

iii *The triumphant return*

The stout of heart,   protector of seamen,   *1 Return to*
swam to the shore;   he rejoiced in the sea-treasure   *the shore*
1625 whose mighty burden   he bore with him;
his noble company   came to meet him,
joyfully giving   their thanks to God
for letting them see   their lord safely returned.
Hastily from the champion   helmet and chainmail   *2 The adventure*
1630 were taken off   — the waters of the tarn   *is ended*
encrusted with gore   lay quiet under the heavens.
Filled with joy   they crossed the fields,   *3 The return*
treading their way   and retracing the footpaths   *with the head*
they remembered;   four of the men,
1635 each of them hardy   and high of spirits,
with difficulty   by prodigious effort
barely managed   on a bloody spear
to carry away   from the sea cliff
the head of Grendel   to the golden hall.
1640 Making their way   across the meadow,   *4 Arrival at Heorot*
presently the Geats   approached the hall,
brave and fearless   the fourteen men
counting their prince   proud in their midst.
Then the brave lord,   leader of his men,   *5 Beowulf enters*
1645 daring in battle,   renowned for his deeds,
entered the hall   to greet Hrothgar.
Then by the hair   the head of Grendel   *6 The head*
was drawn across the floor   where the men drank;   *is shown*
the warriors saw   the awesome sight,
1650 terrifying to the lords   surrounding their lady.

25 · Dialogue of Victory

i *Beowulf's Speech*

The son of Ecgtheow,   Beowulf spoke: *1 "We bring you*
"Lord of the Scyldings,   Son of Healfdane,   *sea treasure*

we have gladly brought you   what you gaze upon,
the treasure of the sea   as a token of victory.

1656 I barely survived   the terrible venture
under the water,   accomplished my work
in grim anguish;   God was my help,
or the savage fight   would have ended suddenly;
Hrunting was not   of any help to me
1660 during the strife   though it is a good sword,
but God the Ruler,   most present Guide
to friendless men,   afforded me the grace
to see an ancient,   gigantic sword
shining on the wall   and to wield it;
1665 then when the time was right   I attacked and slew
the guardians of the place;   then the patterned blade
burned to nothing   in the blood's fierce heat
as it gushed forth;   thence from the fiends
taking the hilt   I avenged the terrible
1670 slaughter of the Danes   with justice due.
I make this promise   that you may in Heorot
sleep free of care   with your company of men,
the young and old   of your people,
and that from that quarter,   King of the Scyldings,
1675 you now will have   no need to fear,
as you did before,   the slaughter of your followers.
When the golden hilt,   ancient work of giants,
was given into the hands   of the gray old hero,
powerful in war,   the work of mysterious smiths
1680 came into the possession   of the king of the Danes;
for after the monsters,   guilty murderers,
the man of hatred   and his mother,
the foes of God,   gave up this world
it came into the keeping   of the mightiest king
1685 who in this world   distributed wealth
between the two seas   in Scandinavia.

ii *Hrothgar's inspired speech (I)*

    King Hrothgar spoke,   gazing upon the hilt,
the ancient relic   on which was written
how strife began   and how later the giants
1690 were drowned in the rush   of the raging flood,
the engulfing waters   sent by the Lord God,
the eternal Ruler, to punish this race

Marginal notes:

2 "I survived with God's help

3 "You need fear no longer."

4 The hilt is given to Hrothgar

1 Hrothgar looks on the hilt

of lawless exiles   who lived by terror;
also on the gold   of the hilt guard
1695 above the melted   serpentine markings
encrusting the sword,   in secret runes
the name of the man   for whom it was made
had been inscribed.   All were silent
when the son of Healfdane   spoke in wisdom:

2 "Beowulf is better than I

1700 "For one grown old   in governing his people
in truth and justice   who recalls time past
it is possible to say   that this prince was born
the better man.   My friend Beowulf,
your glory is lifted   across the land

3 "Beowulf's glory and reward

1705 and everywhere among all people   through patience and prudence of mind
you fully govern your power;   I shall fulfill the promise of friendship
which I made when we spoke before.   You shall become the mainstay
and lasting comfort   of your countrymen
and help to your land.   Heremod was not thus;

4 "You will help your people

5 "Unlike Heremod

1710 he himself prospered   but brought no prosperity
to the Scyldings,   the descendants of Ecgwala,
but rather death   to the Danish people;
in madness he slew   the men closest to him
in feast and war,   until the famous lord
1715 in solitude passed   from the pleasures of men;
although mighty God   supported him in might,
long advanced him   in the delights of power
above all men,   yet his mind was stirred
by growing blood-lust;   he did not give gifts
1720 for the glory of the Danes,   but lived in gloom
to suffer the pain   of a people afflicted
by lingering strife.   May you learn from this
to heed lordly virtue;   this is a lesson for you
from one old in winters.

6 "Give heed to this lesson

iii *God gives: man disposes*

It is wonderful to tell
1725 how mighty God,   Who governs all
in His providence,   apportions wisdom,
prosperity and might   among mankind.
Sometimes He permits   a noble mind
to think with delight   on a life of pleasure,
1730 giving him joy of lordship,   in his native land
to hold the citadel   safe for his people;

1 "All comes from God

2 Man corrupts in self-love

under his rule He places   spacious realms,
such worldly dominion   that in his lack of wisdom
he cannot conceive   that its end will come;
1735   he flourishes in success,   sickness and age
cause him no harm,   no sorrow of heart
darkens his spirit,   no strife anywhere
bursts into war;   because all the world
turns as he wills   he knows nothing worse.

26 · Night Ends the Feast

i *Hrothgar's Speech (II)*

1740   "At last within him   a latent pride   *1 "Man falls*
grows and flowers;   when the guard and protector   *in pride*
of the soul sleeps   in the profound slumber
of worldly occupation   the slayer wickedly
lurks very near   to let loose his arrows;
1745   then heedless of defense   beneath his helmet
he is struck to the heart   by the strange enticements,
the piercing shaft   of the proscribed spirit;
what he has long owned   appears too little,
and in hatred and greed   he does not uphold honor
1750   by giving rich gifts;   because he was once granted
many blessings by God,   the Ruler of Glory,
he is forgetful and careless   of what must come.
By decree of fate   it follows thereafter   *2 His doom is*
that his doomed flesh   falls into decline,   *certain*
1755   and in its frailty perishes;   his fortune will pass
to be inherited by another   who will without heed
disperse his abundance   in reckless abandon.
Beloved Beowulf,   best among men,   *3 "You must avoid it*
illustrious warrior,   guard against wickedness,
1760   choose a better goal,   the good of eternity,
give no heed to pride.   Your heroic glory   *4 "Glory is*
is but of the moment;   soon it shall be   *of the moment*
that sickness or sword   will deprive you of strength,
the grasping fire   or raging flood,
1765   the smiting sword   or flying spear,
or baneful age   when the eye's brightness
will weaken and grow dark;   suddenly, warrior,
it will be death   that will draw you down.

ii *The lesson of his life*

Just so I reigned   over the realm of the Danes,   *1 "I prospered*
1770 held sway under the heavens   and with sword and spear
protected them in war   here in this world
against many nations   so that no foe
could I anywhere find   under the compass of the skies.
Alas there befell me   fortune's reversal,   *2 "Reversal*
1775 lamentation after song   in my native land
after Grendel's attack,   the ancient terror
from whose persecution   I dwelt in constant
grievous sorrow.   Thanks be to God,   *3 "Thanks be to God*
the eternal Lord,   that I have lived   *that I have*
1780 through lingering strife   long enough to look   *survived*
here with my eyes   upon his blood-stained head.
Now take your place,   partake of the feast   *4 "Feast now;*
honored in triumph;   we two will share   *tomorrow you*
many treasures   after morning comes."   *will be rewarded."*
1785 The Geat was delighted,   going at once   *5 Beowulf takes*
he went to his place   as the wise one bade.   *his place*
Then again as before   a feast was prepared   *6 Feasting resumed*
on this second occasion   for the brave company
assembled in the hall.

iii *The concluding night*

The shadow of night   *1 Night brings the*
1790 darkened over the courtiers;   the company arose   *feast to end*
as the gray old king   gave indication
of his wish to retire,   and rest was welcome
to the weary   Geatish warrior.
Directly the retainer,   whose duty it was   *2 Beowulf is*
1795 in courteous service   to supply such comforts   *conducted to bed*
as in those days   were deemed fitting
for seafaring warriors,   conducted on his way
the weary visitor   who had voyaged from afar.
The hero rested   —the roof towered high,   *3 Beowulf sleeps*
1800 carved and gold-encrusted—   the guest slept within,
until the black raven,   blithe-hearted, announced
the bliss of heaven.   Then the bright sun   *4 Daybreak brings*
advanced on its way;   the noble warriors   *the wish to depart*
eagerly hurried,   were ready hastily
1805 to return to their people;   the brave traveler

wished to sail home   upon his ship.
Then the worthy Beowulf   bade that Hrunting   *5 Return of*
be borne to Hunferth,   bade him take back   *Hrunting*
his beloved sword,   thanked him for the loan,
1810 saying he found it   in battle a friend
of goodly strength;   a gracious man
he uttered no words   to disparage the weapon.
Then the warriors   wearing their armor   *6 Audience with*
were ready to leave;   beloved by the Danes,   *Hrothgar*
1815 the noble came   where the king sat;
the brave hero   greeted Hrothgar.

27 · Farewell

i *Beowulf's farewell*

The son of Ecgtheow,   Beowulf spoke: *1 "We wish to*
"Now we seafarers   who have sailed from afar   *depart*
seek to announce   our eager desire
1820 to return to Higelac;   your hospitality
and your welcome here   were all we could wish.
If in any way   I may earn in this world   *2 "I shall*
a firmer place   in your affections   *serve you*
through deeds of war   than I have done already,
1825 my regal lord,   I shall be ready at once.
If I should hear   at home over the seas   *3 "In your need*
that a neighbor attempts   terror against you,   *I will aid you*
as your dire enemies   not long since did,
I will come to your aid   with a company of men
1830 a thousand strong;   I am sure that Higelac,
the king of the Geats,   guardian of his people
though he is still young,   will strive to aid me
in word and deed   that I may honor you well,
and to assist you   I will bring spears
1835 and supporting might   when you have need of men.
Should your son Hrethric   decide to visit   *4 "Hrethric will*
the Geatish court   he will there discover   *find friends."*
many a friend;   foreign countries
can be of much worth   to a man of promise.

ii *Hrothgar's farewell*

1840   In response to him   King Hrothgar said: *1 "You have*
"God in His wisdom   has given you the words   *greatness*

you speak from your heart;   I have never heard
so young a man   manifest such prudence;
you are mighty of strength,   mature of mind,
1845 wise in your speech.   It seems to me   *2 "You would be*
that in the future   if the fierce sword,   *a good king*
the battle spear   or even sickness,
should take Higelac,   the son of Hrethel,
your people's lord,   and you still live
1850 and consent to rule   over the realm,
the Geats would find   no man more fit
to be their king,   keeper of the treasure
and guardian of men.   Dear Beowulf, the more   *3 "You have*
I learn of your character   the more I like it;   *brought peace*
1855 through your accomplishment   it will come to pass
that peace will be shared   by our people,
the Danes and the Geats,   and the strife they endured,
the spirit of enmity,   will be set to rest;
as long as I rule   my spacious realm
1860 our treasures will be shared;   across our shores
many a man will greet   his fellow with gifts,
and ring-prowed ships   will bear riches across the sea
as tokens of peace.   These people I know   *4 "The peace*
abide by tradition,   truly faultless   *will endure."*
1865 in their resolute firmness   toward friend and foe.

iii *Final parting*

Then regal Hrothgar,   the son of Healfdane,   *1 Farewell*
gave him in the hall   another twelve gifts;
he bade him safely   seek his dear people
with his treasures   and swiftly return.
1870 The noble lord   of the Danish nation   *2 Hrothgar's*
clasped in embrace   the best of warriors;   *tearful*
the gray-haired king   granted him his kiss   *farewell*
and burst into tears;   of two eventualities
that might occur   one seemed more likely
1875 to the wise old man,   that they would never again meet
in lofty converse;   Hrothgar so loved him
that he could not restrain   the storm of emotion,
for in his heart's blood   within his bosom
feelingly dwelt   a deep affection
1880 for the beloved man.   Then Beowulf left,   *3 Beowulf leaves*
crossed the greensward   glorying in gold,

exulting in treasure   — the sea-traveler
riding at anchor   awaited its ruler.
Often in leaving   they lavished praise   *4 Praise of*
upon Hrothgar's gifts   — here was a king   *Hrothgar's gifts*
who ruled without flaw   until the ravages of age
deprived him like many   of the pleasures of power.

part two

the hero in age

A Homecoming: *Glory and Doom*

28 · Arrival Home — Hygd

i *Journey home*

<table>
<tr><td></td><td>The heroic band of brave young men</td><td>*1 Arrival*</td></tr>
<tr><td></td><td>came to the shore clad in their coats</td><td>*at shore*</td></tr>
<tr><td>1890</td><td>of close-linked mail; the coastguard observed</td><td></td></tr>
<tr><td></td><td>the return of the company as he had its coming;</td><td></td></tr>
<tr><td></td><td>from the high cliff he did not call</td><td></td></tr>
<tr><td></td><td>to the guests roughly but riding to them</td><td></td></tr>
<tr><td></td><td>said these warriors in shining armor</td><td></td></tr>
<tr><td>1895</td><td>who went to their ship would be welcome at home.</td><td></td></tr>
<tr><td></td><td>The stately vessel stood at the shore</td><td>*2 The laden ship*</td></tr>
<tr><td></td><td>with ringed prow, laden with riches,</td><td></td></tr>
<tr><td></td><td>horses and war gear; over Hrothgar's</td><td></td></tr>
<tr><td></td><td>hord of treasure the mast towered.</td><td></td></tr>
<tr><td>1900</td><td>Beowulf first gave a sword as gift</td><td>*3 Gift-giving*</td></tr>
<tr><td></td><td>to the boat ward who through the worth</td><td>*and departure*</td></tr>
<tr><td></td><td>of the golden heirloom was honored the more</td><td></td></tr>
<tr><td></td><td>on the meadbench. He boarded his ship</td><td>*4 Boarding*</td></tr>
<tr><td></td><td>and left Denmark to cross the deep.</td><td></td></tr>
<tr><td>1905</td><td>The robe of sail with sheetings of rope</td><td>*5 The journey*</td></tr>
<tr><td></td><td>was tied to the mast; the timbers creaked;</td><td></td></tr>
<tr><td></td><td>the wind did not hinder the hastening ship</td><td></td></tr>
<tr><td></td><td>upon its course, and the curved prow,</td><td></td></tr>
<tr><td></td><td>foaming whitely, breasted the flood</td><td></td></tr>
<tr><td>1910</td><td>upon its way across the waters</td><td></td></tr>
<tr><td></td><td>until the cliffs of home, the Geatish headlands,</td><td></td></tr>
<tr><td></td><td>came into sight. Sped by the wind</td><td>*6 Arrival at*</td></tr>
<tr><td></td><td>the ship was beached and rested on the shore;</td><td>*the home*</td></tr>
<tr><td></td><td>the harbor watch who had long waited,</td><td>*shore*</td></tr>
</table>

1915 scanning the horizon   for sight of the beloved,
soon was ready   by the seashore;
he secured with ropes   the ring-prowed vessel
and made it fast   lest the tidal flow
set the lovely ship   loose from the shore.

ii *Hygd*

1920   Beowulf ordered unloaded   the lordly treasure,
the gold and ornaments;   it was not far to go
to find where Higelac,   the son of Hrethel,
the liberal provider,   lived with his men,
for his home was seated   near to the sea

*1 The treasure
is taken to
Higelac's hall*

1925 — the building was splendid,   the king very brave.
Enthroned in the hall   was the youthful Hygd
wise and accomplished;   though for few winters
Hæreth's daughter   had been dwelling
within the stronghold   she was not stingy

*2 The goodness
of Hygd*

1930 or niggardly in giving   gifts of much price
to her Geatish subjects.   A gracious queen
she weighed Thryth's pride   and wretched crimes.
No one close to Thryth   within the court
except her lordly father   was fearless enough

*3 She thinks of
Thryth's evil*

1935 to look upon her   in the light of day;
for the doom of such doing   was the deadly clutch
of the grasping hands;   after he was held
the sword at once   made its settlement
— its patterned blade   announced bloody

1940 sentence of death.   Such deeds no queen
or woman should do   though wondrously fair,
the peace-weaver   deprive of life
a faithful man   for fancied injury.
Offa descended from Hemming   put a halt to this;

*4 These are
not the deeds
of a queen*

*5 King Offa
redeems her*

1945 men drinking ale   spoke of the difference;
how she ceased to be   the malicious source
of grief to her people   after she was given,
adorned with gold,   to the gallant youth
and worthy noble   by her father's wish

1950 and went to seek   across the pale water
the hall of Offa;   here upon the throne
she lived thereafter   the length of her life
famed for the greatness   of her goodness
and her exalted love   for the lord of men,

1955 who was I have heard   of the human race
     the worthiest   in all the world
     between the two seas.   Offa was in truth   *6 The greatness*
     a valiant warrior,   for his victories and gifts   *of Offa*
     widely honored   and for his wisdom in ruling
1960 his native kingdom;   in the kindred of Hemming
     he begot Eomer,   grandson of Garmund,
     skillful in war,   sustainer of warriors.

29 · Return to the Court

i *Beowulf returns*

     The hero stepped   upon the strand,   *1 Beowulf leaves*
     with his company   crossed the shore   *the shore*
1965 and the wide sands   — the world candle
     shone from the South.   Swiftly they went   *2 Approach*
     along the way   which led they knew   *to the hall*
     to the stronghold   where the slayer of Ongentheow,
     their youthful lord   and their leader,
1970 distributed his treasure.   Straightway Higelac   *3 Higelac is*
     was told that Beowulf   was returning,   *informed*
     that his companion   and princely champion
     had safely survived   his battle venture
     and alive and hale   was approaching the hall.
1975 At the ruler's bidding   within the banquet hall   *4 Place is made*
     room was quickly made   for the arriving guests.   *in the hall*

ii *Higelac's Greeting*

     After saluting his lord   with due ceremony   *1 Beowulf greets*
     in manfully graceful   words of greeting,   *Higelac*
     the survivor of peril   took his place by Higelac,
1980 kinsman by kinsman.   In loving kindness   *2 Hygd pours*
     the daughter of Hæreth   within the hall
     directed the mead pouring;   into the men's hands
     she gave the wine cup.   In the high hall   *3 "What did you do*
     Higelac began   graciously to question
1985 his close companion,   curious to hear
     of the adventures   of the Geatish voyagers:
     'My dear Beowulf,   what did you do
     after you suddenly   decided to seek
     across the salt waters   distant warfare

1990 and battle at Heorot?   Were you of help   *4 "Were you*
     to illustrious Hrothgar   in relieving his woes   *successful?*
     so widely bruited?   In my mind boiled   *5 "I had doubts*
     a seething doubt   of my dear man's
     brave enterprise;   long I begged you
1995 to meet in no manner   with the murderous demon,
     to leave to the Danes   themselves to do
     battle with Grendel.   To God I say thanks   *6 "Thank God."*
     that I see you now   safely returned.

iii *Narrative Introduction; Ingeld (I)*

         The son of Ecgtheow,   Beowulf spoke: *1 "I was successful*
2000 "Lord Higelac,   many have learned
     of the meeting   between Grendel and me,
     of the kind of battle   I encountered
     in that very place   where he had visited
     upon the Danes   dire misery
2005 and violent affliction;   this I avenged,
     so that the last   living survivor
     of Grendel's vicious,   sin-enveloped,
     bestial race   may not boast at dawn
     of causing lamentation.   When I came to Denmark   *2 "I was*
2010 I went to the hall   to address Hrothgar;   *welcomed*
     as soon as the illustrious   son of Healfdane
     had ascertained   my mind's intention   *by Hrothgar*
     he had me seated   beside his own son;
     the company was merry,   —I have never met
2015 under heaven's roof   festivity in the hall
     more filled with joy.   The famed queen,   *3 "Wealhtheow*
     securer of peace,   at times crossed the hall   *appeared*
     to greet the warriors   and to give in bounty
     the treasured ring   before returning to her place.
2020 Sometimes Hrothgar's daughter   carried their drink   *4 "I saw*
     in turn to each   of the old retainers;   *Freawaru*
     as she gave the warriors   the golden cup
     I heard the company   call her by the name
     of Freawaru;   to Froda's fair son
2025 the golden princess   has been promised;
     the ruler of the Danes   has arranged this,
     for the nation's protector   counts it politic
     to try through the woman   to settle by truce

the bloody feud.   Though the bride be fair
2030 the fall of a king   is seldom followed
by enduring rest   of the deadly spear.
A youthful Dane   will conduct the maiden
into the hall,   arousing hatred
in the heart of the king   and his Heathobards
2035 who at the feast   will in fury watch
a Dane wearing   the damascened sword,
the hardened heirloom   treasured by the Heathobards
while they wielded power   with such weapons.

*5 "Such attempts
are futile*

*6 "I prophesy
disaster*

30 · Foreboding and Fame

i *Ingeld prophecy (II)*

But at the last   they lost in battle
2040 their beloved comrades   and their own lives.
Then an old warrior,   seeing the weapon
and remembering   the murderous slaughter,
will speak at the feast   —his heart is fierce—
and bitterly start   to stir up trouble,
2045 sounding out the spirit   of a young soldier
by awakening remembrance;   he'll speak these words:
'My friend can you recognize   your father's sword,
the valued blade   he bore into battle
when wearing his helmet   he went to war
2050 for the final time   and the Danes felled him,
the valiant Scyldings   who were victorious
after Withergild died   and our warriors fell?
Now a son of someone   who slew your father
troops into the hall,   gloats over the treasure,
2055 and boasts of the murder   by bearing the sword
which you by reason   and by right should wear.'
On every occasion   he will recall and provoke
with terrible words   until such time
as the maiden's escort   will be murdered
2060 and, blood-encrusted,   will die by the blade
for his father's deed;   the other flees,
escapes alive   knowing the country well.
A savage hatred   will surge in Ingeld,
2065 and in waves of sorrow   his love for his wife
will turn colder,   and the sworn truce

*1 "The Heathobards
were defeated*

*2 An old warrior
will say, 'See
your father's
sword*

*3 'See the
affront given.'*

*4 "The words will
be effective*

*5 "The truce will
be broken*

will then be broken   by both of the sides.
Therefore I consider   the peace uncertain   *6 "Thus I doubt*
between Heathobards and Danes,   the alliance doubtful   *the peace"*
and their friendship unsteady.

ii *Narrative: Grendel*

                 "Bestower of bounty,   *1 "I return*
2070 I now return   to my tale of Grendel   *to my story*
that you may discover   what came to pass
in the combat of hands.   After heaven's jewel   *2 "Grendel slew*
had coursed the earth   the demon came,   *Hondscioh*
terrible in the night,   to track us down
2075 where as yet unharmed   we guarded the hall;
there for doomed Hondscioh   the deadly attack
was to be fatal   —he was the first to fall,
girded for battle;   Grendel slew him
and with greedy mouth   gulped down the body
2080 of the illustrious warrior,   young and beloved.
The bloody-toothed slayer   mindful of slaughter   *3 "He attacked me*
was not prepared   as yet to depart
from the golden hall   with empty hands,
for he tested me   with terrible strength,
2085 gripped me with his hands;   he carried a glove
of marvelous size   and strangely clasped,
which had been made   by ancient magic
and demon cunning   from dragon skins;
into its depths   the fierce devil
2090 for no crime I did   wished to cram me
and many another;   he could not manage it
after I stood upright,   stirred to anger.
It would take too long   to tell how I repaid   *4 "I was victorious*
the people's foe   for the evils he perpetrated;
2095 the deeds I did there   redounded, my lord, ,
to the glory of your people;   he got away,
and a little while   enjoyed life,
yet his right hand   remained in Heorot
to mark his retreat;   in abject misery
2100 mournfully he sank   to the bottom of the mere;
for the bloody conflict   the king of the Scyldings
rewarded me with treasure,   a wealth of gold
in mighty abundance.   After morning passed   *5 "Next day we*
and we took our places   to partake of the feast   *celebrated*

2105 there was song and story;   the old Scylding
      well-founded in lore   told of far-off days;
      sometimes the warrior   made the harp's wood
      rejoice at his touch,   at times telling
      a tale of sorrow,   at time recounting
2110 a mysterious legend;   the magnanimous lord,
      grizzled warrior,   sometimes would begin,
      bound down with years,   to speak of his youthful
      strength in battle;   his wise heart stirred
      as he remembered much   of his many winters.
2115 Thus in that place   we took our pleasure   *6 "There was joy*
      the entire day   until the darkness of night   *until nightfall*
      came again to man.

      iii *Narrative: Grendel's dam*

                          "Grendel's mother   *1 "Grendel*
      in her sorrow   was soon ready   *was avenged*
      to revenge her son,   violently murdered
2120 by Geatish might;   the monstrous woman
      avenged her child,   with heroic valor
      killed a warrior;   there the wise counselor,
      the old lord Æschere,   parted from life.
      After morning came   the Danes could not   *2 "Æschere could*
2125 do as they wished   for him who lay dead,   *not be buried*
      give him to consuming fire,   set the beloved
      upon the funeral pyre;   in her fiendish embrace
      she had taken his body   into the waters of the tarn;
      to Hrothgar this grief   was the greatest
2130 of all those that long   had afflicted this lord.
      The king in sorrow   called upon me   *3 "Hrothgar*
      as I held you dear   nobly to dare   *appealed to me*
      the raging waters   and risk my life
      to win glory   —he vowed to reward me.
2135 Then as is widely known   I went to find   *4 "I completed*
      the grimly terrible   guardian of the deep;   *the feud*
      for a time we closed   in single combat
      —the sea welled with blood;   in the battle hall
      with a huge sword   I cut off the head
2140 of Grendel's mother;   with great hardship
      I managed to survive   and remain undoomed
      —the lord Hrothgar,   son of Healfdane,
      rewarded me   with wealth of treasure.

31 · Fortune's Reversals

i *Narrative conclusion; gift-giving*

"Thus the nation's king   observed good custom;   *1 "Hrothgar was*
2145 I did not lose   from his largesse   *generous*
in rewarding my strength,   for the son of Healfdane
weighed by my delight   the wealth of his gifts.
Heroic lord,   I desire lovingly   *2 "I bring his*
to give them to you;   still of your grace   *gifts to you*
2150 I hold all I have;   except Higelac for you
I count not many   as close kinsmen."
He had the armor   brought to the hall,   *3 "Hrothgar asked*
the boar standard,   the battle helmet,   *me to tell*
the splendid sword,   and spoke these words: *the story of*
    the armor."
2155 "Hrothgar gave me   this gear of war;
the wise ruler   wished specially
that first I tell   the tale of his gift;
he said that for long   the lord of the Danes,
King Heorogar,   held it as his own,
2160 yet had no wish   to give Heoroweard,
his own brave son,   the breast armor
though he was faithful;   enjoy it to the full."
As I have heard,   next to have place   *4 The remaining gifts*
were the four mares,   swift and matching
2165 in apple-dark hue;   he gave to Higelac
war gear and mares;   thus men should act
and should not weave   webs of malice
with dark cunning   to contrive the death
of near comrades.   The nephew was completely   *5 Beowulf and*
2170 loyal to Higelac,   his valiant lord,   *Higelac are true*
and each paid heed   to the other's happiness.
I heard he gave   to noble Hygd   *6 Gift to Hygd*
three graceful horses   with handsome saddles
and the wondrous necklet,   Wealhtheow's reward,
2175 he gave to her;   thereafter the gem
graced her breast   with its golden beauty.

ii *Reversals in Beowulf's life*

Thus did Beowulf   reveal his bravery;   *1 Present glory*
a warrior famed   for his worthy deeds   *as God's gift*
he strove for glory;   in his cups he never slew
2180 his hearth companions,   for his heart was not savage;

the precious gift   God had given him
of greater might   than any man's
he guarded with valor.   He was long unvalued;   *2 Inauspicious*
the sons of the Geats   considered him unworthy,   *beginning*
2185 and their royal lord   did not lavish on him
much attention   upon the meadbench,
for they assumed   he was a slothful
and feeble prince.   Change of fortune   *3 Fortune*
with blessing of fame   banished his misery.   *brings fame*
2190 Protector of nobles,   renowned in battle,   *4 Transfer of*
Higelac called   for Hrethel's heirloom   *Hrethel's sword*
adorned with gold   — among the Geats
no treasured sword   was more esteemed;
he gave it to Beowulf,   laid it on his bosom
2195 and made him master   of a domain
of seven thousand hides;   both of them held
in the nation   native estates
and inherited land;   to one went lordlier
and greater realm   as befitted his rank.

iii *Future doom*

2200   In days to come   in clashes of battle   *1 The cycle of doom*
this came to pass: first Higelac was killed,
then King Heardred   under cover of shield
was slashed by swords   wielded by the Swedes
whose fierce soldiers   slew him in war
2205 when they advanced   upon the victorious Geats
and violently harried   the son of Hygd.
After this the rule   of the broad realm   *2 Beowulf*
was rested in Beowulf;   he reigned righteously   *reigns*
for fifty winters,   a wise old king
2210 protecting his land.   But at the last began   *3 The dragon*
in the dark nights   the rule of the dragon
who guarded the hoard   on the high heath
in a lofty stone barrow;   a path lay below
unknown to the people.   Some nameless man   *4 The cause of the*
2215 creeping inside   close to the hoard,   *dragon's anger*
clutched in his hands   an ornamented cup
encrusted with treasure;   the dragon, tricked
as it lay sleeping   through the thief's skill,
did not lie quiet   — in the neighboring land
2220 the folk discovered   that he was swollen with fury.

B — *Battle with the Dragon*

32 · The Dragon and the Treasure

i *Violation of the hoard*

In provoking the dragon   and violating the hoard
he did not act wilfully   or by his own wish,
but through necessity;   he was someone's slave,
guilty of something,   who sought to escape
2225 the scourge of the lash,   and lacking shelter
forced his way in.   A terrible fear
gripped the intruder   as soon as he entered,
yet it befell   that the poor fugitive
made good his escape   from his great peril;
2230 quickly fleeing   before disaster fell
he carried off the cup.

1 The act was
unpremeditated

2 Escape with
the cup

ii *The ancient burial*

The earthen cave
was filled with other   fabled treasure,
the precious riches   of a noble race,
its enormous legacy,   just as some unknown
2235 had hidden it   with heedful care
in distant days.   Death long before
had taken them all;   the surviving retainer,
the last of his nation,   the longest to live
mourning his kinsmen,   was mindful that he
2240 would also not live   long to enjoy
the hoarded treasure.   A barrow on a headland
near the seashore   had been newly prepared
and made secure   through skillful concealment;
the keeper of the hoard   carried inside
2245 the richest portion   of the princely treasure
of beaten gold;   he spoke briefly:
'Oh earth, now hold   what heroes could not keep,
the warriors' treasure   once wrested from you
and now returned;   the terror of war
2250 has murderously taken   every last man,
and all my race   that revelled at the feast
have departed this life.   I have no one left
to carry the sword   or cleanse the cup,

1 The treasure

2 The last survivor

3 "I give the
treasure to the
earth

4 "All are dead

the bejewelled bowl,   —the noble band has gone;
2255 the sturdy helmet   will be stripped of gold
and decorated plating,   —the polishers are sleeping
who kept the helmets   clean and shining;
the coat of mail   is decaying too
and will go no more   to guard in battle
2260 from the bite of blade   after the shield is broken
—no longer now   will the leader wear it
standing with his men.   There is no sweet song   5 "Joy is gone."
from the joyous harp;   no goodly hawk
flies through the hall;   no swift horse
2265 stamps in the courtyard   —accursed death
has made depart   these many men."
Thus the survivor   in sadness of heart,   6 His death
lamenting his grief,   mournfully wandered
by day and night   until the waters of death
2270 overwhelmed his heart.

iii *The dragon*

          The happy treasure   1 Seizure by
was found unguarded   by the ancient foe,   the dragon
the scaly dragon   which scours the land
in search of barrows   and bound in flames
flies in the night;   it is greatly feared
2275 by dwellers in the land;   it lives to search
for the buried hoard,   where hoary in age
it guards heathen gold   though it gains nothing.
Thus the threatening foe   for three hundred winters   2 Violation
held the treasure   in an earthen house
2280 of rugged strength   until aroused to fury
by a single man   who sought the king
with the golden cup   to gain settlement
with his master.   When the wretched man   3 Beowulf sees
was granted his petition   after gaining entrance   the cup
2285 and stealing the hoard   then the king saw
the ancient treasure   for the first time.
When the dragon stirred,   strife was renewed;   4 The dragon
it sniffed the stone   and starkly found   aroused
the track of the foe   who had trodden too near
2290 the dragon's head   by hidden way;
thus when guarded   by the Master's grace
a man may survive   misery and exile

untouched by doom.   The protector of the hoard   *5 He searches*
eagerly searched   and sought to find   *for the cup*
2295 the man who had sorely   afflicted it sleeping;
burning with rage   around the barrow
it circled repeatedly   — no man appeared
in the desert waste   to sate its wish
for the work of battle;   returning to the barrow
2300 it searched for the cup   and soon discovered
that a man in truth   had tampered with its gold,
its heaped-up treasure.   The guardian of the hoard   *6 He attacks*
direly waited   for dusk to come;
the bitter foe,   keeper of the barrow,
2305 fiercely craved   fiery reprisal
for the precious cup;   when day had passed
as the dragon wished,   it would not wait
long by the barrow,   but ready for the burning
it went forth with fire;   as the beginning was fearful
2310 for the people of the realm,   so for the royal provider
a sore conclusion   was soon to come.

33 · The Dragon Attacks: Beowulf Responds

i *Attack and return*

Vomiting flames   the firedrake began   *1 The dragon*
to burn the bright houses   — the blaze arose   *attacks*
to men's horror;   the monster in its flight
2315 intended to leave   no one alive;
the Geatish folk   both far and near
were widely aware   of the violent war
the dragon waged   in deadly hate
with broad devastation.   At break of day   *2 It returns to*
2320 after it had wrapped in flame   and blazing fire   *its stronghold*
the human inhabitants   it hurried to the hoard
buried in the cave;   it trusted in its courage
and its barrow fastness   — its faith proved false.

ii *Beowulf's reaction*

The terrible truth   thereafter was told   *1 Beowulf is told*
2325 to Beowulf hastily,   that his own home,
the splendid hall   which held his throne,
was wasted by flames.   To the wise worthy   *2 He is unsure*

the greatest sorrow   troubling his soul
was that he felt   he had offended the Ruler,
2330 transgressed ancient law   and made the Eternal Lord
bitterly angry;   within his breast
his thoughts were clouded   by unaccustomed doubt.
The firedrake with flames   had destroyed the fastness,   *3 He plans*
the nation's stronghold   and all the neighboring   *revenge*
2335 land by the sea   —for this the lord of the Geats,
the valiant king,   devised revenge.
The leader of warriors,   protector of lords,   *4 The shield*
commanded the making   of a marvelous shield
entirely of iron;   he knew in truth
2340 that linden wood   would be worthless
against the flames.   Great for so long,   *5 But Beowulf*
the worthy would die,   would end the days   *is doomed with*
of transitory life   along with the dragon   *the dragon*
who long had held   the wealth of the hoard.
2345 The generous prince   proudly disdained   *6 Beowulf's*
to hunt the far-flyer   with a host of men   *confidence*
or large company;   he did not fear the encounter,   *in his heroic*
nor valued at all   the might and valor   *past*
of the dragon   because since the day
2350 when in combat   he had crushed Grendel
and his horrible race   and cleansed the hall
where Hrothgar ruled   he had survived
with victory blessed   many other battles
and much peril.

iii *Beowulf remembers war*

                One of the mightiest   *1 Higelac's death*
2355 of his single encounters   came on the occasion
of Higelac's death   when the son of Hrethel,
the Geat's beloved king,   was killed in Frisia
in furious battle   through the fatal drink
of the biting sword.   Thence Beowulf came   *2 Beowulf's*
2360 through his own strength,   took to the sea;   *escape*
he bore in his arms   the battle-gear
of thirty men   when he turned to the main;
in their foot battle   the Hetware who bore
their shields against him   had no reason
2365 for exultation   —few succeeded
in returning home   after encountering this hero;

solitary and bereaved   the son of Ecgtheow
came back to his people   across the sea's expanse.
Then Hygd offered him   hoard and kingdom,
2370 treasure and throne,   for she could not trust
her son to safeguard   his ancestral sovereignty
against a foreign host   now Higelac was dead;
but neither she   nor the destitute nation
had any success   in persuading the hero
2375 to assent to their wish   that he ascend the throne
instead of Heardred,   Higelac's son,
but supported   the youthful prince
in loyalty   and loving counsel
until he was of age.   Seeking Heardred's help
2380 Ohthere's exiled sons   crossed the sea;
they had revolted   against the Swedish ruler,
lord Onela,   the most illustrious
of the sea kings   who in Sweden
allotted treasure.   This led to the death
2385 of Higelac's son,   the hapless Heardred,
who was fatally struck   by slashing swords;
after he was slain   Ongentheow's son, Onela,
sought to return   to his home in Sweden
and permitted Beowulf   to mount the throne
2390 as ruler of the Geats   —this king was good.

*3 Offer and
refusal of
throne*

*5 Heardred embroiled
in Swedish wars*

*6 Onela slays
Heardred, gives
throne to Beowulf*

34 · Approach to the Dragon

i *Beowulf remembers (II)*

For his prince's death   Beowulf planned repayment
in coming days   and became to Eadgils
the exile's friend.   Thereafter in armed force
the son of Ohthere   across the wide sea
2395 advanced with his men   and in revenge
killed Onela   his uncle and king.

*1 Beowulf plans
revenge*

*2 Revenge
accomplished*

ii *Beowulf's doom*

Thus Ecgtheow's son   was successful
in all his deadly   dangerous battles
and heroic deeds   until the day
2400 when he dared battle   against the dragon.
In angry passion   with eleven companions

*1 Beowulf triumphed
until he met
the dragon*

2 He seeks the dragon

the lord of the Geats   went to look at the dragon;
he had discovered   the cause of the slaughter
and wakening of the feud   when by the informer's hand
2405 the illustrious cup   came to his bosom.

3 The thief
is guide

The members of the troop   were made thirteen
by the man who was cause   of the conflict;
the despised serf,   though in sorrow
and unwillingly,   had to show the way
2410 because only he   had come to the cave
and its sunken hoard   near to the surge
and fall of the sea.   Within it was full

4 The treasure
and its guardian

of gold and gems;   the ungoodly guardian
and ancient warrior   held watch over the treasure
2415 buried in the earth   —by no easy bargain
could any man   make it his own.

Munificent and courageous,   the ruler of the Geats

5 Beowulf
broods

sat on the headland   while he said farewell
to his hearth companions;   his grieving heart
2420 was restless with death.   The doom was near

5 His doom
approaches

which soon would meet   with the old man,
seek his soul's treasure,   sunder in two
life and body;   not much longer
would the hero's being   be bound in flesh.

iii *Beowulf's memorial farewell (I)*

2425   The son of Ecgtheow,   Beowulf spoke:
"In the days of youth   I endured the storms

1 "I remember
my youth

of many battles   —I remember it all.
I was seven   when the sovereign lord,
comfort of his people,   Hrethel the king,

2 I was nurtured
by Hrethel

2430 received me from my father   and with festal gifts,
mindful of kinship,   maintained and kept me;
I was while he lived   no less misliked
as a man in his stronghold   than were his sons,
Herebeald and Hæthcyn   and my own Higelac.
2435 A bed of murder   was made for the eldest

3 "Hrethel's
inconsolable
grief

by unkindly act   of more than kin
when Hæthcyn killed   his beloved Herebeald,
by misadventure   missing the mark
with an arrow shaft   shot from his bow
2440 and slaying his brother   with the bloodied bolt;
it was wrongful strife   not to be settled,

wearing the heart;   without hope of revenge
the noble lord   ended his life.
He mourned as does   an old man enduring
2445 in aged grief   the death on the gallows
of his young son;   he chants his song
of grief and lamentation   while the raven delights
in the hanged son;   he may not help
through aged wisdom   in any way;
2450 every morning   he remembers the death
of his departed   — past endurance
is any thought   of another heir
to hold the hall   except for him
whose deeds are ended   through death's necessity;
2455 in sorrow he looks   upon his son's dwelling,
the wineless hall,   the windy and joyless
place where he rests   — the riders and warriors
sleep in darkness—   there is no sound of harp,
no pleasure in the house   as in days past."

4 "Like the grief of the father of a son on the gallows

35 · Onset of Battle

i *Memorial farewell (II)*

2460 "He goes to his bed   alone in grief
to lament the lost one;   his home and lands
seem all too wide.   So sorrow welled
within the heart   of king Hrethel
for his son Herebeald;   he could not seek
2465 settlement of the feud   from the slayer,
nor with violence   could he be revenged
upon lord Hæthcyn   though he loved him not;
because of a grief   too great to bear
he left man's joy   and chose the light of God;
2470 when he passed from life   as a prosperous man
he left to his sons   his land and city.
After Hrethel died   mutual hostility
and savage war   was awakened
between Swedes and Geats   across the wide sea
2475 when the stalwart   sons of Ongentheow
became eager for war;   not wanting peace
they crossed the sea   to bring to the country
around Hreosnaburh   horror and death;

1 "To which there is no solution

2 "Thus Hrethel died of grief

3 "Hrethel's death was followed by Hæthcyn's in Sweden

my dear uncles   did famous deeds
2480 in avenging   the vicious feud,
though in grim bargain   one of them gave
the price of his life   —for prince Hæthcyn,
king of the Geats,   the conflict was fatal.
In the morning Higelac,   as I have heard,
2485 avenged his brother   with blade of sword,
for king Ongentheow   who had killed him
was himself slain   when Eofor did not stay
his feud-minded hand   from the fatal blow
and hewed the helmet   of the hoary Swede.
2490 As fate appointed   I repaid in battle
Higelac's bounty   with my bright sword;
he settled upon me   native estates
for my pleasure;   he never was pressed
by necessity   to seek at a price
2495 a lesser champion   in the land of the Gifthas,
of the Scyldings   or of the Swedes.
My place was always   at the point of battle
to stand alone   before my lord,
and ever will I battle alone   while this blade endures
2500 which often served me   before I slew Dæghrefn,
the Frankish champion,   in fatal combat
with manly strength   and has often served me since;
he could not carry   the rich collar
and lay it on the breast   of his Frisian lord,
2505 for the hero bravely   fell in battle
guarding the standard,   yet not my sword
but my battle grip   crushed his bones
and burst his heart   —now will the hand
and the hard edge   fight for the hoard."

ii *Vow and command*

2510   Beowulf spoke   his battle vow
the final time: "In my youth I faced
many tests of war;   in my age I remain
guardian of my people,   determined to gain
glory from the feud   if the foul ravager
2515 will come from his barrow   to seek me in battle."
Then he addressed   his dear companions,
each of his worthy   helmeted warriors,
for the last time: "I would not take

*4 "Higelac was
avenged*

*5 "Higelac was
bountiful and
I repaid him
in service*

*6 "I never faltered
and will not now."*

*1 "I will hold
my old course."*

2 "I must go armed

sword against the dragon   if I could see
2520 any other   honorable way
of gripping this adversary   as I did Grendel;
but because I must face   the fiery blast
of poisoned flame   I have put on armor
and taken a shield.   I shall not retreat   *3 "I shall not retreat;*
2525 from the dragon   —dominating fate   *Fate will decide*
will determine   what will take place
at the stronghold   —I am resolved
and boast no further   against the battle flyer.
You men in armor   protected by your mail   *4 "I must go alone"*
2530 attend on this hill   which of us two
will best survive   the bloody wounds
of murderous violence;   it is not your venture,
nor within the means   of any man but me
that he dare measure   this adversary's might
2535 or do this worthy deed.   I shall win the gold   *4 "I shall win*
with bravery,   or death in battle,   *death or gold."*
terrible slaughter,   will take your lord."

iii *Onset of battle*

The hero arose   helped by his shield,   *1 He advances*
brave and helmeted   bore his chainmail
2540 toward the stone cliff;   in one man's strength
alone he trusted   —no coward's attempt.
The gallant man   who had managed to survive   *2 View of*
many battles,   mighty clashes   *the barrow*
of warriors in combat,   saw by the wall
2545 the stone arch rising   from whence a stream
broke from the rock,   a rushing burn
of murderous fire;   not for a moment
could a man come   close to the hoard
without being burned   by the dragon's fiery blast.
2550 Relentless in purpose   the lord of the Geats   *3 Challenge*
swollen with rage   roared his challenge   *and response*
from out his breast,   the sound of battle
resounding clearly   within the gray cliff;
hate was aroused,   the hoard keeper knowing
2555 a human spoke;   little time was spent
in bid for amity;   first came a blast
from out the stone,   —the sound shook the earth—
the adversary's breath   enflamed for battle

burned in the cave.   The king of the Geats
2560 turned with his shield   toward the alien terror;
the coiled serpent's   heart was incited
to seek battle.   The bold warrior king
had already drawn   his ready-edged sword,
the ancient inheritance;   in their hostility
2565 each of them felt   awesome fear of the other.
With his lofty shield   the great leader
manfully stood   and waited in his mail.
Quickly the dragon   gathered its coils
and came to attack   coiled and flaming,
2570 hurried to its fate.   Unhappily the shield
protected his life   for less a time
than was pleasing   to the famed prince,
for it befell   that fate decreed
that for the first time   he must this day fight
2575 without gaining victory.   The lord of the Geats
lifted his hand,   with his sword hewed
the encrusted horror;   the blade crumpled
bright upon the bone,   bit without power
when the nation's king   had need of it,
2580 hard-pressed in battle.   The blow aroused
the barrow keeper   to bitter fury;
it flung deadly fire   — the flames of war
encompassed all.   The generous king
boasted of no triumph,   for his naked blade
2585 had failed in the test   as does not befit
a long-trusted sword.   There was no sweetness
for the celebrated   son of Ecgtheow
in departing   from his place on earth,
to inhabit   away from here
2590 a different home,   leaving time's day
as all men must.   The adversaries again met
without time of respite.   The keeper of the treasure
was emboldened,   and a renewed blast
surged from its breast;   victorious Beowulf,
2595 enveloped in flames,   suffered fiercely.
No company   of his comrades,
sons of nobility,   stood about him
in warlike valor,   for they had fled to the woods
to save their lives.   One of them felt sorrow
2600 welling in his heart   — who holds to right
will never betray   the ties of kinship.

*4 He turns toward
the dragon*

*5 They face
each other*

6 He faces the attack

7 The dragon attacks

8 The shield fails

9 The sword fails

10 The dragon attacks

*11 Beowulf is not
victorious*

12 Beowulf will die

13 Renewed attack

*14 The dragon
is emboldened*

*15 Beowulf's
men flee*

16 Except for one

36 · Wiglaf Joins the Battle

i *Wiglaf*

This worthy warrior   was called Wiglaf;
he was of Swedish descent,   the son of Wihstan
and related to Ælfhere;   he saw his lord
2605 masked by his helmet   suffering the heat.
Remembering what his lord   had lavished upon him
—the Wægmunding home   and noble hall,
all the folkland   his father owned—
he could not restrain   his hand from seizing
2610 his linden shield;   he unsheathed the sword
that once Eanmund,   the son of Ohthere,
had inherited;   this hapless exile
was slain by Wihstan,   Wiglaf's father,
in deadly combat;   he carried to Onela
2615 the burnished helmet,   the mailed byrnie,
the giants' sword;   the king gave him.
the battle dress   and death-ready gear
stripped from his nephew,   nor spoke of feud
though Wihstan had slain   his brother's son.
2620 Many years Wihstan   kept the treasures of war,
the sword and the armor,   until his son
was able to do   deeds like his father's;
when aged Wihstan went   his way from life
he gave to his son   among the Geats
2625 a wealth of armor.   The young warrior
for the first time   was now to follow
his beloved king   into the clash of battle;
his courage did not falter;   his father's sword
did not fail him   —the dragon found
2630 the truth of this   after the two met.

1 Wiglaf sees Beowulf's distress

2 He recalls Beowulf's gift

3 Wiglaf's inheritance

4 Wiglaf's first test

ii *Wiglaf speaks*

Wiglaf appealed   to his companions
with truth greatly   from his grieving heart:
"I remember the day   when we drank the ale
on the mead bench   and made our boast
2635 that when he had need   as now he does
we would repay   our generous prince
for rewarding us   with war armor,
helmets and swords;   holding us honorable
and trusting us   he gave us treasure;

1 "I remember our promises

2640 considering us warriors   worthy to bear
     helmets and swords   he selected us
     for this mission;   yet our mighty protector
     was already determined   alone to attempt
     the heroic deed   as he had always done,
2645 being without rival   in recklessly reaching
     for dangerous glory.   The day has now come   *2 "Repayment*
     that our great king   stands gravely in need   *is now due*
     of good warriors;   let us go to aid
     our leader in battle   however baneful
2650 the flaming horror.   God knows I feel   *3 "I am resolved"*
     it is for the best   that my body
     be embraced in flames   with my bountiful lord;
     I think it shameful   to carry our shields
     back to our homes   without having
2655 protected the life   of the nation's lord
     and killed the enemy;   I know clearly
     that the debt we owe   would still be due
     if we abandon him   to do battle
     and to die alone;   he and I at least
2660 will stand together   with sword and armor."
     In helmet mask he dashed   into the deadly smoke   *4 He advances*
     to succor his lord;   he spoke briefly: *saying, "I will*
     "Beloved Beowulf,   be bold for the right,   *support you."*
     for you once said   in the summer of your youth
2665 that while you lived   you would never allow
     your glory to fade;   famed for your deeds,
     resolute lord,   you must protect your life
     with all your power;   I will support you."

iii *Battle resumed*

        As Wiglaf finished,   the fiendish dragon   *1 Second attack*
2670 encrusted in flames   in evil fury   *of the dragon*
     for the second time   fiercely attacked
     its hated foe;   the fire burned
     his shield to the boss,   and his byrnie
     offered no succor   to the spearman,
2675 but the young kinsman   quickly hastened
     to share his kinsman's   when his own shield
     was consumed by fire.   The king again struck   *2 Beowulf's*
     with mighty force,   remembering fame   *sword snaps*
     he drove his sword   into the dragon's head

2680 with grim violence;   iron gray and ancient
Nægling snapped   — Beowulf's sword
failed in battle.   Fate did not grant
that blade of sword   should be of help
to him in battle   — his hand was too strong;
2685 as I was told   his stroke overtaxed
every weapon   so that in waging war
he was none the better   for the strongest blade.
For the third time   the terrible firedrake,
the nation's foe,   remembering the feud
2690 rushed upon the hero   when it was given room;
grimly blazing   it gripped his neck
with baneful fangs;   Beowulf was blood-stained;
his life in waves   welled from his wounds.

3 No sword availed him

4 The third, fatal attack

37 · The End of Battle

i *The dragon is slain*

Then as I was told   in the king's extremity
2695 the noble at his side   made known his strength,
bravery and heroism   that were his by birth;
in his coat of mail   courageously the man
helped his kinsman;   he did not aim at the head
but struck the middle   of the baneful monster,
2700 burning his hand   as the blade penetrated,
dearly encrusted   — the fire became
thereafter weaker.   The war king again
recovering his senses   from his coat of mail
drew his deadly,   battle-sharp dagger;
2705 the king cut deeply   into the dragon's middle.
They slew the foe,   — it was slain heroically —
the noble kinsmen   both cut it down,
the two together   — so should a retainer act
in time of need.   This triumph was the last
2710 the king was to win   through his own works
and deeds in the world;   then as the wound
given by the dragon   began to swell
and to fester,   he felt very soon
deep in his heart   how the deadly poison
2715 perniciously welled.   The lord then went
beside the wall   and seating himself

1 Wiglaf strikes

2 Beowulf strikes with his dagger

3 Together they were victorious

4 Beowulf is near death

5 Beowulf looks on the barrow

gazed in wisdom   on the work of giants,
the imperishable grave   supported within
by stone arches   set upon pillars.
2720 The worthiest of retainers,   Wiglaf, with his hands   *6 Wiglaf revives*
bathed with water   his blood-stained lord,   *him*
the battle-weary   illustrious Beowulf,
and unclasped the helmet   of his beloved king.

ii *Beowulf's last commands*

Beowulf spoke   despite the pain   *1 "I have no son*
2725 of his fatal wound   in full knowledge
that in his life's span   no days were left
for earthly pleasure;   to the past belonged
the number of his days   —death was most near:
'Now I would give   my war armor
2730 to my own son   if such an heir
begotten of my body   had been granted
to me by fate.   For fifty years   *2 "I recall*
I ruled my people;   of the powerful kings   *peaceful reign*
of neighboring lands   there was not one
2735 who was rash enough   to raise against me
the menace of war.   The working of Fate   *3 "I did no*
I awaited in my land   and protected it well;   *treachery*
I never contrived   treacherous quarrel
with many false oaths.   Mortally wounded   *4 "I was never a*
2740 I find in this   a final comfort   *fratricide*
as life leaves body   that the Lord of men
will have no cause   to accuse me
of the death of kinsmen.   My dear Wiglaf,   *5 "Wiglaf must*
go without delay   to look at the hoard   *enter the cave*
2745 within the gray stone   now the dragon is stretched
in the sleep of death   despoiled of his treasure.
Be of good speed   that I may see   *6 "I seek solace*
the golden wealth   and wondrous gems   *from the treasure."*
of the treasure hoard;   because I have it
2750 I now may leave   my life more easily,
relinquish the lordship   I have long possessed.

38 · Beowulf's Death

i *Wiglaf views the treasure*

Then as I have heard   Wiglaf hastened,   *1 Wiglaf enters*
obedient to the wishes   of his wounded,   *the cave*
battle-torn master;   in coat of mail
2755 he made his way   within the mound.
Once past the seat,   the proudly exulting   *2 He looks at*
young retainer   saw the massed treasure   *the treasure*
of jewels and gold   gleaming upon the ground
in the den of the ancient   night-flying dragon,
2760 saw marvels on the wall   and the cups that men
of old had owned,   deprived of ornaments
and left unpolished,   helmets in plenty,
old and rusted,   many rings for the arm
cunningly twisted.   (Treasure of gold   *3 (The power*
2765 covered by the earth   may easily conquer   *of treasure)*
any human,   hide it who will.)
He also saw   a golden standard   *4 The golden standard*
high over the hoard   woven by hands
with the greatest skill;   light gleamed from it
2770 so that he could see   the surface of the floor
and gaze upon the treasure;   there was no trace
of the dragon,   for it had died by the sword.
Then I heard that one man   plundered the hoard,   *5 He takes*
the ancient wealth,   the work of giants;   *the treasure*
2775 he placed upon his bosom   the plates and cups
he himself chose;   he took the standard,
the brightest of beacons.   The iron blade   *6 The dragon*
of Wihstan's sword   had wounded to death   *was slain*
the protector   of the treasure
2780 which for a long time   in fiery terror
fiercely flaming   had fought for the hoard
in the middle of the night   until it met its death.

ii *Beowulf dies*

Eager to return   to show the treasure   *1 Wiglaf returns*
Wiglaf hastened,   urgently wishing
2785 to discover   if the king of the Geats,
his courageous prince,   his powers failing,
were still alive   where he had left him.

Laden with treasure   he found his lord
covered with blood,   and with death closing

2 *Beowulf speaks:*
"I thank God for
the treasure

2790 on his illustrious king   he began to cast
water upon him   until words burst
from his breast-keep;   Beowulf spoke,
sorrowful and gray,   looking upon the gold:
'I give my thanks   to the King of glory,
2795 the sovereign Ruler   Who rules in eternity,
that He granted   my gaining here
for my people   before my death
the great riches   on which I gaze.
For the treasure   I have traded

3 *"I give my*
people to
your keeping

2800 my aged life;   it is left to you
to lead my people.   I may stay no longer.
After I am burned   have my chiefs build

4 *"I command a*
barrow to be built."

a stately mound   by the sea at Hronesness
as a memorial   to my people;
2805 towering high   above the headland,
Beowulf's Barrow   will be its name,
called this by sailors   who steer their ships
from far away   over the dark flood."
The valorous king   unclasped from his neck

5 *"You are the*
last survivor."

2810 his golden collar;   this and his coat of mail
and gold-encrusted helmet   he gave to the spearman,
the young warrior,   bade him use them well:
'Wiglaf you are   the last Wægmunding,
our sole survivor;   Fate has swept away
2815 in destiny's decree   all my kinsmen,
noble of fame,   and I must follow after."
Thus for the last time   the old hero unlocked

6 *He dies*

his thought in words   before the waves of fire
consumed him on the pyre   — his soul departed
2820 to seek the esteem   of those sure of judgement.

39 · The Dead

i *The dead adversaries*

Then it remained   for the young man
in sorrow to look   upon his beloved
lying on the earth   his life ended,

1 *Wiglaf looks*
on Beowulf

pitiable in death.   The earth dragon,
2825 his dread slayer,   also lay dead,
crushed and lifeless;   the coiled serpent
no longer would rule   over the ring hoard,
for near the treasure   it had toppled to earth,
finished by the stab   of the sharp sword
2830 beaten on the forge   to battle hardness;
stilled by its wounds   the wide flyer,
glorying in possessions,   would never again
make an appearance   at midnight coursing
the clouds in flight,   for it had fallen,
2835 struck at the hands   of the heroic king.
(As I was told   no man in truth,
however mighty,   ever met success
if undaunted   by the danger
he braved the venemous   breath of the ravager
2840 to rifle the hoard   in the treasure house
and found the dragon   which dwelled within
awake in the barrow.)   For Beowulf's death
the treasure in part   was repayment;
through both their doing   it had brought an end
2845 to their transitory lives.

2 And on the dragon

3 (None had survived battle with the dragon)

4 Death and the treasure

ii *Wiglaf and the deserters*

In a little while
the craven men   came from the woods,
the traitorous   cowardly ten
who were afraid   to fight with spears
beside their prince   in his great peril;
2850 only now in shame   they carried their shields
and harness of war   where the old hero lay
— they looked upon Wiglaf.   In weariness
the warrior sat   beside his king
with useless water   trying to waken him;
2855 his great longing   could never give
further life on earth   to his warrior lord
or in any way alter   the Ruler's will
— the doom of God   dominated all
the doings of men   as yet it does.
2860 In bitter reproach   the youth blamed them
for having abandoned   honor in battle;
looking at them   he no longer loved

1 The deserters approach

2 Wiglaf tries to restore life to Beowulf

3 "Beowulf has wasted his gifts on you

the son of Wihstan　　spoke in sorrow;
"Lo, this he may say　　who speaks truly
2865 that the soldierly dress　　in which you now stand
　　— the treasured gifts　　of the great king
　　bountifully given　　at the ale bench
　　to you his retainers　　attending in the hall,
　　your helmets and mailshirts,　　the most splendid
2870 that he could find　　whether near or far —
　　this war armor　　he grievously wasted
　　suddenly and as soon　　as he was beset in battle.
　　The nation's king　　had no need to boast
　　of his comrades in arms,　　yet the King of victory
2875 the Lord granted　　that alone with the sword
　　he revenged himself　　when he needed valor.
　　I could lend him　　little succor,
　　protection in battle,　　yet I attempted
　　beyond my powers　　to support my kinsman;
2880 the savage foe　　pierced by my sword
　　grew ever weaker,　　the flame welling
　　from his head with less fury;　　too few defenders
　　pressed about their lord　　in his peril.
　　Now the grant of treasure,　　the gift of sword,
2885 delight and comfort　　in their country,
　　your kinsmen must lose;　　each man must leave
　　the home of his race　　and his possessions
　　in the native land　　after the powerful lords
　　hear from afar　　news of your flight,
2890 your infamous deed　　— death is better
　　for every lord　　than life of shame.

4 "Beowulf was
betrayed

5 "I alone helped him

6 "Their shame and
its consequences.

C — *Aftermath*

40 · Forebodings

i *Announcement of Beowulf's death*

Then he bade the news   of the battle be brought   *1 Wiglaf sends a*
over the cliffs to the keep   where the company   *messenger to*
of noble warriors   waited in sadness   *the city*
2895 the entire morning   in expectation
either of the death   of the dear one
or of his return.   Of his terrible news   *2 "Beowulf is dead*
he kept nothing hidden   after he rode up the hill
and related the truth   to all the listeners:
2900 "Now the gracious   benefactor of the Geats,
the nation's ruler,   rests in the clutch
of death's murderous bed,   slain by the dragon.
His mortal foe   remains beside him   *3 "And the dragon*
slain with the dagger;   with sword he could not
2905 manage to wound   in any way
the adversary.   The son of Wihstan,   *4 "Wiglaf keeps watch*
Wiglaf, is seated   at Beowulf's side,
the living noble   by the head of the unliving,
holding the watch   over the hated
2910 and beloved dead.

ii *The Frankish threat*

Now our nation lives   *1 "The Frankish*
in fear of war   after the fall of our king   *threat*
is widely bruited   and brought to the hearing
of the Franks and Frisians.   The feud with them   *2 "Higelac*
had its grim beginning   when Higelac brought   *began the feud*
2915 his fleet to raid   the Frisian land;
the Hetware   harrying him in battle
triumphed swiftly   by strength of numbers;
the mailed warrior   was made to bow,
to fall amidst his troop;   no treasure was given
2920 by that lord to his men;   the Merovingians
thereafter gave   no sign of good will.

iii *The Swedish threat (I)*

Nor do I expect   any peace or truce

from the Swedish nation,   for it is widely known

that at Ravenswood   royal Ongentheow

2925 cut down Haethcyn,   the son of Hrethel,

when a Geatish army   in arrogance

first launched attack   on Swedish land.

At once the wise Ongentheow,   the father of Ohthere,

old and terrible,   counterattacked,

2930 slew King Hæthcyn   and recaptured the old

mother of Onela   and of Ohthere,

his royal consort   robbed of her gold;

then he closely followed   his mortal foes

until at last   without leader

2935 they barely reached   the cover of Ravenswood.

With his army he beseiged   the sorely wounded

whom the sword had left;   the whole night long

he vowed the destruction   of the stricken company;

he said in the morning   he would kill many

2940 and give the rest   to the gallowstree

for the bird's delight.   Relief appeared

along with the dawn   to the downcast men

after they heard   Higelac's horn

and trumpet winding   as the worthy

2945 followed their track   with a troop of retainers.

Margin notes:
1 "Feud with Swedes also began with invasion
2 "Ongentheow's counterattack
3 "And seige of the Geat
4 "Rescue by Higelac

41 · Foreboding and Preparations

i *The Swedish threat (II)*

The bloody track   of terrible slaughter

of Swedes and Geats   was widely seen,

awakening the feud   between the two forces.

The wise and worthy   Ongenthcow went

2950 in great sadness   to seek his citadel,

the king retreating   with his kinsmen;

he had experienced   the battle prowess

of daring Higelac   and doubted he could

offer resistance   to the sea men,

2955 or from invading warriors   defend his wife,

his children and treasure;   the old man retreated

Margin notes:
1 "Blood and the feud
2 "Ongentheow retreats

behind his earthen works.   To the Swedish warriors   *3 "The citadel*
pursuit was given,   and Higelac's standard   *is overrun*
advanced to overrun   the place of refuge
2960 as the son of Hrethel   pressed to the stronghold;
there the gray-haired   Ongentheow was held
and brought to bay   by blade of sword;
the king had to submit   to be judged in combat
by Eofor, son of Wonred.   His brother Wulf   *4 "Ongentheow's*
2965 had angrily struck   Ongentheow with his sword;   *death*
because of the blow   the blood under his hair
streamed from his veins,   but the ancient Swede
was not afraid,   and fronting him
the nation's king   quickly repaid
2970 the daunting blow   with deadlier return;
Wonred's brave son,   Wulf, could not give
any countering thrust   to the old king,
for Ongentheow had hacked   through helmet to head;
encrusted with blood   he was forced to bow,
2975 to fall upon the ground   though not fated to die
for he was healed   though hurt by the wound;
after Wulf, his brother,   was beaten to the ground
the hardy Eofor,   Higelac's retainer,
with giant sword,   despite the shield,
2980 cleaved the giant helmet   of great Ongentheow
and struck to the quick   the ancient king.
While many bound   his brother's wounds,   *5 "The booty*
raised him up quickly   when they had room
through gaining possession   of the battle ground,
2985 Eofor seized   upon Ongentheow
and stripped him   of hard-hilted sword,
of shirt of mail   and helmet mask
and carried to Higelac   the old king's armor.   *6 "Higelac's*
Accepting the gift,   the king of the Geats,   *repayment*
2990 proud Higelac,   graciously promised
to repay them both   upon his return,
and true to his word   he rewarded
Eofor and Wulf   with abundant wealth;
he lavished on each   land and treasure
2995 valued in the hundred thousands,   — no man inhabiting the earth
could blame his rewarding them   for bravery in winning glory — —
in pledge of faith   he favored Eofor
with his only daughter   to adorn his home.

ii *The deadly consequences*

    "This is the feud,   the foemen's emnity,   *1 "Only the king*
3000 the savage hatred   that the Swedish people,   *kept us safe*
as I expect,   will now repay
after they learn   that lord Beowulf
has lost his life   who long protected
throne and treasure   against every threat;
3005 after the death   of daring warriors
his princely deeds   even surpassed
his prudence in counsel.   Now our best course   *2 "Who now must*
is in haste to look   upon the nation's lord   *be burned*
and bear aloft   our bountiful king
3010 to the pyre.   Every portion   *3 "Along with*
of the hoard must be burned   along with the hero;   *the treasure*
the gold beyond count,   grimly purchased,
the riches bought   with his own body
in his last adventure,   the flames must devour,
3015 the fire cover;   no noble will clothe himself
with ornaments in memory,   no beautiful maiden
clasp on her neck   adorning collar,
but stripped of gold   must go in sadness
into lingering exile   in foreign land
3020 now the leader in war   has laid aside laughter,
song and pleasure.   Therefore, many a spear   *4 "Coming slaughter."*
cold in the morning   fingers must clasp
and hands must raise;   the song of the harp
will never rouse the warrior,   but the black raven
3025 settling on the doomed   will have much to say
in relating to the eagle   his luck at the feast
while he and the wolf   worried the corpses."

iii *Viewing the dead; the curse of the treasure (I)*

    Thus the bold man   gave his message,   *1 He spoke*
the evil tidings;   he spoke truly of what was   *the truth*
3030 and of what was to come.   The company arose,   *2 Approach to*
went beneath Earnaness   with welling tears   *Beowulf*
in sadness to look   upon the strange sight;
they found him on the earth   who in former times
had given them bounty,   his body without soul
3035 lying in rest;   now the last day
of the worthy had come;   the warlord of the Geats,

their king, had died   an awesome death.
First they had seen   the strange creature,   *3 The dragon*
the loathsome dragon,   lying opposite
3040 upon the field;   where it was felled
the fire drake lay   scorched by the flames,
monstrously horrible   and measuring the length
of fifty feet;   once it flew joyously
in the dark sky   and in the day returned
3045 to its den below;   now fast in death
it had come to the end   of its use of caves.
Beside it were placed   goblets and pitchers,   *4 The treasure*
and plates were heaped   by precious swords   *and its curse*
eaten through with rust   of the thousand years
3050 of their burial   in the bosom of earth;
for the heritage left   by legendary men
was made secure,   enclosed by a spell,
so that no man   might violate
the treasure house   unless the True God,
3055 the victorious King   Who protects mankind,
gave permission   to such a man
as He saw fit   to open the hoard.

42 · The Treasure and the Hero

i *The curse of the treasure (II)*

Then it was seen   that he did not succeed   *1 The dragon's*
who unrighteously   kept the riches   *avarice*
3060 secretly under the wall;   the keeper slew
one like few others;   the feud was ended
with furious vengeance.   It is a fated mystery   *2 Death is*
where the mighty hero   will meet the end   *a mystery*
of his destined life,   live no longer
3065 to dwell in the meadhall   with his dear kinsmen.
So it was for Beowulf   when he sought in battle   *3 As is the death*
the keeper of the hoard;   he did not himself know   *of Beowulf*
how his life's course   would come to an end.
For famous lords   had solemnly laid   *4 As is the curse*
3070 upon the buried treasure   this ban until doomsday,   *of the treasure*
that any man   who plundered the mound,
attainted by sin   in the devil's temple,
horribly tormented,   would be chained in hell

unless he had first   with certainty found
3075 the favor of God,   the Giver of gold.

ii *Wiglaf's lament*

The son of Wihstan,   Wiglaf lamented: *1 "Self-will*
"Often must many   through one man's will   *brings misfortune*
suffer such misfortune   as has befallen us.
We had no success   in persuading   *2 "We could not*
3080 our beloved lord,   protector of the land,   *persuade him*
not to give battle   to the keeper of the gold,
to let it lie   in the den where it lived
and might continue   till the end of time;
he held to his destiny   and the high fate,
3085 the relentless doom,   which drove him on.
The treasure was revealed   and grimly taken;   *3 "The hoard*
the way within   the earthen wall
was not easily come by,   but when I could
I entered the cave   and cast my eyes
3090 on the riches of the hall,   then hastily loaded
into my hands   a heaping burden
of the treasure   and took it there
where my lord waited.   He was still alive   *4 "Beowulf's*
sage and aware;   old in sorrow   *dying wish*
3095 he spoke of much   and gave command
that you fashion   on the funeral field
a great barrow   high and glorious,
befitting the works   of the worthiest
king and warrior   in the wide world
3100 while still he enjoyed   his stronghold's wealth.
Hastily again   now let us go   *5 "Let us enter*
under the wall   to look on the wealth   *the barrow*
of the wondrous hoard;   I will show the way
which will lead you   to look directly
3105 at the bright gold;   now shall the bier
be made ready   for when we return
to carry hence   our dear king
and beloved lord   to his last home
where he will rest   in the Ruler's protection.
3110 The brave warrior,   the son of Wihstan   *6 "Beowulf will be*
ordered that many   householders and men   *given to*
be given command   that they gather   *the flames."*
wood from afar   for the funeral pyre

of the good ruler: "Now the flames will rise,
3115 the black fire consume   the soldier's prince
who often withstood   the iron storm
when feathered shafts   in barbed flight
were shot with violence   over the shieldwall
and in dense showers   did their duty."

iii *Emptying of the battle field*

3120   Then next Wiglaf,   Wihstan's son,   *1 Entrance into*
called together   from the company   *the barrow*
seven of the best   who served the king;
with these warriors   he went beneath
the hostile roof;   one held in his hands
3125 a lighted torch   to lead the way.
No need to select   one of them by lot   *2 Stripping the*
to strip the hoard,   for all of them saw   *hoard*
that unprotected   the entirety rested
and mouldered in the hall;   no one mourned
3130 their quick dispatch   in carrying out
the dear treasure.   Next they tumbled   *3 Burial of*
the dragon over the cliff,   let the waves take,   *the dragon*
and flood engulf   the keeper of the gold.
The countless whole   of the hoarded wealth   *4 Hoard and Beowulf*
3135 was loaded on a wain;   the old warrior   *are carried*
and noble lord   was borne to Hronesness.   *to Hronesness*

43 · The Pyre and the Barrow

i *The pyre*

Then upon that ground   the Geatish people   *1 The pyre*
prepared for him   a mighty pyre;
they hung about it   helmets and shields,
3140 shining corselets,   as he had required;
the men lamenting   laid in the midst
their illustrious king,   beloved lord.
On the hill the warriors   then began to awaken   *2 The burning*
the greatest funeral fire;   above the flames
3145 the black smoke rose;   the roaring blaze,
stirred by the wind   mingled with weeping,
crumpled in its heat   the bonehouse of the heart
and at last subsided.   Comfortless they lamented   *3 Lamentation*

with doleful grief   the death of their king;
3150 so too with bound hair,   bitterly oppressed
by grief of heart,   a Geatish woman,
remembering Beowulf,   sang mournful lament
of her sore dread   of evil days,
of mounting slaughter   and warrior's savagery,   *4 The smoke*
3155 shame and captivity.   Heaven swallowed the smoke.   *vanished*

ii *The barrow*

Then upon a headland   the Geatish people   *1 The barrow*
built a barrow,   lofty and broad,
widely visible   to voyagers at sea,
and completed building   the hero's beacon
3160 within ten days;   in a tomb they walled
the remains of the flame,   finding for the work
men of foremost skill   to make it most splendid.
Inside the barrow   they set the gems   *2 The hoard*
and the treasure   that men had taken
3165 out of the hoard   with angry hearts;
they left the gold   and lordly wealth
to earth and dust   where yet it dwells
as worthless to men   as it was before.
Then noble youths,   twelve in number,   *3 Burial rites*
3170 brave in battle   rode round the barrow;
they wished to lament   and mourn their king,
to sing his dirge   and speak of the man;
they praised his glory   and greatly honored
his heroic deeds,   as is the right duty
3175 of a man to praise   his prince in words
and love him in heart   when he must leave
his dwelling here   in the house of his body.
Thus the Geatish people   and his hearth companions   *4 Praise of*
made final lament   for the fall of their lord;   *Beowulf*
3180 they said he was   of the kings of the world
the most gentle   and the mildest of men,
most kind to his people   and keenest for glory.

Notes to the Translation

The point of departure for the following notes is Klaeber, 121–230, 453–59, 465–70.

33. "Icily … rested," is a flat translation of the evocative phrase, *isig ond utfus*. The denotation of *isig*, which is unique, is probably something like "covered with ice," but its metaphoric connotation is the cold of death, nature's ultimate threat to fallen man; *utfus* is frequently attested with the connotation of "death journey." See *Web of Words* (Chapter Two, note 7), pp. 35, note 2, and 82.

62. For lack of anything better I have accepted Kemp Malone's reading, *Studies in Heroic Legend and Current Speech* (Copenhagen, 1959), pp. 124–41, with its emendation and identification of Onela as Yrse's husband. I am mindful, however, of the objection raised by Norman Eliason, "Healfdane's Daughter," *Anglo Saxon Poetry* (Chapter Two, note 23), pp. 3–13, and base no conjecture on the reading.

68–70. Although I have stuck with Klaeber's emendation in the translation, I find Fred Robinson's defense of the MS reading persuasive, "Two Non-cruces in *Beowulf*," *Tennessee Studies in Language and Literature* 11 (1966): 151–55.

84. "Daughter's husband" translates *aþumsweoran*, literally, "son-in-law and father-in-law," which involves emendation of the MS *aþumswerian*, Klaeber considering this a scribal error, conflating *ath*, "oath," and *swerian*, "to swear." It is likely that word play is involved. The burning of Heorot, 83–84, must be the result of events later narrated in the Ingeld prophecy, but Norman Eliason, "The Burning of Heorot," *Speculum* 55 (1980): 75–83, denies such reference as being "inept as it is dubious, for it anticipates a conflict not mentioned in the poem until almost 2,000 lines later," p. 76. He argues, instead, somewhat unconvincingly, for a different emendation of line 84 which would have the line refer to Grendel's ensuing attack. In defense of the conventional reading represented in the translation it should be observed that the habit of suspended reference is characteristic of the narrative method of the poem, and that there is an implied reference to the burning of Heorot in lines 781–82, *nymþe liges fæþm / swulge on swaþule*, finally, that the ultimate doom of Heorot does provide, in the manner of the poem, a satisfactory transition to Grendel's attack.

90–101. The translation reflects a difference from the usual punctuation of the passage, as in Klaeber's edition, where the Song of Creation is ended at 98, with 99 beginning a new period, *drihtguman*, "lordly men," being taken to refer to the Danes and *feond on helle*, 101, "fiend in hell," to Grendel, *se grimma gæst*, "grim demon," 102. With either punctuation the problem of suspended reference remains, the inevitable result of the poet's method of narrative disjunction. (See Chapter One, note 2.) The linking sign, however, is most clearly the repetition of *gæst* (*ellengæst*, 87, *grimma gæst*), 102. Furthermore Grendel is not literally the *feond on helle*. To be sure, he is frequently designated as *feond*, even *feond moncynnes*, 164, 1276, and he is called *helle gæst*, 1274, but specifically in the context of his fated destination as the result of his battle with Beowulf, foretold in 852, "hell received him," *him hel onfeng*. The obvious referent for *feond on helle* is not Grendel, then, but the devil himself. The referent for *drihtguman* is more ambiguous; indeed, if the immediate context of the word were the Danes feasting in the hall, there could be no doubt that it must refer to them. The immediate context, however, is not the listeners in the hall, but the song which recounts the creation of life "to every kind of animate creature," *cynna gehwylcum þara ðe cwice hwyrfaþ*, p. 98. In such a context the reference of *drihtguman* to the first humans in Eden is required as the inevitable sequence to the mention of animate creation. Equally natural in this sequential context is the stirring in hell of Satan's revenge, the archetype of Grendel's. Christoper Bell, *"Beowulf,* 99–101," *Notes and Queries,* New Series 18 (1971): 163, independently arrived at the same punctuation. Marijane Osborn, "The Great Feud: Scriptural History and Strife in *Beowulf,"* (Chapter Two, note 2) sees the passage as an exemplification of "the classical figure of *synchesis,* liquid syntax …. Through this hovering reference the poet has offered an archetypal referent for Grendel that is accessible to us but not to those in the story," p. 975. The use of the device she cites is easy to attest in Old English poetry, although it here may seem to impose over-strenuous demands on the reader. If *synchesis* is involved, it would strengthen the point I am trying to make; however, the figure defies my attempts at translation.

136. "lawless feud," *fæhðe ond fyrene.* The designation of Grendel's attack as "feud" provides another example of thematic interweaving of human and monstrous. The motif is elaborately developed, for example, ll. 154–58, where the "lawlessness" of Grendel's feud is ironically described in terms of his refusal to accept wergild or to pay it. The concept of feud is what itself is monstrous; in the feud man and monster both reflect Satan's archetypal revenge.

168–69. The translation of this notoriously ambiguous passage attempts to suggest its metaphoric irony. The outlaw Grendel is no loyal retainer of Hrothgar, serving at his throne, a recipient of his love; rather he has usurped the throne from which he dispenses only the gifts of hate and murder like another Heremod, or, more precisely, like his demonic master who, as the first exile from God, could not approach His throne into eternity. John Gardner, *Construction of Christian Poetry* (Chapter Four, note 1), p. 63, gives a perceptive reading: "Grendel can occupy the literal meadhall, but as a creature eternally exiled from God's favor, he can never 'know his desire' in the cosmic meadhall, or approach the treasure throne of God." W. F. Bolton, *Alcuin and Beowulf* (Chapter One, note 2), p. 122, arrives at a similar reading. All three readings were arrived at independently. Betty Cox, *The Cruces of Beowulf* (The Hague: Mouton, 1971), pp. 56–79, strains the limits of an allegorical, rather than metaphorical, reading in equating *gifstol* and *maþðum* to the Ark of the Covenant. She goes beyond what I would venture although she refers to me as being "the most explicit persuader" for her method, p. 57. For an alternative reading, which I find unconvincing, see G. Storms, "Notes on Old English Poetry," *Neophilolugus* 61 (1977): 439–40. See also Joseph Baird, " 'for metode': *Beowulf* 169," *English Studies* 49 (1968): 418–23. Marijane Osborne, "The Great Feud: Scriptural History and Strife in *Beowulf* " (Chapter Two, note 2), puts the matter into clear perspective of the "double vision" offered in the poem, pp. 90–101.

175–79. See Anne Payne, "The Dane's Prayer," (Chapter Two, note 2).

202–3. "The lords of the council were easily persuaded." Their willingness seems natural enough in view of the favorable "omens" and their knowledge of Beowulf's credentials as a slayer of monsters (see lines 419–24). Curiously enough, however, much later in the poem it is learned that Higelac was not of their mind and, indeed, pleaded with Beowulf not to attempt the venture, 1992–97. What we have here is not an example of Homer nodding, but of the poet's characteristic manner of narrative movement development through backward-interlace (see note to line 84); there is an implicit irony in Higelac's fear of the recklessness of his champion and in his own recklessness in venturing on the raid against the Franks.

237–85. H. W. Tonsfeldt, "Ring Structure in *Beowulf*" (see Chapter Four, note 2), p. 445, calls attention to the chiastic ("ring") pattern of the coastguard's challenge and Beowulf's reply.

250–51. My translation is based on the MS reading *næfre,* usually emended to *næfne.* My reading, though independently arrived at, is confirmed by Fred Robinson, "Two Non-Cruces" (see note to lines 68–70).

305-6. The reading here follows Carleton Brown's emendation, *"Beowulf* and the Blickling Homilies," *Publications of the Modern Language Association* 53(1938): 905-16.

316. "by decree of grace," *mid arstafum*, a word found only in *Beowulf* and *Riddle* 26 is again used by Hrothgar in reference to Beowulf's venture, 382, 458. It underscores Beowulf's role as providential agent of God's design. The counterpoint is provided by *facenstafas*, 1018, "fated treacheries," and *endestæf*, 1753, "the decree of fate," which is written through the will of the proud man. (So also *runstæf*, 1695.) Here the poet in his creative lexicon establishes the contrast between Providence and Fate (see Chapter Two, notes 2, 12, and 25).

425. E. G. Stanley, "Two Old English Phrases," pp. 672-82 (see Chapter Three, note 1), casts doubt on the customary legal connotation given to *gehegan* and the stylistic deductions drawn therefrom; my translation accordingly has been rendered as neutral as possible. I draw no stylistic conclusions, although I consider it likely that the legal metaphor of the feud is suggested here.

431-32. My translation finds independent confirmation by John Niles, *"Beowulf* 431-2 and the Hero's Civility in Denmark," *Notes and Queries* N. S. 27 (1980): 99-100.

499. *Unferth.* Because of the alliterative pattern the MS *Hunferð* cannot be right. As Klaeber explains, "the consistent scribal error is perhaps influenced by other Hun-compounds; he notes further that the name means "mar-peace" and points to his role in Hrothgar's court, 148-49. Without denying Unferth's role, Lewis Nicholson, "Hunlafing and the Point of the Sword," *Anglo-Saxon Poetry: Essays in Appreciation for John C. McGalliard* (Chapter Two, note 23), p. 50, attempts an interesting but not convincing defence of the reading, *Hunferth.* That Unferth is an emblem of festering strife is convincingly argued by James Rosier, "Design for Treachery: the Unferth Intrigue," *Publications of the Modern Lasnguage Association* 77 (1962): 1-7. Rosier's argument is developed and extended by Joseph Baird, "Unferth the Thyle," *Medium Aevum* 39 (1970): 1-12. He finds that "Unferth seems to have been, somewhere in the dark matrix whence the poem arose ... a Wodensman, a thyle, and vestiges of this Wodenism are still discernible in the poem as we have received it .... But the poet did, I believe, recognize and knew his audience would recognize the dark associations surrounding Unferth. The ambivalent attitude presented toward him is a symptom of this recognition. [There is a] necessary expression of Christian sentiment with regard to a character of sinister connections. With the attitude clear, the basic character can be allowed to remain," pp. 9-12. Robert Finnegan, "Beowulf at the Mere (and elsewhere)," *Mosaic* 11, No. 4 (1978): 49, puts the matter simply, "The poet has suggested a number of things about Unferth, all of them bad." Adelaide Hardy, "Historical Perspective and the *Beowulf*-Poet," (Chapter Two, note 2), pp. 442-43, pushes Baird's argument to what appears to me a self-defeating extreme by putting him in league "against God's warrior with devils who can and do acheive their evil ends." Geoffrey Hughes, "Beowulf, Unferth and Hrunting," *English Studies* 58 (1977): 383-95, in a balanced reconsideration, concludes that as a warrior of importance Unferth cannot be a mere jester, that his contention with Beowulf must be taken seriously and that he is, if only indirectly, involved in the treachery of Hrothulf. W. F. Bolton, *Alcuin and Beowulf* (Chapter One, note 2), pp. 117-22 also finds Unferth an insidious character. The view which finds Unferth to be part of a design for treachery appears to me consistent with his portraiture in the poem, and this view finds convincing exposition by Stanley Greenfield, "The Extremities of the Beowulfian Body Politic," *Saints, Scholars and Heroes,* edited by Wesley Stevens and Margot Kent (Collegeville, Minn.: Monastic MS Library, 1979), pp. 1-14. However, a blander view of Unferth has been argued, if unconvincingly, by J. D. A. Olgilvy, "Unferth: Foil to Beowulf," *Publications of the Modern Language Association* 79 (1964): 370-75 and by Carol Clover, "The Germanic Context of the Unferth Episode," *Speculum* 55 (1980): 444-68. A more impressive, if not more persuasive, argument is presented

by Norman Eliason, "The Thyle and Scop in *Beowulf*," *Speculum* 38 (1968): 267–84. He agrees with Rosier that Unferth is a "scurrilous jester," 268, but argues that his encounter with Beowulf is simply "part of the evening's festivities," and that "The two speeches are not to be taken in dead earnest," p. 271, indeed that Unferth "made up the swimming match [?] out of whole cloth" and that Beowulf retorted in kind, p. 272. See also Fred Robinson, "Elements of the Marvelous in the Characterization of Beowulf," *Old English Studies in Honor of John C. Pope* (Toronto: Toronto University Press, 1974), pp. 130–32. Robert Bjork, "Unferth in the Hermeneutic Circle: A Reappraisal of James L. Rosier's 'Design for Treachery: the Unferth Intrigue'," *Papers on Literature and Language* 16 (1979–80), provides a survey of the controversy and concludes on linguistic grounds that Rosier's hypothesis on the connotation of *thyle* is unsound, but he does not address himself to the more significant question of Unferth's role as reflecting the disorder within Heorot, which is supported by internal evidence. Finally, Jane Roberts, "Old English UN-'Very' and Unferth," *English Studies* 61 (1980): 289–92, inconclusively attempts to make Unferth into a "magnanimous" character.

506–81. The contention with Breca has traditionally been regarded as a swimming match, an inherent absurdity which is explained by reference to folk-lore sources. Recently, this traditional assumption has been demonstrated to be unfounded. James W. Earl, "Beowulf's Rowing Match," *Neophilologus* 63 (1979): 283–90, cogently observed that it is "rowing," not "swimming," which is specified in lines 512 and 540, and that *sund*, 507, 517, taken to mean "swimming" is a secondary, not a primary meaning of the word, which is "water"; further that *glidon*, 515, is as appropriate to rowing as it is to swimming, and that *fleotan*, 542, is more likely to mean "sail" than "swim." His argument, although developed independently, confirms the earlier arguments of Fred Robinson, "Elements of the Marvellous," (see note to 499) and "Beowulf's Retreat from Frisia," *Studies in Philology* 62 (1965): 1–16, as well as Karl Wentersdorf, "Beowulf's Withdrawal from Frisia: a Reconsideration," *Studies in Philology* 68 (1971): 395–415. One must feel grateful that this and other absurdities (see notes to 1495 and 2359–67) have been removed through the attention to detail of these scholars. My translation reflects their conclusions.

612–38. André Crépin, "Wealhtheow's Offering of the Cup to Beowulf: A Study in Literary Structure" (see Chapter Four, note 6), pp. 45–58 provides a rhetorical analysis of the structure of this passage.

703. "The warriors slept." Understood literally, the sleep of the Geats under the circumstances appears improbable, but in *Beowulf* the literal is frequently a metaphoric veil. What is significant is the symbolism of their sleep and Beowulf's wakefulness; in his homily, 1740–44, Hrothgar makes explicit use of the metaphor of spiritual sleep.

745–49. The passage is ambiguous and has occasioned much conjecture. In general the translation follows the exegesis of Calvin Brown, "Beowulf's Arm-lock," *Publications of the Modern Language Association* 55 (1940): 621–27.

768–69. "death was pouring its cup," *ealuscerwen*, "ale sharing." The word seems best understood as related to the motif of the *poculum mortis*, "the cup of death," see line 2358 and Carleton Brown, "*Poculum mortis* in Old English," *Speculum* 15 (1940): 395–96. For an objection to this reading see Edward Irving Jr., "Ealuscerwen: Wild Party at Heorot," *Tennessee Studies in Literature and Language* 11 (1965): 66–67, who is apparently troubled by the fact that no literal death is occurring. More recently, Harvey De Roo, "Two Old English Fatal Feast Metaphors: *Ealuscerwen* and *Meodoscerwen*," *English Studies in Canada* 5 (1979): 249–61, has argued persuasively for the reading I have adopted, and shows its thematic importance, "The key to its [*ealuscerwen's*] meaning lies, I believe, in its being part of a larger metaphor of the fatal feast ... as a prelude to death.... It is used to convey an anti-social and monstrous behaviour inherent in Grendel ... [who in tracing his descent from Cain] may be seen as perpetuation of a heroic feud," pp. 255-58.

901-13. The Heremod analogue is ambiguous because it makes allusion to unexplained events. However, the thrust of the story of a hero fallen through pride seems clear (see the later use of Heremod as example, 1709-22). The time of trouble brought by Heremod is presumably that from which the Danes were rescued by Scyld.

942-46. The echo of Luke 11:27, along with other biblical allusions, should not be read as establishing Beowulf allegorically as a type of Christian hero. What must be kept in mind are the two aspects of Beowulf's typology: as God's agent he has typological correspondence, for example, to David; as pagan hero he has no such significance (see Chapter Two, note 13).

1020. "The sword of Healfdane," *brand* is frequently emended to *bearn*, as by Klaeber, to refer to Hrothgar. A defense of the MS reading by Hertha Marquardt, *Anglia* 50 (1931): 391ff., as a refence to Hrothgar by metonymy is unnecessary; rather as object, not subject, it refers to Hrothgar's gift of the patrimonial sword to Beowulf as Sherman Kuhn convincingly argued, "The Sword of Healfdane," *Journal of English and Germanic Philology* 42 (1943): 82-95, and 76 (1977): 231-37. The reference to the sword in 2154 adds further, conclusive evidence.

1066-68. Norman Eliason, "The Thyle," (see note to line 499, Unferth) by admittedly "awkward" punctuation makes an unconvincing attempt to have the lines refer to Hrothulf.

1063-1162. The Finnsburh Tale bristles with difficulties including the problem of where it begins. I am finally convinced by Klaeber's view that lines 1068-70 constitute an introductory announcement of the subject, the tale proper beginning with 1071. For a reasoned view of the entire tale and an excellent survey of the literature, see Donald Fry, *Finnsburh* (Chapter Four, note 22). With Fry's reading I am in general agreement, and the outline of the story, as I see it, is given in Chapter One. In line 1068, "through Finn's followers," *Finnes eaferum* in considered a comitative dative by R. A. Williams, *The Finn Episode in Beowulf* (Cambridge: University Press, 1924), pp. 20-21, who translates, "the sons of Finn fell," and notes that the scop begins in the middle of things "and wishes to recall events that precede." Accepting Williams' opinion that the story begins in the middle, Fry (p. 37, note) on the authority of Alfred Wyatt, (*Beowulf*, revision of R. W. Chambers, Cambridge: University Press, 1920), considers the phrase best translated as instrumental, "through Finn's followers." As Fry rightly insists the story is given in indirect discourse and quotation marks should not be employed.

1072. "enemies' faith," *eotena treow*, Fry, pp. 13-14, points out, "no sentence in Finnsburh scholarship has caused more trouble than this one." He provides, pp. 14-16, an excellent survey, persuasively concluding, "Whoever the *eoten* are, they are probably not Danes and not subject to Hengest." He tentatively accepts the argument of Robert Kaske, "The *Eotenas* in Beowulf," *Old English Poetry*, edited by Robert Creed (Providence, R.I.: Brown University Press, 1967) that *eoten*, meaning giant, is an "insulting figurative epithet for 'enemies'," and is thus a hostile term for the Frisians, pp. 286ff. His argument is convincing and I have translated accordingly. Kaske also suggests the possibility that the Frisians were actually considered to be giants and that there is a traditional hostility between the Danes and the Frisians.

1082-85. The translation reflects the reading of the lines by Joseph Baird, "The 'Nor-clause' of *Beowulf*, 1084-85," *Modern Philology* 69 (1971): 133-35.

1126-59. "Home" is the key word of the paragraph. The Frisians, leaving Finn with his hall retainers, seek their "land and dwellings," *wica ... Frysland*, 1125-26. Hengest remains "in the houses of Finn's stronghold," *hamas ond heaburh*, 1127, though he remembers his own country, *eard*, 1129; he remains until spring comes to earth, *geardas*, 1134. He thinks to leave the "guesthall," *gist of geardum*, 1138, but is bent on revenge which results in the death of Finn "in his own home," *æt selfes ham*, 1147; the treasure of Finn, king of the land, *eorðcyninges*, 1155, is taken from his *ham*, 1156, and his queen is returned to her own people, 1158-59. As in my translation, Fry, pp. 21-22, construes *hamas ond heaburh*, 1127, as object of *wunode*, 1128; that is Hengest "remained", *wunode* in the homes and city of Finn. This appears to me the only solution to the problem raised by the singular *heaburh*, which can only refer to Finn's stronghold and which would not then be in Frisia if taken as the object of *geseon*, line 1126. Roy Leslie, "Editing of O. E. Poetic Texts," *Old English Poetry*, edited by Daivd Calder (Berkeley: University of California Press, 1979), pp. 111-25, defends the conventional reading, but without explaining the difficulty avoided in Fry's reading.

1129. "of his own will," *unhlitme*, is a nonce word best related to *hlyp*, "lot," and thus "unalloted," that is, "unforced," Fry, pp. 20-22. John Vickrey, "The Narrative Structure of Hengest's Revenge," *Anglo-Saxon England* 6 (1977): 91-103, provides a different connotation for the word on the basis of which he interprets 1131-37 as symbolically implying the completion of Hengest's revenge. His argument is ingenious, but is not nearly as convincing as Fry's simple explanation that "instead of sailing home, Hengest waits for the opportune moment to launch a surprise attack on Finn," p. 22. In Fry's explanation there is no need to attribute a modern indecision to Hengest (as does Arthur Brodeur, *The Climax of the Finn Episode*, Berkeley: University of California Press, 1943, pp. 329-30); rather he is a retainer waiting to accomplish the sacred duty of revenge in complete disregard of compact and vow. The story thus understood, it should be added, finds significant counterpart in the account of Beowulf's treacherously awaiting his chance to be avenged on Onela which is reinforced by the repetition of the key word, *gemunde*, in referring to Hengest's plan of revenge, 1129, 1141, and to Beowulf's, 2391.

1163-68. The expanded lines correspond to the text. The device, used rather sparingly in the poem, serves as elsewhere to underscore an important motif, here the theme of future disaster concealed by the apparent peace of the heroic present.

1174. "Now you intend," *þu nu hafast*, presents difficulties which have been much discussed and have led to several emendations. The phrase is best considered to be elliptical, as does Klaeber who doubtfully relates it to the preceding sentence, while considering that a line has been omitted. It appears to me best related to the following sentence, "I've been told ...," *me man sægde*, 1175, with something like "have in mind" as the understood object of *hafast*; thus the translation, "men tell me you intend."

1197-1201. The story of Hama is shrouded in the mist of legend. Klaeber seems correct in observing that the poet's version of the story springs from a "Christianization of the legend, in which Hama carries his treasure to a monastery," 178-79, the "gleaming stronghold," where the "eternal good" is found, the cloister being an emblem of the heavenly Jerusalem. Since Ermanric is the pagan type of the evil king, Hama is his true Christian antitype, not Beowulf, as John Gardner incorrectly posits in "Guilt and the World's Complexity" (Chapter Three, note 2), p. 16. Only on the false heroic scale is Beowulf the antitype of Ermanric and Heremod.

1229. "protects his king" is the reading of Kemp Malone, "Some Beowulf Readings," *Franciplegius*, edited by Jess Bessinger and Robert Creed (New York: University Press, 1965), p. 120.

1257-67. The punctuation differs from Klaeber's which connects "For a long time after the murder," *Lange þrage / æfter guðceare*, with the slaying of Grendel although as Klaeber notes "long time" is an exaggeration not borne out by the story (p. 180). As I read it, the phrase provides an anticipatory reference to Cain's murder of Abel, 1262, the murder through which Cain becomes the progenitor of the race of Grendel. The legend of Cain's progeny here and in 102-14 is related to the apocryphal Book of Enoch by Robert Kaske,

"*Beowulf* and the Book of Enoch," *Speculum* 46 (1971): 421–31. His findings are supported and developed by Ruth Mellinkoff, "Cain's Monstrous Progeny in *Beowulf*," *Anglo-Saxon England* 8 (1979): 143–62 and 9 (1980): 183–97. Stephen Bandy, "Cain, Grendel, and the Giants of *Beowulf*," *Papers on Language and Literature* 9 (1973): 235–49, emphasizes the role of St. Augustine in the formulation of the "standard exegesis of the history of Cain, a story filled with monsters and prodigies," 235–37; this promising beginning, however, produces disappointingly vague results.

1357–76. The echoes of the *Aeneid* and of apocrypha are noted by Klaeber (182–83). See Carleton Brown, "*Beowulf* and the *Blickling Homilies*," *Publications of the Modern Language Association* 53 (1938): 905–16.

1409–10. An echo of the *Aeneid* 11, 524, which is also found in the O. E. *Exodus* 58, where the context is the flight of the Hebrews from Egypt, a symbol of the release from the bondage of the world. The effect of the line in *Beowulf* is to stress the mysterious peril of Beowulf's adventure. Compare the easy visit to the tarn after the first battle, 853–56.

1471–72. The contrast between Unferth and Beowulf, like that between Heremod and Beowulf and unlike that between Ermanric and Hama, is based on the false scale of heroic glory.

1495. "Then it was day," *Đa wæs hwil dæges*, is usually rendered as "Then it was the space of a day," but the reading in the translation first suggested by S. O. Andrews, *Postscript on Beowulf* (Cambridge: University Press, 1948), p. 94, has been convincingly established by Fred Robinson in "Elements of the Marvelous in the Characterization of Beowulf," (note to line 499), pp. 119–24. He carefully examines the other uses of the phrase in Old English poetry as an index of time and clinches his argument by noting the indices of time, 1311, 1445, 1600 and 1789–90.

1522–28. For the significance of the sword failure see Sylvia Horowitz, "The Sword Imagery in Beowulf," (Ph.D. dissertation, State University of New York at Binghamton, 1978), pp. 62–92.

1687–98. The hilt of the giant sword with its runic inscription is one of the most evocatively beautiful motifs of the poem. Its cruciform shape has led to an interesting conjecture on its Christian significance by Kjell Meling, "Cruciform Runes in the Manuscripts of Some Old English Poems," (Ph.D. dissertation, State University of New York at Binghamton, 1972), pp. 207–11. Sylvia Horowitz, *Sword Imagery* (note to lines 1522–28), pp. 113–31, sees the name on the sword as that of Magog, which she backs with valuable evidence, particularly in the light of Jane Leake's findings (Chapter One, note 1.) Robert Hanning has placed the sword brilliantly in a thematic context, "*Beowulf* as Heroic History" (Chapter Two, note 20), "The hilt is a metaphor for the heroic poem itself: a beautifully wrought testimony to the past and its deeds, sundered from its cutting edge, and thus recalling the break in time and outlook between the heroic age and its audience. Hrothgar's imperviousness to the hilt's message exemplifies the ignorance of providence which separates the pre-Christian past from the Christian present."

1705–08. The expanded lines give emphasis to a crucial statement. In effect, Hrothgar's prediction becomes a test by which Beowulf's final bringing of disaster to his people may be judged. As Sarah Smith has observed, "*Folce to frofre*: the Theme of Consolation in Beowulf," *American Benedictine Review* 30 (1979): 191–204, the phrase "has predominantly Christian connotations," p. 194, and she shows that "the nature of the comfort Beowulf brings illustrates his limitations as a pagan king," p. 202, and undercuts Hrothgar's prophecy that Beowulf will be a comfort to his people. She further points out that "in the second half of the poem the language of 'consolation' is conspicuously absent ... in an inversion of the order of the Latin *consolatio* .... The entire section is a kind of dirge," p. 203. The Geats are left without comfort, and their grief is "a final refutation of the efficacy of consolation in this life .... There is not even left the comfort of a true funeral oration, and the poem concludes with a portrait of a barren world outside any scheme of human or divine consolation," 204. (See also Chapter Two, note 21.)

1807-10. The lines have been given an unlikely reading as referring to Unferth's gift of the sword to Beowulf which James Rosier, "Design for Treachery," (note to line 499) convincingly dismisses.

1931-32. The translation is based on Kemp Malone's "Hygd," *Modern Language Notes* 56 (1941): 356-58. Norman Eliason, however, "The 'Thryth-Offa' Digression in *Beowulf*," *Franciplegius* (note to line 1239), pp. 124-38, argues that Hygd alone is the subject. She, by strained conjecture, Eliason presumes to have been married to Offa before her marriage to Higelac. He translates, "Hygd was ever haughty," p. 126. Bruce Moore, "The Thryth-Offa Digression in *Beowulf*," *Neophilologus* 64 (1980): 127-133, answers Eliason's objection to the introduction of Thryth as too startling by pointing out that such "startling shifts of perspective are typical of the movement of Beowulf," p. 127, which is particularly true of the episode of the homecoming. Much earlier Adrien Bonjour in *The Digressions in Beowulf* (Oxford: University Press, 1950), pp. 53-55, has observed the resonance between the Thryth and Heremod analogues as part of a pattern of comparison.

2183-88. Norman Eliason, "Beowulf's Inglorious Youth," *Studies in Philology* 76 (1979): 101-8, argues that the lines do not refer to Beowulf, but to Higelac. His argument is unconvincing and involves a reading, as he admits, "stylistically ... less satisfactory than the traditional one," p. 106. If further defense of the traditional reading is needed, Beowulf's inglorious youth is in context entirely appropriate to the theme of *edwenden*, "reversal," which ties together the fitt.

2210. "at the last," *oð ðæt*; note the echo of foreboding openings of fitts *26* and *30*.

2228-31. Damage to the MS makes the reading purely conjectural. For "it befell," line 2228, see Kemp Malone, "Some *Beowulf* Readings" (see note to line 1239), p. 121.

2288. "sniffed," *stonc*. Hans Schabram. "*Stonc, Beowulf* 2228," *Festgabe für Hans Pinsker*, edited by R. Acobian (Vienna, 1979), pp. 144-56 has shown this to be the correct meaning, rather than the usual "hasten."

2297-99. My translation is free, but responds to what I think is meant. The lines present difficulties which I wish I could believe are solved by Alfred Bammesberger, "Three *Beowulf* Notes," *English Studies* 61 (1980): 481-82.

2345. "proudly disdained," *oferhogode*. The verb has connotations of heroic pride. (See Chapter Two, note 16.)

2359-2367. The usual reading, in spite of the almost comic improbability involved, has Beowulf swim home towing thirty suits of armor. This view was challenged by Kemp Malone, reviewing Hoops, *Commentar*, in *English Studies* 15 (1934), p. 151. His view has recently been confirmed and broadened by Fred Robinson, "Beowulf's Retreat," and by Karl Wentersdorf, "Beowulf's Withdrawal," (see note to lines 506-81); also Fred Robinson, "Elements" (see note to 499). My translation is based on their reading.

2385. "hapless," keeps the MS reading *orfeorme*, which is emended to *(f)or feorme* by Klaeber. See *Web of Words*, pp. 19, 180.

2457. "the riders ... sleep"; in the father's "reveries" (Klaeber, p. 213) the riders are perhaps suggested by their absence at the son's inglorious funeral in contrast to their featured role in that of Beowulf.

2472-74. Beowulf's perception that the death of the aged Hrethel led to Swedish aggression appears biassed since the messenger says that the Geats "in arrogance," 2926, were the aggressors. Their slaying of aged Ongentheow will eventually lead to the resumption of the feud when the aged Beowulf dies.

2559a. The reading is that of Carleton Brown (note to lines 305-06), p. 916.

2808. "from far away," a translation of *feorran* independently supported by John Hermann,

"Beowulf, 2802-08," *The Explicator* 37, No. 3 (1979): 24-25, who points out the significance of the adverb as yet another index of the difference between Beowulf's expectations and reality.

2820. "esteem," *dom* is the reading suggested by Tolkien's discussion, "*Beowulf. The Monsters and the Critics*," *Proceedings of the British Academy*, 22 (1936): 245-95, reprinted in *An Anthology of Beowulf Criticism* ed. Lewis E. Nicholson (Notre Dame, Ind.: University of Notre Dame Press, 1963), pp. 51-103; see especially pp. 95-96 in the latter volume.

2844-45. The translation is indebted to Alfred Bammesberger's "Three Beowulf Notes," pp. 482-83 (see note to lines 2297-99), who convincingly defends the MS reading *æghwæðre*, 2824, as instrumental with the referent being "treasure in the preceding clause." This reading serves to point up the thematic function of treasure.

3074-75. These lines echo the conclusion to the preceding fitt *41*, and as Adeline Bartlett has observed, *The Larger Rhetorical Patterns* (Chapter Four, note 6), pp. 28-29, "we have in line 3051-3057 a statement that no one was to touch the ring-chamber unless (*nefne*) God should grant permission .... We come back then, with lines 3069-3075, to a restatement of 3051-3057: Whoever plundered the hoard would have been held accursed, guilty of sin, unless [reading *næfne*, 3074] the grace of God had first favored him." Her translation of 3074-75 appears a little free but seems to me responsive to the meaning demanded by the repetitive phrasing, with its implication that the barrow was entered at Beowulf's direction without God's dispensation so that the curse became effective. (Both passages are introduced by "for," a free translation of *swa* to suggest the connection between the passages.) The proposed reading finds support in G. V. Smithers' "Five Notes on Old English Texts," *English and Germanic Studies* 4 (1951-52): 75-84, who has established the meaning of *goldhwæte* as "gold-bestowing," and A. J. Bliss, "Beowulf, lines 3074-3075" (Chapter Two, note 23), who confirms the meaning of *Agendes est* as "God's favor." Bliss, on the basis of Smithers' reading of *goldhwæte*, his own of *Agendes est* and Bartlett's observation, has sought to find a chiastic pattern in the entire passage, 3051-75 which does not withstand scrutiny, first because it is not supported by the rhetorical signals confined, as they are, to the incremental repetition of 3054-56--3074-75; second, because it makes an impossible unit of the end of one fitt and the first paragraph of the next; finally because it is too complicated to carry conviction. He concludes that the lines do establish Beowulf's motive in attacking the dragon, a conclusion that is clearly right, however one may disagree with his rhetorical analysis.

3151. "Geatish." The translation is based on the reading of the MS by John Pope, *The Rhythm of Beowulf* (New Haven: Yale University Press, 1942), p. 232. Lines 3150-54 are badly damaged in the MS and must be heavily reconstructed.

3163-68. G. V. Smithers, *The Making of Beowulf* (Durham: University of Durham, 1961), p. 19, has perceptively observed that the burial of the gold as gravewoods (as with Scyld) is historically accurate though viewed from a Christian perspective.

The Hero in the Earthly City: A Reading of Beowulf presents a coherent view of the theme and structure of *Beowulf* in the context of the poet's Augustinian frame of reference, and an authoritative translation of the poem. The intensive study and the lively, graceful translation offer both a deep appreciation of *Beowulf* as poetic masterpiece and a stimulus to further study.

Huppé opens with a clear and full summary of the Beowulf story, then proceeds to a discussion of thematic polarities — Christian/pagan and Christian/heroic especially — and analyzes their antitheses, interaction, and reconciliation. The chapter on narrative polarities deals densely and richly with contrapuntal development seen in the use of words, points of view, narrative voice, and descriptions of nature within the poem. In a brilliant discussion of structure, Huppé reviews and then rejects solutions proposed by Klaeber and others in favor of a carefully worked out design which encompasses and resolves previous disparities and which illustrates the essential unity of the whole poem. He supports his structural argument by careful analysis of the parts, episodes, fitts, and paragraphs of *Beowulf*, and provides a chart to illustrate his points.

The last chapter is the translation itself, which is both the justification for and the end result of Huppé's study. Taken together, the study and translation provide a cohesive and compelling reading of *Beowulf* which, however controversial, will have to be taken into account in all future discussions of the poem.

Bernard F. Huppé, Distinguished Service Professor Emeritus of English at the State University of New York at Binghamton, was founder and co-director of the Center for Medieval and Early Renaissance Studies from 1968 to 1976. He was Fulbright Fellow (Vienna, 1955–56). Among his numerous publications are *The Old English Homily and Its Background* (co-edited with Paul Szarmach, 1978); *The Web of Words* (1970); *A Reading of the Canterbury Tales* (1964: now available direct from MRTS); *Fruyt and Chaff: A Study in Chaucer's Allegory* (with D. W. Robertson, Jr., 1963; 1976); *Doctrine and Poetry* (1959); and *Piers Plowman and Scriptural Tradition* (with D. W. Robertson, Jr., 1951; 1969).

mRts

medieval & Renaissance texts & studies
is the publishing program of the
Center for Medieval & Early Renaissance Studies
at the State University of New York at Binghamton.

mRts emphasizes books that are needed —
texts, translations, and major research tools.

mRts aims to publish the highest quality scholarship
in attractive and durable format at modest cost.